Illustrator:
Jose L. Tapia

Editor:
Janet Cain, M. Ed.

Editorial Project Manager:
Ina Massler Levin, M.A.

Editor-in-Chief:
Sharon Coan, M.S. Ed.

Art Director:
Elayne Roberts

Cover Artist:
Sue Fullam

Production Manager:
Phil Garcia

Imaging:
Hillary Merriman

Publishers:
Rachelle Cracchiolo, M.S. Ed.
Mary Dupuy Smith, M.S. Ed.

Interdisci
Early Humans
Challenging

Author:
Michelle Breyer, M.A.

Teacher Created Materials

Teacher Created Materials, Inc.
P.O. Box 1040
Huntington Beach, CA 92647
©1995 Teacher Created Materials, Inc.
Made in U.S.A.

ISBN-1-55734-572-4

Table of Contents

Table of Contents *(cont.)*

Introduction

Early Humans contains an exciting, whole language, interdisciplinary unit about the development of the Earth and early humans. This unit has 224 captivating pages that arc filled with a wide variety of lesson ideas and reproducible pages designed for use with intermediate and middle school students. This learning-about-the-past theme is connected to the curriculum with activities in reading, language arts (including written expression), science, social studies, math, art, music, and life skills. Many of these activities encourage cooperative learning.

This unit is divided into the following sections to allow for easy thematic planning: How We Learn About the Past; Earth, the Early Years; Early Humans; Literature Connection: *Maroo of the Winter Caves*. The lessons are designed so that they can be used in conjunction with social studies and science textbooks.

This interdisciplinary unit includes the following:

- **Bulletin Board Ideas**—providing time-saving suggestions and plans for bulletin boards

- **Curriculum Connections**—correlating the theme to curriculum areas, such as language arts, math, social studies, and science

- **Visual and Performing Arts**—providing opportunities for students in the areas of music, dance, art, and drama

- **Writing Ideas**—supplying writing suggestions and activities that cross the curriculum

- **Articles**—providing informational articles with related questions

- **Literature Connection**s—suggesting lessons for use with literature selections related to the theme

- **Group Projects and Activities**—fostering cooperative learning

- **Hands-On Activities**—providing opportunities for students to be active learners

- **Research Activities**—suggesting ideas that can be used to extend and enrich learning

- **Assessment**—providing opportunities to evaluate students' understanding

- **Technology**—suggesting technology that is correlated with the theme and can be integrated throughout the unit

- **Bibliography**—suggesting additional literature related to each section of the theme

Bulletin Board Idea

Use the following bulletin board idea to introduce *Early Humans*. The patterns shown below and on page 6 make the bulletin board quick and easy to create. Begin by covering the background with butcher paper. Use yarn or string to create the illusion of a staircase. Then use an opaque projector to enlarge and copy the patterns. Place the early humans in the following order on the staircase: (starting at the bottom step) Australopithecus, Homo Habilis, Homo Erectus, Neanderthal, Cro-Magnon, Modern Human. Label the early humans under the steps. Finally, create the title "Early Humans."

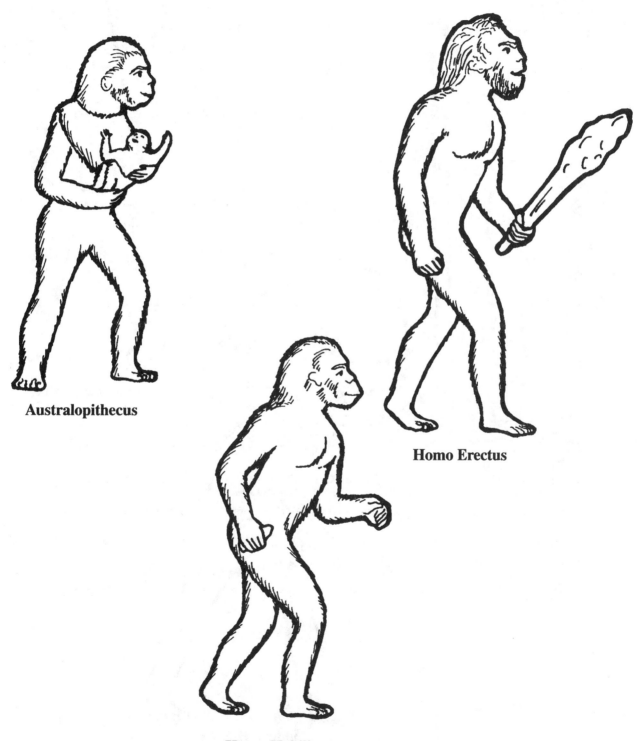

Australopithecus

Homo Erectus

Homo Habilis

Bulletin Board Idea *(cont.)*

Cro-Magnon

Neanderthal

Modern Human

6

Teacher Generated Artifact Hunt

This hands-on activity will help motivate students as they learn how archaeologists use a variety of sources as clues to understand the past.

Preparing for the Lesson:

1. Bring a variety of items from your home that give clues about your family (hobbies, activities, interests, etc.). Try to include some written sources of information (postcards, diary entries, letters, etc.), as well as non-written sources (objects, special clothing, photographs, etc.). There should be about eight items so that small groups of students can examine one item at a time.

2. Reproduce the Artifact Hunt Recording Sheet (page 8) for students.

Teaching the Lesson:

1. Set the stage for this activity by telling students to pretend that it is the year 2550. Explain that you have just returned from a remarkable excavation site believed to be a family dwelling that existed during the 1990's. Tell students that you have brought back a few items, or artifacts, for them to examine and evaluate so they can determine what life was like then. You may wish to ask students to make generalizations about the people based on their evaluation of the artifacts.

2. Divide the class into cooperative learning groups. Have each group pick a student to be the recorder. The recorder's job is to make a written record of the group's observations and ideas.

3. Distribute copies of the Artifact Hunt Recording Sheet (page 8).

4. Provide each group with one artifact. Allow 5–10 minutes for the groups to examine the artifacts and discuss their findings. Monitor group interaction. You may need to guide students' discussions by asking the following questions: How is this artifact special? What does it tell you about the family who owned it? What purpose did the artifact serve? Are there any clues that tell you how old the artifact is?

5. Ask groups to trade artifacts every 5–10 minutes until each group has examined at least four.

6. Discuss the findings. Hold up an artifact, and allow students to respond with their observations. Then tell what you know about the artifact, why you chose it, and what it "says" about your family. Record any misinterpretations made by students. Continue this process with each item.

7. Use the following questions for a follow-up discussion:

   Why weren't you 100% accurate in your evaluation of an artifact? (not enough information, read too much into the artifact, did not see the room it came from, did not see what else was buried near it, etc.)

   What kinds of artifacts did you use as sources of information? (written, non-written, objects, photographs, etc.)

   Why do historians and archaeologists draw different conclusions about the past? (different points of view, different background experiences, might examine and interpret the clues differently, studying the past is not an exact science, the historians and archaeologists were not there, etc.)

   What responsibilities do historians and archaeologists have when telling about he past? (to examine sources carefully to check for accuracy; to try to get as much first-hand information as possible from people who were there; to get as many points of view as possible; etc.)

Artifact Hunt Recording Sheet

Carefully examine each artifact. Then record your observations and ideas on the following chart.

What does it look like? What do you think it is used for?	What can you tell about its owner? (Male or female? Young or old? Not enough information.)	What does it tell you about the life style of the person?

Student Generated Artifact Hunt

This activity is a great way to get students to know each other and appreciate their similarities and differences. It also reinforces their understanding of the different types of sources and methods that historians and archaeologists use to piece together clues about the past.

Preparing for the Lesson:

1. Reproduce the Artifact Hunt Recording Sheet (page 8) for students.

2. Make an overhead transparency of the Types of Sources Graph (page 10).

3. Have each student bring a personal item that the class can pretend is an "archaeological find." Be sure students understand that the items they bring must be appropriate for school. Remind them that the items can be written or non-written sources and should reveal something about their owners. Ask students to bring the items in plain brown paper bags.

Teaching the Lesson:

1. As students enter the classroom, have them place their paper bags containing the artifacts on a shelf or table that is located in the back of the classroom. Randomly number the bags.

2. When you are ready to start this activity, remind students that the objectives of the lesson are to review the different types of sources historians use and to reveal information about the owners. Point out that this is not just a game to guess who brought in each item. Then review the rules for viewing the artifacts: Talk quietly while discussing an object. Handle each object with extreme care. Keep each object with its numbered bag for identification. Do not tell others which artifact is yours.

3. Distribute the bagged artifacts around the classroom. Before taking the artifacts out of the bags, ask the class to predict which type of source was brought in the most. Record their predictions on the chalkboard.

4. Give students the copies of the Artifact Hunt Recording Sheet (page 8). Then have them carefully take the artifacts out of bags.

5. Set a time limit of about 15–20 minutes for students to walk around the classroom and examine and evaluate the different artifacts. Tell students to be sure to write their observations and ideas on their recording sheets for at least five artifacts. Make extra recording sheets available for students who have time to examine more than five artifacts. Monitor on-task behavior.

6. When the time limit is up, have students return to their seats to discuss their findings. Hold up the artifacts, one at a time. Briefly discuss the artifacts, and help students note discrepancies between the information recorded by the class and the information given by the owners.

7. Display, complete, and discuss the transparency of the Types of Sources Graph (page 10).

8. To conclude the activity, discuss how important it is for historians and archaeologists to do research and not just make speculations. Decide, as a class, which types of sources offer the most accurate information. Ask students why they think interpreting sources of information from prehistoric times would be so difficult.

Types of Sources Graph

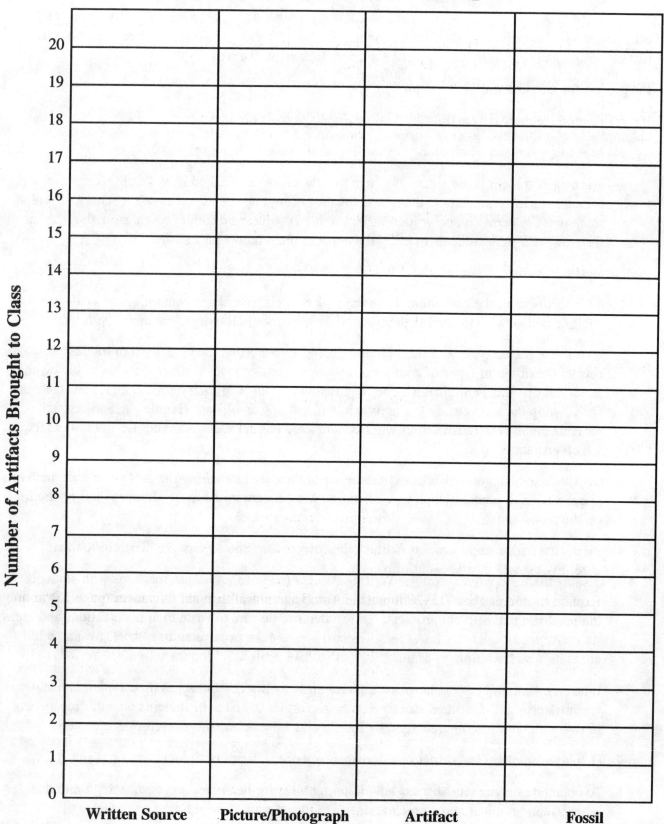

Number of Artifacts Brought to Class

20
19
18
17
16
15
14
13
12
11
10
9
8
7
6
5
4
3
2
1
0

Written Source   **Picture/Photograph**   **Artifact**   **Fossil**

Types of Artifacts

Oral History Autobiographical Incident

Oral history, or learning about the past through stories, myths, and legends, is an important source of information for historians. During prehistoric times, the time before written language, all history, including religious beliefs and ceremonies, hunting practices, knowledge of plants and animals, and family stories, was passed down from generation to generation by word of mouth.

Have your students experience the oral tradition for themselves by researching their past through their parents, grandparents, and other relatives. Then have them transform this research into an organized written composition.

Preparing for the Lesson:

1. Have students discuss their lives as young children with family members. Ask students to select one memorable incident from their past.

2. Create overhead transparencies for The Writing Process (page 13) and the Editing Checklist (page 14).

3. Reproduce the Editing Checklist (page 14) and the Autobiographical Incident Organizer (page 12) for students.

Teaching the Lesson:

1. Remind students to use the following format when writing their compositions:

   - Start with an introduction that states the main idea and tells the reader the purpose of the composition.

   - Be sure that the body of the composition gives plenty of supporting details that are arranged in a logical order. Elaborate, using metaphors, figurative language, similes, descriptions, examples, adjectives, adverbs, prepositional phrases, etc.

   - At the end, write a conclusion that summarizes the main idea of the composition.

2. Display the transparency for The Writing Process (page 13). Discuss the steps with students. Explain to students that they will use the Autobiographical Incident Organizer (page 12) to do the prewriting stage.

3. Display the transparency for the Editing Checklist (page 14). Help students understand how to use this to improve their compositions. Be sure students understand that they should edit their own compositions first, then have two other students act as editors, and finally give the compositions to you so you can give them feedback.

4. Distribute the copies of the Autobiographical Incident Organizer (page 12). Review the directions with students. Allow students to ask questions about the assignment.

5. Explain to students that they will use their organizers to write compositions. Tell them that they will use the compositions to give speeches to the class.

Autobiographical Incident Organizer

We all have special memories of being young children based on stories told to us by our parents and/or older family members. These memories may include embarrassing moments, funny events, accidents, special outings, or holidays.

Use this page to organize your information about a memorable incident from when you were a young child. Be sure the reader understands what happened during the incident, when and where it happened, the reactions and feelings of the people involved in the incident, and why this incident is especially memorable to you or your family.

Introduction—Opening Statement—The opening statement lets the reader know what you are going to talk about. You can restate the prompt adding in your event, or be creative and start with some action from your story. Make sure it is clear that you understand the prompt.

_____

_____

_____

_____

_____

Specific Supporting Details—Sequence Statements—This is the majority of your piece. It must include a clear sequence of what happened, the setting of the event, and the reactions and feelings of the characters involved. Write a brief description of the sequence.

1. _____

2. _____

3. _____

4. _____

5. _____

Conclusion (Summary Statement)—Concluding Statements—Wrap it up by describing at least three reasons why this event was especially memorable to you or your family. Then give a strong closing sentence.

_____

_____

_____

_____

_____

The Writing Process

PREWRITE

Cluster, outline, brainstorm, draw, and discuss your ideas.
Then make a plan to organize your ideas.

↓

FIRST DRAFT WRITING

Write down your ideas. Skip every other line. Use the information you recorded
on your prewriting plan to organize your ideas in a logical manner.
Do not worry about spelling, capitalization, punctuation, or grammar.
Read over your first draft to be sure it makes sense.

↓

RESPONSE

Read your composition to a partner and get feedback to help clarify ideas.
Have your partner help you identify the strengths and improve the weaknesses in
your composition.

↓

REVISION

Add details and descriptive words or phrases to your composition.
You may need to change the sequence of sentences in order to clarify the ideas.

↓

EDITING AND REWRITING

Have a second partner read your composition and help you make any grammatical
and mechanical (spelling, capitalization, punctuation) corrections.

↓

EVALUATION

Be sure you and your partners use the editing sheet to evaluate your composition.

↓

PUBLISHING

Type or use your best handwriting to recopy your composition.
Check it over again before turning it in to the teacher.

Editing Checklist

Name _____

Title _____

✓ = No changes needed   ✱ = Just okay   X = Problem. Editor will help make corrections.

	1st Editor *listen and revise*	2nd Editor *read and revise*	Teacher's Comments
Proper format? (introduction, supporting details, conclusion)			
Specific supporting details? (Use of metaphors, figurative language, similes, descriptions, examples, adjectives, adverbs, prepositional phrases, etc.)			
Correct sentence structure, grammar, and word use?			
Correct spelling?			
Correct punctuation? (periods, commas, quotation marks)			
Correct capitalization? (proper nouns, sentence beginnings)			
Strengths of composition?			
Weaknesses of composition? (editors help make corrections)			

_____   _____
1st Editor   2nd Editor

Autobiographical Speech

After students have researched and written their autobiographical incidents, have them transform their written work into oral history itself by creating speeches.

Preparing for the Lesson:

1. Make an overhead transparency or chart of the Speech Organizer (page 16).

2. Reproduce the Speech Organizer (page 16) and the Speech Evaluation Form (page 17) for students.

Teaching the Lesson:

1. Using the overhead transparency or chart for the Speech Organizer (page 16), explain how to organize a speech.

2. Review the Speech Evaluation Form (page 17) so that students thoroughly understand what you expect from them during their speeches.

3. Distribute the copies of the Speech Organizer (page 16). Have students note that their speeches will be based on the autobiographical incidents that they wrote. Explain to students that when giving their speeches they cannot read their compositions word for word. Suggest that they use index cards to write outlines of their speeches. Point out that the speeches should include the following parts:

    - Start with an introduction that will get your audience interested in your speech. This could be a probing question, trivia information, a joke, or a dramatization that is related to your topic. Be sure the audience knows what topic your speech will cover.

    - During the body, or main part, of your speech, follow a clear sequence of events. Give specific supporting details that will help give your audience mental pictures of the events.

    - Conclude your speech with a short summary. You may wish to end with something that gives your audience something to think about or that makes them laugh.

    - Tell students to practice giving their speeches at home in front of mirrors, so they will be able to easily recall what they want to say and will not be embarrassed to speak to the class. They should time themselves while practicing so their speeches are 3–5 minutes long.

4. Assign a due date for the speeches. You may wish to schedule a few presentations each day over several days rather than having all students give their speeches in one day.

5. As students give their speeches, fill out their evaluation forms, writing as many comments as possible. At the end of the speeches, take time to briefly discuss the evaluations. You may also wish to have two students from the audience evaluate the speeches. Be sure to make extra copies of the evaluation forms if you choose to do this.

6. After all the speeches have been completed, discuss the importance of the oral tradition and the power of clear oral communication. You may wish to have students write additional speeches for other assignments they are given.

Speech Organizer

Name _____

Use this organizer to prepare a speech for the class.

Your speech is due: _____

I. **Introduction**—get audience interested—question, trivia, joke, dramatization

_____

_____

_____

_____

_____

_____

II. **Body**—clear sequence of events, points with supporting details

_____

_____

_____

_____

_____

_____

_____

_____

III. **Conclusion**—summarize and state points, end with strong closing statement

_____

_____

_____

_____

Review your Speech Evaluation Form (page 17) for the criteria of this assignment.

Speech Evaluation Form

Speaker _____

✓ = No changes needed   ✱ = Just okay   X = Problem. Editor will help make corrections.

Place an evaluation mark in each category, along with some constructive comments.

SPEECH FORMAT:

❑ Introduction (background to gain interest) _____

❑ Body (specific supporting details) _____

❑ Conclusion (summary and closing statement) _____

SPEAKING TECHNIQUE:

❑ Voice Expression (volume, speed, and inflection) _____

❑ Sentence Structure (clear and complete sentences, without run-ons) _____

❑ Correct Grammar _____

❑ Eye Contact (look at audience) _____

❑ Appropriate Hand Gestures _____

❑ Visual Aids (props, pictures) _____

❑ Prepared and Rehearsed (smooth delivery) _____

❑ Time Limit (3–5 minutes) _____

Best part of the speech? _____

_____

_____

_____

Suggestions for improvement? _____

_____

_____

_____

Evaluator _____

Advertisement Evaluations

We learn about the world around us in a wide variety of ways, such as television, newspapers, radio, and movies. Similarly, historians gather and evaluate many sources to form their ideas about past events. Therefore, it is important to be able to distinguish among facts, reasoned judgments, and opinions. Use the following lesson to help students explore the world of advertising to determine whether they should believe everything that they read.

Preparing for the Lesson:

1. You will need a variety of magazines with many types of advertisements that can be cut up.

2. Gather glue, scissors, thin black markers, and 12" x 18" (30 cm x 46 cm) pieces of construction paper that are light colors.

Teaching the Lesson:

1. Write the following example on the chalkboard or on an overhead transparency to review the difference between facts, reasoned judgments, and opinions.

   Fact—a statement that can be proven by direct observation, written sources, or findings
   Magic Johnson is no longer playing basketball with the Lakers.

   Reasoned Judgment—a statement that is based on fact but has not yet been proven
   The Lakers will probably not do as well without Magic Johnson since he was their star player.

   Opinion—a statement of personal preference, feelings, or ideas
   I still think the Lakers are the best basketball team!

2. Distribute the magazines and allow students to select advertisements. Remind students that the ads should include plenty of written information as well as pictures.

3. Have students analyze the ads to see whether their claims are facts, reasoned judgments, or opinions.

4. Pass out the pieces of construction paper. Ask students to turn the papers so that they make long vertical rectangles. Have them glue the ads onto the bottom section of the pieces of construction paper. Then, using the thin black markers, have them write on the top part of the papers which portions of the ads are facts, which are reasoned judgments, and which portions are opinions.

5. Invite students to share their findings with the class. Then display the magazine evaluations on a bulletin board.

6. To wrap up the lesson, discuss the importance of using only facts or reasoned judgments to interpret findings from the past when trying to understand our world's history.

Artifact Mystery Game

Many artifacts discovered by archaeologists are very unusual and difficult to interpret. It is up to the individual archaeologists to use their prior knowledge and clues from the excavation site to make a reasonable interpretation of the item and its use. The following activity allows students to use their imaginations and critical thinking skills to uncover the true identities of home artifacts.

Preparing for the Lesson:

1. Ask students to search their homes for a very unusual artifact that is appropriate to bring to school. Point out that the artifacts can be whole objects or parts of an object. Tell students that they must know what the artifacts are and what purpose they serve. You may wish to allow each student to bring more than one artifact for this activity.

2. Have students bring their artifacts to school in bags so that no one will see them.

3. Provide index cards and markers for each student.

4. Divide the class into an even number of teams with about four students on each team.

Teaching the Lesson:

1. Tell students that their team members will be presented with an artifact and four different descriptions of that artifact that have been written by another team. The object of the game is to try to uncover the true identity of each artifact. Tell students that teams will earn one point for each correct guess. The team with the most points wins.

2. First, have each team secretly work together away from the other teams. Some teams may need to quietly work in the hallway or the library.

3. Have each team examine their artifacts and select only four to use for the game.

4. Give each team 16 index cards, four for each artifact, and some markers. Tell them to follow these instructions for filling out the index cards: Starting with the first artifact, clearly write on the index card what it is and what purpose it serves. On the other three cards, make up this information. Do the same for the other three artifacts. Remember, you are trying to stump the other team, so be convincing!

5. Once the teams have all of their index cards complete, pair up the teams to play the game. It is best to have one team sit across a table or set of desks from the other team. The game begins with an artifact being placed on the table, along with the four descriptions. The team owning the artifact clearly reads each description for the other team. The guessing team is allowed three minutes to discuss their ideas about which card has the correct description. Then the guessing team picks up the card with the description that they think is correct. If the card they selected is the correct one, they keep the card. The play alternates back and forth across the table until the identity of each of the eight artifacts has been revealed. The team holding the most correctly guessed cards at the end of the game is the winner.

6. After all the teams are finished playing the game, ask students to share their experiences with interpreting and evaluating artifacts.

Classroom of the Mysteries

The following lesson is intended to be used with the humorous tale about an archaeological discovery in David Macauley's book, *Motel of the Mysteries*. After reading the story, students will choose a common classroom object to interpret, write about, draw, and form a plaster casting of, just as if they were out at an excavation site. You may wish to assign some of the writing and drawing as homework projects. Invite a parent volunteer to help students create their plaster casting imprints.

Preparing for the Lesson:

1. Obtain a copy of David Macauley's book *Motel of the Mysteries* (Scholastic Inc., 1979).

2. Gather 9" x 12" (23 cm x 30 cm) pieces of white construction paper for the drawings, white lined paper for writing (or computer paper if students will be typing their information), and any color of 12" x 18" (30 cm x 46 cm) construction paper to display the finished products.

3. To make the pictures, students will need pencils, erasers, thin permanent black markers, and crayons, markers, or colored pencils.

4. To make the casting imprints, you will need enough modeling clay for each student to have about a golf ball size or larger portion, depending on the size of their objects.

5. To fill the casting imprints, you will need a box of white tile grout. (Plaster of Paris does not work well because it becomes brittle.)

6. Have plenty of paper towels to lay the castings on until they are dry.

Teaching the Lesson:

1. Tell students that you are going to read them a story about a magnificent archaeological discovery from the year 4022. Ask them to listen carefully to the interpretations of the findings by the historian, Howard Carson, who based his conclusions purely on clues found at the excavation site. Note the similarities of this story to that of Howard Carter's discovery of King Tut's Tomb. Throughout the story, discuss the findings and other aspects of the excavation which relate to how we interpret the past.

2. Read aloud, show the illustrations, and discuss the story.

3. Introduce the lesson, Classroom of the Mysteries, using the following information:

    Tell students that again it is the year 4022, and just like Howard Carson they are traveling along Usa during their 116th Cross-Continental North American Catastrophe Memorial Marathon. However, as they fall down a shaft near an abandoned excavation site, they are not faced with the entrance to a motel room, but rather the entrance to this very classroom. (If you have a room number on your door, try to use that information in your introduction.)

    As they open the door and examine the interior, they decide that the contents and configuration of the room could only imply that this was once a place where the ancient Yanks of North America worshipped their gods (a church, temple, synagogue, etc.). Therefore, every item in the classroom must have had some religious significance, such as being used during rituals, sacrifices, offerings, communicating with the gods, etc. (You may need to help some students understand that they are interpreting the object and changing its original purpose to that of a religious nature.)

Classroom of the Mysteries *(cont.)*

4. Have students select a small object from their desks, or from other places in the classroom, that they can interpret, draw, write about, and for which they can make a plaster casting. Some suggestions include crayons, paper clips, staple remover, markers, pencil sharpener, etc.

5. First, have students examine the object carefully and brainstorm all of the possible religious interpretations. Have them interpret any of the writing or symbols on the object as well.

6. It is usually easiest to begin with the drawing of the objects first, since students can be examining them while they draw. Distribute the white construction paper and instruct students to draw their objects with as much detail as possible. Point out that students will want to draw them as large as the paper will allow so that every aspect of the objects can be included.

7. Have students show you their finished drawings so that you can give them feedback. After you have approved their pencil drawings, have students outline them, using thin permanent black markers. Then ask students to color in their drawings. Tell students to complete their drawings by labeling the different parts.

8. Next review The Writing Process (page 13) with students. Ask them to write a diary entry describing their artifacts. You may wish to review the pictures and descriptions of the treasures from the story to help inspire your students.

    Tell students that the written portion should be a narrative, and it should include the following: **an opening**—describing how they came to be there; **a full description of their object**—what it is, how it looks, dimensions, and how it was used by the Ancient North American Yanks in their religious ceremonies; **a closing**—describing their feelings and future aspirations for this excavation site

9. Finally, have students create plaster castings by following these directions: First flatten the modeling clay onto a paper towel. Then press the object into the clay. Remove the object carefully and fill the depression with mixed tile grout. Once dry, remove the plaster cast from the clay. Gently scrape off any excess clay with a paper clip or blunt scissors.

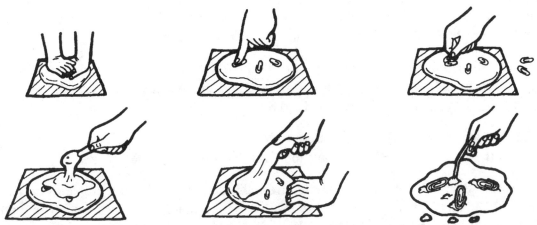

10. Display students' drawings, written descriptions, and plaster casts in a learning center entitled "Classroom of the Mysteries." Allow time for students to share and discuss their archaeological interpretations and what they have learned from this lesson.

Digging Up the Past

Archaeology is the study of people and things from the past. The artifacts, bones, fossils, and ruins discovered by archaeologists help them to learn more about how the people from long ago lived, what they ate, how they were affected by disease, and even how their culture came to an end. The following activity helps students learn about the many facets of archaeology by having them recreate an excavation site of their own.

Preparing for the Lesson:

1. Divide the class into archaeological teams with about four students per team.

2. Gather large shoeboxes (one per team), thick black markers, hole punchers, heavy yarn or string to make a grid on the shoeboxes, and damp sand for filling the shoeboxes.

3. Ask students to bring to class some small, common household objects to bury in their excavation sites. Have them bring "tools," such as spoons, stiff paintbrushes, etc.

4. Reproduce the article about archaeologists (pages 23–24), so each team has at least one copy.

5. Reproduce Make a Shoebox Excavation Site (page 25) so each team has at least one copy.

6. Reproduce the Excavation Grid Sheet (page 26) so that you have one for each student plus one more for each team to use for their master plans. (You will want to make extra copies in case students make mistakes and they need to start over.)

Teaching the Lesson:

1. Distribute the copies of Archaeologists (pages 23–24) to each team. As a class, read the passage and discuss what an archaeologist does.

2. Have each team outline the steps needed to excavate a site. Check for understanding.

3. Then give each team a shoebox, hole puncher, black marker, and yarn. Have the teams assemble their excavation sites according to the directions on page 25.

4. Have students carefully place their "artifacts" (household items) in their excavation sites. Tell them to use the grid sheets (page 26) to record where items are located.

5. After all the teams have assembled their excavation sites, have them exchange shoeboxes with another team and take turns digging for artifacts. Each student should carefully record his or her team's findings on an Excavation Grid Sheet (page 26).

6. When all the teams are done excavating their shoeboxes, ask them to compare their findings against the master copy of the Excavation Grid Sheet made for their boxes.

7. As a class, discuss what students learned from this activity. Ask what problems they encountered and how they attempted to resolve those problems. Have them tell about the discoveries they made and what they liked and disliked about the activity.

8. To extend this lesson, have students research some famous excavation sites and archaeologists.

Archaeologists

Imagine walking across a vast plain where no humans have lived for thousands of years. Yet, at one time, a complex village existed in that very area. After the village was abandoned, the only signs of a once prosperous civilization are a few ruins and artifacts that were left behind. Time passes, and soil covers the site. Within a few centuries, the village goes undetected. Covered by grass and trees, its secret is sealed below layers of earth.

So how do we eventually come to learn about this buried village? Some evidence of the village may appear through the natural process of erosion. This erosion can be caused by animals digging for a meal, plants growing and uprooting the soil, or heavy winds and rain. However, we might discover the village as we make changes to meet the needs of our modern world, such as clearing the site for new buildings or roadways. Regardless of how this village is found, once it is revealed it is put into the hands of capable archaeologists who examine the site and compile an archaeological record.

Who are archaeologists? Archaeologists are scientists who want to know what life was like for people who lived long ago. They use artifacts (things made or used by people), bones, fossils, and ruins as clues to the past. Their job requires both skill and diligence as they look for potential sites to have archaeological digs. Archaeologists are also usually anthropologists, scientists who study the origin, culture, and values of different peoples. It is often helpful for archaeologists to be trained in other fields of science, such as biology, chemistry, geology, paleontology, and zoology. Before the archaeologists can make their archaeological record of a site, they must do research to learn about the people who are believed to have lived in that region. As a result, the archaeologists try to find information about the following aspects of the people's lives:

1. Culture—how the people lived, the ways of living they had in common

2. Community—where the people lived, the social structure and buildings

3. Communication—how the people exchanged ideas, language, pictures, gestures

4. Religion—what they valued or worshipped

5. Traditions—the actions and beliefs handed down from the past

In most cases, information about the people of a region lies buried under Therefore, archaeologists must use excavation, or digging, to examine the determined, the archaeologists carefully map out the area. Then a grid is surface into squares and labeling the coordinates. Finally, the archaeolog brush away dirt to reveal relics from the past.

Modern Human

Archaeologists *(cont.)*

It is important that the archaeologists be patient and careful workers so that fragile and valuable objects are not damaged. The tools they use depends on what type of job needs to be done. Usually, archaeologists begin digging with a large tool, such as a shovel or pick. When they come to what they believe is an artifact, bone, or fossil, they switch to a finer tool such as a trowel, ice pick, or firm brush to clear away loosened dirt. The soil that has been loosened must then be sifted through a wire mesh sieve so that tiny objects are not overlooked. Every object, no matter how small or seemingly insignificant, is carefully labeled and recorded. A grid map is used to mark the exact location where each object is found. Eventually, the finds are taken back to a laboratory for further examination. Sometimes, plaster castings are made of bones or fossils that are too difficult to move. Once at the laboratory, the items are pieced together and studied. Sometimes the archaeologists perform tests, such as radiocarbon dating, on the objects in an attempt to determine their ages.

Bones, fossils, and artifacts are all examples of items found at an excavation site. Some of the most difficult items for archaeologists to interpret are artifacts, or objects that have been made or modified by humans. Occasionally, it is difficult to tell whether a stone found at a site is just an ordinary stone or an artifact that has been chipped or shaped in some particular way by a person who lived long ago. In addition, when the archaeologists are excavating a site they often find only a portion of an artifact. Frequently, an artifact is broken or was made from material that did not survive the test of time. Arrowheads are commonly found artifacts since they are usually made from stone or bone. Often, when archaeologists find these arrowheads, the leather, wood, and sinews that were once attached have disintegrated. However, in some dry caves these ancient weapons and tools have been preserved intact. These rare finds have given archaeologists a better understanding of the people who made these arrowheads. For example, if the archaeologists find arrowheads made from flint in an area where flint does not occur naturally, they can infer that the people of the area may have found the flint while traveling or got it when they traded with or were attacked by people from another region where flint can be found.

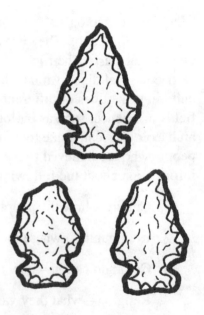

Archaeologists also use stratigraphy to help them interpret their findings and uncover clues about different periods in history. Stratigraphy is a method of determining the age of artifacts by keeping track of the layers of soil in which they were found. The layers, called strata or beds, are actually a number of layers of rock separated from the next strata by a distinct change in the surface. For thousands of years, countless generations might have inhabited a particular site. As old homes fall into ruin, new ones were built in the same spot. Over time the objects that were discarded or lost by the different generations form a series of layers. These layers create a "tell," or mound. As the archaeologists excavate the mound, they usually find the newest objects at the top and the oldest ones at the bottom. Unfortunately, with the passage of time the layers can be disturbed and things from different ages may be buried together. Therefore, it is important for archaeologists to use a variety of techniques to date and interpret their findings in order to make a clear and accurate archaeological record for the excavation site.

Make a Shoebox Excavation Site

Now that you have read about the work that archaeologists do, it is time for you to be an archaeologist. In this activity you will get to create your own excavation site!

Materials:

- large shoebox, without a lid
- damp sand
- hole puncher
- yarn

- digging tools, such as spoons and stiff paintbrushes
- marker
- "artifacts" (common household items) to bury
- copies of the Excavation Grid Sheet (page 26)

Directions:

1. First, make a grid across the top of your shoebox. Do this by punching holes in the top edge of the box and tying pieces of yarn in the holes to form the lines of the grid.

2. Next, use the marker to label the coordinates of the grid.

3. Using the marker draw the stratigraphy on the outside of the box and label the time periods. Remember to leave a space on the top.

4. Pour damp sand into the box. Carefully follow your plan as you bury the artifacts in the sand. Be sure to tightly pack the sand for best results.

5. After you have packed all of your artifacts, exchange boxes with another team and begin excavating the site that they have created. Be sure to take turns digging for the artifacts. Record your findings on a copy of the Excavation Grid Sheet (page 26).

6. Compare your findings with the Excavation Grid Sheet that shows where the other team buried their artifacts.

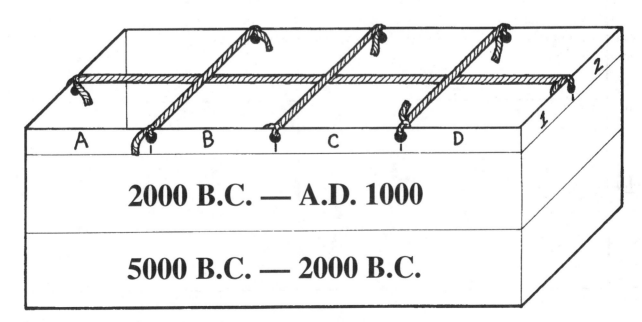

Excavation Grid Sheet

Draw and label the artifacts in the appropriate locations on the grid. Next to each artifact write the time period during which you think it was used based on the stratigraphy.

	1	2
A		
B		
C		
D		

Make a Fossil

Fossils are the remains of traces of living things from ancient times that have been preserved in the layers of sediments composing rocks. In this activity, students will make their own fossils.

Preparing for the Lesson:

1. You will need enough pottery clay (whitish-gray) for each student to have a piece that is about 4" x 4" x 2" (11 cm x 11 cm x 5 cm).

2. You will need paper towels to place the fossils on when they are wet, stiff paintbrushes, and brown tempera paint that has been diluted by water to make the fossils appear to be very old.

3. Ask students to collect leaves, small twigs, shells, acorns, etc., to make their fossils.

4. Gather samples of real fossils, or find books with pictures of different types of fossils.

Teaching the Lesson:

1. Review with students the different types of fossils that are described below. Show the samples of real fossils or the pictures of fossils found in books.

   Molds—These are impressions that are left in sediment by the hard parts of living organisms. Over time, the parts decay or change form, but the impressions remain. (This is the type of fossil students will be making.)

   Casts—These are made when molds are filled with sediment and minerals. Casts preserve the shape of the molds by making exact impressions of living organisms.

   Trace Fossils—These show where living things were once active. The organisms are completely gone. Dinosaur footprints and worm burrows are examples of trace fossils.

2. Distribute the clay and paper towels. Have students press the various items into the clay, making sure they do not cover the items with the clay. Have students place their molds on paper towels and write their names next to their molds. Put the molds in a safe place to dry.

3. Allow the clay to dry overnight. (If you have a kiln, you may wish to fire the clay. Be sure to let the clay dry for a couple of days before firing.)

4. After the clay is dry, have students carefully peel the items out of the clay. Tell them that this represents the decaying of those organisms over long periods of time. Allow students to use the firm paintbrushes to carefully clean out any material that sticks to the mold. Warn them not to gouge the clay or make any stray marks.

5. Have students paint the dried fossils so that they will look very old.

6. Invite students to examine the molds and guide a discussion using these questions: What does the clay represent? *(layers of sedimentary rock)* Why would heat and pressure affect fossils? *(organism decays so quickly, it does not leave a mold)* If the Precambrian time is 7/8 of Earth's history, why do we not have more fossil evidence from this period? *(some were destroyed by earthquakes, volcanoes, erosion, humans; animals from that time had few hard parts to be fossilized)*

Creation Stories

Every culture, since the beginning of time, has had their own beliefs about how the Earth was created. This lesson allows students to explore scientific and legendary theories related to Earth's creation.

Preparing for the Lesson:

If possible, obtain copies of the book and magazine suggested below. They will prove to be invaluable resources for this lesson, as well as for the entire unit.

> *Keepers of the Earth, Native American Stories and Environmental Activities for Children* by Michael J. Caduto and Joseph Bruchac; Fulcrum, Inc.; 1988.

> *National Geographic*, "1491 America Before Columbus" Vol. 180, No. 4; October, 1991.

Teaching the Lesson:

1. Together, as a class, brainstorm the different theories on how the world began. Write each theory and its components on the chalkboard or overhead transparency. The three most common theories students might have heard about are shown below.

    Big Bang Theory—There was a big explosion out in space, and the Earth is merely a fragment from that explosion.

    Dust to Planet Theory—Minute dust particles out in space slowly joined together until eventually the planet Earth was formed.

    Creation Theory from the Old Testament—God created the Earth in seven days, putting all forms of life on the planet. You may wish to read aloud a version of this theory.

2. Explain that there is not enough evidence to prove any of the theories about how the Earth was created. However, some people have strong feelings about the creation of the Earth and humans due to their cultural and religious backgrounds. Therefore, it is important that we respect each individual's opinions and beliefs. Point out that you will be presenting a variety of scientific information, as well as some beliefs from ancient peoples, to provide students with the opportunity to learn about different ideas. Be sure students and their parents clearly understand that you are not trying to tell students what to believe but rather to provide them a variety of information. You may wish to send home notes to parents addressing this issue.

3. Tell students that regardless of the origination theory in which they believe, scientists have been able to ascertain certain facts about the Earth. They know that the planet is approximately 4.5 billion years old. That means over 4 billion years ago the hot, molten rock of the Earth's crust cooled and formed water vapor which in turn produced the first atmospheric weather with clouds and rain. Eventually, large land masses and bodies of water formed.

4. Point out that ancient peoples had many different ways to explain the beginning of time on Earth. Have students read two stories told by ancient Americans (pages 29-30). Have students discuss or write answers to the questions at the end of each story. Then ask them to compare and contrast the theories that are proposed in these stories.

5. Write a summary of these theories on the chalkboard or overhead transparency with the others. Have students discuss the features of these theories that are similar and/or different.

Grandfather Rock

A Sioux, or Great Plains Indian, Story of Creation

The ancient Sioux people say that in the beginning of time all that existed was in the mind of the Great One, Wakan-Tanka. All things which were to be created existed only as spirits without any physical body at all. Every day those spirits floated about in space, seeking to find a place where they could manifest themselves. They traveled high and low, searching until they reached the sun. They wondered if they should settle there. However, the burning rays from the sun reached out, and together the spirits decided that this was not a good place to begin creation, for it was much too hot.

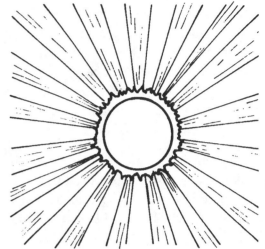

So the spirits took up their travels until they came to the Earth. The Earth was without life and covered only with great waters. The spirits circled the Earth, searching for some spot of dry land upon which life could begin. Suddenly, out of the great waters, an enormous burning rock arose. It made the dry land slowly appear. Clouds formed from the great steam that the rock created as it emerged from the waters. The spirits decided that now life on Earth could begin.

So it is that the rock is called Tunka-shila, or "Grandfather Rock;" it is the oldest one and the beginning of life on Earth. Because of that, all rocks must be respected. The Sioux men meet in the sweat lodges for special ceremonies, and as the water strikes the heated stones and the mist rises once again, it reminds them of that special moment of creation. For this reason, the people of the Sioux tribe sing praises to Tunka-shila, the Grandfather, the Old One.

Questions:

1. Why did the spirits decide not to begin creation on the sun?

2. What event occurred that made the spirits choose the Earth to begin life?

3. How do the members of the Sioux tribe celebrate the creation of the Earth?

The Earth on Turtle's Back

Creation Story of the Northeast Woodlands Indians

In the beginning, before this Earth existed, there were only great waters covering the planet. In the great waters lived many kinds of birds and animals who were happily swimming around. Far above the waters, up in the clouds, was the Skyland. In this Skyland grew a great and beautiful tree. It had four long white roots, and its branches grew many fruits, seeds, and flowers. There was an ancient chief who lived in Skyland, and he had a young and beautiful wife. One night the chief's wife dreamed that the great sky tree must be uprooted. In the morning she told her husband of her powerful dream. He sadly agreed that it was clearly a dream of great importance, and they must do all that was in their power to make the dream come true. Therefore, the sky chief called together the other young men and ordered that the tree be uprooted.

The roots of the great tree were so strong and deep that the young men could not budge it. Finally, the sky chief himself approached the tree and with one great effort uprooted it and placed it on its side. A giant hole was left where the tree once stood, and the chief's wife was curious about it. She peered down into the hole and thought she saw glittering water. As she leaned out further, she lost her balance, falling into the hole. She clutched at the tree to save herself, but only succeeded in stripping off a handful of seeds as she fell down, down, down.

Far below, swimming in the great waters, some of the birds and animals saw the woman falling. "Someone comes," they said, "and we must help her!" Two swans flew up and gently caught the sky woman between their wide wings. Slowly, they began to fly her down towards the great waters where the other birds and animals were waiting and watching.

"She is not like us. How will she live in the great waters?" the animals pondered.

Just then a water bird spoke up. "I have heard stories told that there is Earth far below the great waters. If we dive down and bring the Earth to the surface, she will have a place to live."

One by one, the animals and birds tried to pull up the Earth but never succeeded. Finally Muskrat dove into the waters, determined to bring up the Earth. When she returned, she held out her tightly shut paw to reveal the precious Earth. Turtle swam up from the depths and offered his back as the place to spread the Earth. Muskrat placed her paw against Turtle's giant shell. To this day, all turtles bear the markings on their shells made by Muskrat's paw. The tiny bit of Earth spread over Turtle's back and grew larger and larger until it became the entire world. Then the two swans brought the sky woman down. She stepped onto the new Earth and carefully opened her hand, spilling the seeds from the sky tree. From those seeds grew the first trees and grass. Life on Earth had begun.

Questions:

1. How did the sky woman end up in the water with the animals and birds?

2. Why do you think the animals felt it was important for them to help the sky woman?

3. Do you think that the sky tree's seeds were really the beginning of life on Earth? Explain.

Outline the Eras

Although different written sources have conflicting numbers, there are some basic time periods that students can learn to fully understand and appreciate the history of our planet. This lesson helps students explore geological time while practicing how to make outlines.

Preparing for the Lesson:

1. You will need to decide whether you want individual students to create outlines or cooperative learning groups to create group outlines.

2. Reproduce the Chart of Earth's History (pages 32-34) for each student or group of students.

3. Gather scissors and glue to cut and paste pictures.

Teaching the Lesson:

1. Review how to make an outline using Roman numerals, capital letters, and Arabic numbers. Point out that outlines should contain words and phrases rather than complete sentences.

2. Distribute the Chart of Earth's History (pages 32-34), and ask students to take out lined paper. Have students note the sections that would be written next to Roman numerals (Precambrian Era, Paleozoic Era, Mesozoic Era, Cenozoic Era) and the sections that would be written next to capital letters (the periods and epochs). Tell students to use Arabic numbers to briefly list the important aspects for each time span.

3. As students make their outlines, they can cut out the pictures from the Chart of Earth's History (pages 32-34) and glue them next to the appropriate spaces.

4. After students finish their outlines, lead a discussion using the following questions:

   • What is the longest era? (*Precambrian*)

   • What was happening during that time? (*Earth was forming*)

   • When did the dinosaurs exist? (*Mesozoic Era*)

   • Did humans live during the age of the dinosaurs? (*no*)

   • How long have humans been on the Earth, compared to the dinosaurs? (*3 million years as opposed to about 65 billion years*)

   • Where did the first signs of life appear? (*the oceans*)

5. You may wish to have students work in groups to write their own questions. Have the groups exchange questions. Then allow them to answer each other's questions.

6. As an extension to this lesson, divide the class into four groups and have them make a bulletin board display showing the four main eras of the Earth's history. Create the title "Earth's History" for the bulletin board.

7. In addition, you can follow up this activity with the time analogy activities (pages 36-40) and the time line activities (pages 41-43).

Chart of Earth's History

This geological time scale outlines the development of the Earth and its life forms. The Earth's earliest history appears at the bottom of page 34, and its most recent history appears at the top of this page. You may wish to tape the pages together to make one continuous chart.

	Period/Epoch	Years Ago	Description	Pictures
The Cenozoic Era—Age of Mammals (65 million years ago—present day)	Holocene Epoch	10,000	Modern humans developed agriculture and domesticated animals. They used metals, coals, oil, gas, and other resources. They used the power of wind and rivers.	
	Pleistocene Epoch	2 million	Homo habilis developed and survived with later human species during the ice ages. Mammoths, woolly rhinos, and other giant mammals flourished but died out near the end of the epoch.	
	Pliocene Epoch	5 million	Sea life became much like today's. Birds and many mammals became like modern kinds and spread around the world. The first human-like Australopithecus appeared. The Great Lakes formed.	
	Miocene Epoch	24 million	Apes appeared in Asia and Africa. Other animals included bats, monkeys, whales, primitive bears, and raccoons. Flowering plants and trees resembled modern kinds.	
	Oligocene Epoch	37 million	Primitive apes, camels, cats, dogs, elephants, horses, rhinos, and rodents developed. The Grand Canyon formed.	
	Eocene Epoch	58 million	Birds, amphibians, small reptiles, and fish were plentiful. The first bats, camels, cats, horses, monkeys, rhinos, and whales appeared.	
	Paleocene Epoch	66 million	Flowering plants became plentiful. Invertebrates, fish, amphibians, reptiles, and small mammals were common. The Alps, Himalayas, Pyrenees, and Rocky Mountains came into existence.	

Chart of Earth's History *(cont.)*

	Period/Epoch	Years Ago	Description	Pictures
The Mesozoic Era—Age of Dinosaurs (270 million–65 million years ago)	Cretaceous Period	144 million	The first flowering plants appeared. Invertebrates, fish, and amphibians were abundant. Dinosaurs with horns and armor became common; yet, all forms of dinosaurs died out by the end of this period.	
	Jurassic Period	208 million	The giant dinosaurs ruled at this time. Cone-bearing trees were plentiful, and sea life included shelled squid. The first birds appeared; yet many mammals were still small and primitive.	
	Triassic Period	245 million	The first turtles, crocodiles, and dinosaurs appeared along with the first small mammals. Many fish resembled modern kinds, and insects were plentiful.	
The Paleozoic Era (570 million–270 million years ago)	Permian Period	286 million	The first seed plants appeared in the form of cone-bearing trees. Fish, amphibians, and reptiles were plentiful. Trilobites and other ancient invertebrates died out at the end of this period.	
	Pennsylvanian Period	320 million	Fish and amphibians, along with scale trees, fans, and giant scouring rushes, were abundant. The first reptiles appeared, and giant insects lived in forests where coal later formed.	
	Mississippian Period	360 million	Very few trilobites existed. Crustaceans, fish, and amphibians were plentiful. Many coral reefs were formed. The Appalachian Mountains pushed up again to reach the heights of the modern Alps.	

Chart of Earth's History *(cont.)*

Period/Epoch	Years Ago	Description	Pictures
Paleozoic Era—Age of Ancient Plants and Animals (570 million–270 million years ago) Devonian Period	408 million	The first forests grew in swamps. Many kinds of fish evolved including sharks, armored fish, and lungfish. The first amphibians emerged on land along with insects.	
Silurian Period	438 million	The first coral reefs formed. Spore-bearing land plants appeared. Trilobites and mollusks were common.	
Ordovician Period	505 million	Trilobites and mollusks were plentiful. Tiny animals called graptolites lived in branching colonies along with brachiopods. The Appalachian Mountains first formed.	
Cambrian Period	570 million	Fossils were plentiful for the first time. Shelled animals, called trilobites, and some mollusks were common in the sea. Jawless fish appeared and land plants evolved.	
Precambrian Era Age of Earth Forming	4.5 billion	Coral, jellyfish, and worms lived in the sea about 1.1 billion years ago. Bacteria lived as long as 3.5 billion years ago. Before that, no living things are known. Over 4 billion years ago the hot molten rock of the earth's crust cooled. This produced water vapor which in turn produced the first atmospheric weather with clouds and rain. Eventually, large land masses and bodies of water were formed.	

Place-Value Bingo

Did you know that the Earth is about 4,500,000,000 years old? Pretend that you are a scientist and practice using numbers in the billions as you play this game with a partner.

Materials: Number cubes

Directions: Roll a number cube, and call out the number. Try to create the highest number possible by filling in each digit as you roll. Be careful where you place each number, because once it is written down, you cannot change its place value! After you have rolled a number and written it down, ask your partner to take a turn. After you have filled in all of the digits, practice reading aloud the number. The winning student is the one with the highest number for each round. Good Luck!

Game 1— ___, ___ ___ ___, ___ ___ ___, ___ ___ ___

Game 2— ___, ___ ___ ___, ___ ___ ___, ___ ___ ___

Game 3— ___ ___, ___ ___ ___, ___ ___ ___, ___ ___ ___

Game 4— ___ ___ ___, ___ ___ ___, ___ ___ ___, ___ ___ ___

Game 5— ___, ___ ___ ___, ___ ___ ___, ___ ___ ___

Game 6— ___ ___ ___, ___ ___ ___, ___ ___ ___, ___ ___ ___

_____

Now practice working with numeration in the billions.

Write the following numbers.

1. twenty-three billion, eight hundred sixteen million, fifty thousand, two hundred twenty-six

2. seven hundred eighteen billion, five hundred two million, seventy-eight thousand, six hundred thirty-nine

3. The nebula Trans-x is eighteen billion, six hundred million miles further from the Earth than the nebula Nova. If the nebula Nova is three hundred fifty-eight billion, two hundred eighty-five million, seven hundred forty-one thousand, one hundred six miles from the Earth, how far is nebula Trans-x from the Earth?

Time Analogy

Since 4.5 billion years is quite difficult to comprehend, these three time analogies give students pictorial representations of the very brief time that humans have spent on the Earth.

Preparing for the Lesson:

Reproduce the Time Analogy Charts (pages 38-40) for students. You may also wish to make overhead transparencies of these pages to help guide the lesson.

Teaching the Lesson:

1. Review with students the four main time eras—Precambrian Era when the Earth was forming, Paleozoic Era when ancient plants and animals existed, Mesozoic Era when dinosaurs existed, and the Cenozoic Era when mammals and humans existed. Tell students that the eras are alphabetized in chronological order.

2. Distribute the Time Analogy Charts (pages 38-40).

3. Begin with the clocks on page 38. Have students fill in the information as you read. Model on the overhead if you made a transparency of this page.

    • Based on many different scientific studies, the earliest humans are said to have existed as long ago as 5 million years. The earliest modern humans, are believed to have existed as long as 500,000 years ago. We are going to represent modern human existence with this 24-hour clock. When you change 500,000 years into 24 hours, one hour would equal about 20,833 years. One minute would equal about 347 years.

    • From 12:01 a.m.-11:30 p.m., only prehistoric hunters and gatherers roamed the Earth. The first farmers existed around 11:30 p.m. Civilizations, such as Egypt and Sumer, came around 11:45 p.m. At about 11:50 p.m., Hammurabi of Babylon wrote the first laws. Caesar ruled Rome at about 11:54 p.m., and Columbus discovered America at about 11:58 p.m. The American Revolution was fought just 30 seconds before midnight.

4. After discussing the analogy of modern human existence, call students' attention to the Sears Tower (page 38) located in Chicago to get an overview of Earth's History. Have students record the names of the eras as you read the following passage.

    • If the Sears Tower were to represent the 4.5 billion-year history of Earth, the following would be true: From the ground floor to number 1 would be Precambrian Era when the Earth was forming and no signs of life were present. Number 1 marks the beginning of ancient forms of plants and animals in the seas, or the Paleozoic Era. As you reach number 2, fish, amphibians, and reptiles are abundant. You are about to reach the age of the dinosaurs. Number 2 marks the beginning of the most famous era, the Mesozoic Era, with its Cretaceous, Jurassic, and Triassic Periods—the time when dinosaurs ruled the Earth. In just a short while, the dinosaurs are extinct and we move into number 3, the Cenozoic Era. Finally, mammals appear and dominate this era. The football represents the time all humans have existed on the Earth.

Time Analogy (cont.)

5. The final analogy compares the entire Earth's history to a 12-month calendar. You may wish to fill out the calendar, make an overhead transparency, and reveal each section as you read. Explain that one calendar day would be approximately 13,000,000 years.

January—By the end of the month, the Earth emerges as a red-hot, molten mass.

February—The molten earth begins to cool.

March—As it cools, steam forms, rises, cools, condenses, and falls, only to rise again as steam and vapor from the bubbling-hot earth below. This process repeats itself as the planet cools.

April—By April 15, there are large land masses and giant bodies of water but no life.

May—In small pools on the land there appear protein-like molecules and complex chemical chains that are capable of reproducing themselves.

June—Still no signs of life exist.

July—Living creatures first appear as microscopic virus-like forms. They make their own food.

August—Further expansion of microscopic virus- and bacteria-like life is in the oceans.

September—At the beginning of September, small ocean animals evolve that are similar to jellyfish, worms, and coral. Plants with hard parts, similar to algae, appear by the 15th. Only rarely are fossils formed in rock. By the end of the month, one of the early ice ages occurs.

October—As this month begins, great mountain ranges form in what is now the Great Lakes and Grand Canyon regions. Invertebrates dominate the ancient seas for the last week in October and the first week in November ending the Precambrian Era.

November—The Paleozoic Era begins with the first trilobites. The invertebrates develop since the majority of planet life is underwater from the last ice age. By the third week, half of North America is a shallow sea. Coral reefs are formed. The first vertebrates appear, and the first forests grow in swamps with many kinds of fish. The land is still barren. Three days before Thanksgiving the first amphibians move onto land and the first insects appear. By the end of the month the Earth's crust changes. The eastern coastline of North America moves and forms the Appalachian Mountains.

December—With the first days of December come the reptiles. Giant insects live in forests where later coral swamps form. Three days later the first seed plants appear and the trilobites die out marking the end of the Paleozoic Era. By December 8th, the first turtles, crocodiles, and dinosaurs appear. The Mesozoic Era begins. By the 14th, dinosaurs are king, and the first birds appear. Mammals are small and primitive. Giant dinosaurs are replaced by smaller forms with horns and armor by the 18th and are extinct by the 20th. Now it is the Cenozoic Era, and flowering plants and the Rocky Mountains appear. From the 21st through 25th, birds, amphibians, small reptiles, and mammals are developing. Mammals become the dominate land animals by the 26th. On the 27th, the Alps, Himalayas, and Pyrenees mountains are formed. On the 28th primitive apes and horses appear. On the 29th, the Colorado River starts forming the Grand Canyon, and the Great Lakes are taking shape. By the 30th, most sea life is much like today's. The end of the day on the 31st marks the arrival of the first humans.

Time Analogy Charts

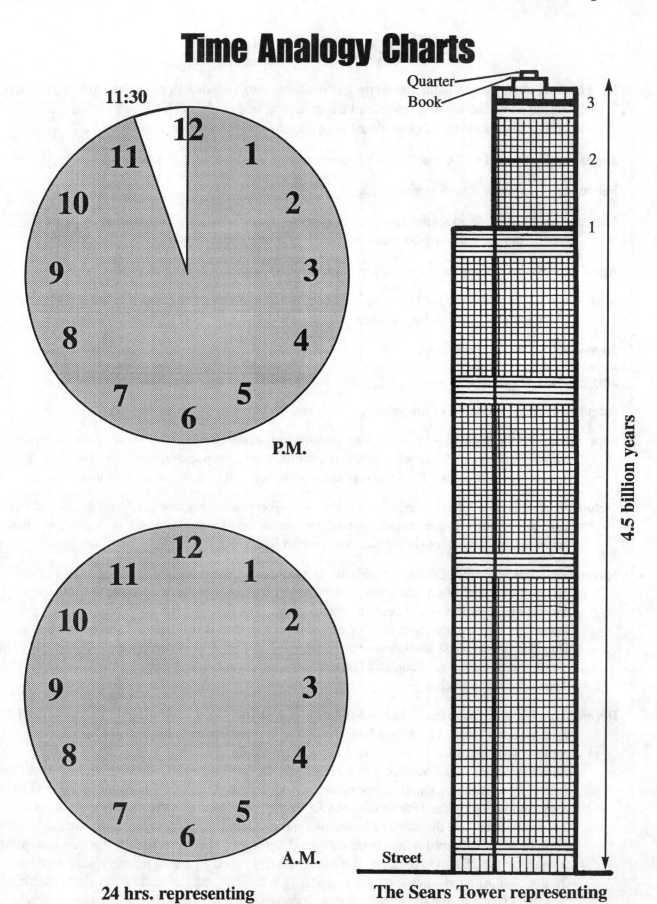

**24 hrs. representing
Man's Existence on Earth**

**The Sears Tower representing
Geological Time**

Time Analogy Charts *(cont.)*

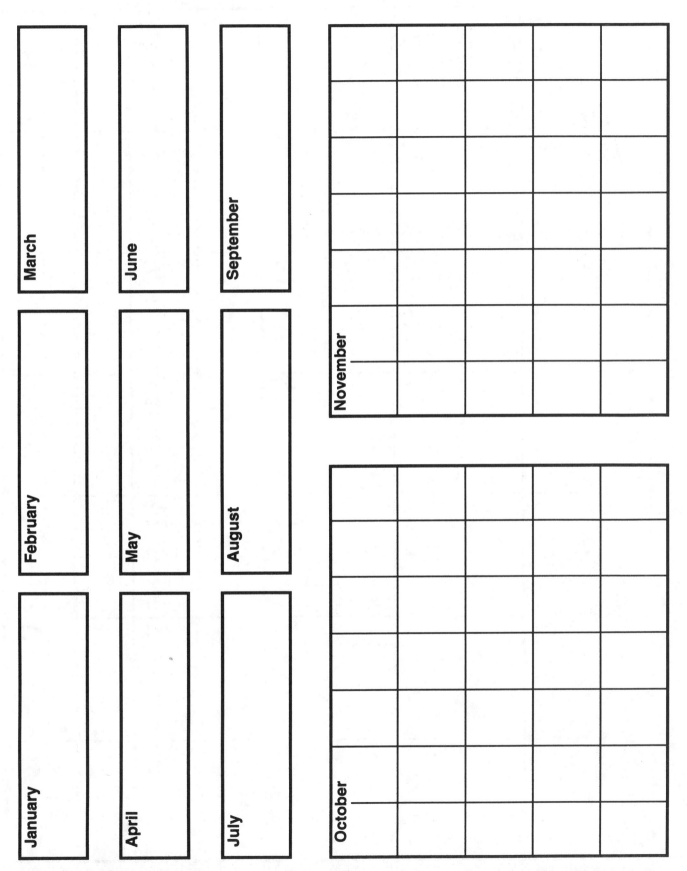

January

February

March

April

May

June

July

August

September

October

November

Time Analogy Charts *(cont.)*

December					
1	2	3	4	5	6	7
8	9	10	11	12	13	14
15	16	17	18	19	20	21
22	23	24	25	26	27	28
29	30	31				

Walk a Geological Time Line

Walking a time line allows students to visualize the great age of the Earth and to discuss the immense impact people have had on the environment in the short time we have inhabited the planet. You may wish to have a group of more capable students, who can work independently, create the time line. Then invite the entire class to "walk" the time line and read the information.

Preparing for the Lesson:

1. The time line will require 45 meters (148 feet) of string or yarn, four different colors of index cards, scissors, markers, a metric tape measure or meter stick, and tape.

2. Reproduce Make a Geological Time Line (page 42) for the group making the time line.

Teaching the Lesson:

1. Distribute the materials and chart for making the time line.

2. Assign a deadline for when the time line should be finished and monitor the group's progress. Provide help as needed.

3. Once the time line is completed, have the group stretch it out on the blacktop or field with all of the index cards facing up so they can easily be read.

4. Take the entire class out to the time line after it has been set up. As you walk the time line with students, stop at each point and have them take turns reading the cards that describe the geological events. When you get near the end and are standing close to the point representing present time, allow time for students to appreciate the short period people have been inhabiting the planet. Point out that the Earth has undergone a great amount of change caused by people even though we have not been here very long.

5. When you return to the classroom, lead a discussion using the following questions. You may wish to assign some of the questions as written homework.

   • How long has there been life on the Earth?

   • What fraction of geological time has there been life on Earth?

   • For about how many years have humans inhabited the Earth? What is our fraction of geological time?

   • What force seems to have changed the planet the most in the shortest amount of time? What evidence do we have?

   • Based on the geological time line, what might happen in the next million years? the next billion years?

   • What do you consider to be the three most significant events in the Earth's history? Why?

6. After students have completed this activity, encourage them to make a personal time line (page 43). Invite them to share their personal time lines with the class.

Make a Geological Time Line

Use the following directions and chart to make a geological time line.

Materials: metric tape measure or meter/yard stick, string or yarn, scissors, colored index cards, black marker, tape

Directions:

1. Use a tape measure or meter/yard stick to measure 45 meters (148 feet) of string or yarn. Keep in mind that one centimeter (0.4 inch) will equal one million years. Make sure you are not stretching the string or yarn as you measure it.

2. Using index cards and markers, clearly label each card according to the chart shown below. Use different colored index cards for each era. Be sure to keep the cards in order as you work.

3. Once the cards are completed, carefully measure and tape them onto the yarn in the appropriate order. The cards will get very crowded at the end, near present time.

ERA	EVENT	YEARS AGO	POSITION
Cenozoic	1. present day	0	the end
	2. industrial revolution	100	0.0001 cm
	3. birth of Christ/the calendar	2,000	0.002 cm
	4. last ice age ended, the farming revolution began	10,000	0.01 cm
	5. oldest known remains of modern humans	300,000	0.3 cm
	6. earliest humans	5 million	5 cm
	7. first elephants and apes	40 million	40 cm
	8. primitive horses, cats, whales, and monkeys appeared	60 million	60 cm
	9. small mammals exist	65 million	65 cm
Mesozoic	10. dinosaurs died out	70 million	70 cm
	11. small dinosaurs with horns and armor are common	140 million	1.40 meters
	12. first birds and flowering plants	160 million	1.60 meters
	13. dinosaurs reached their largest sizes	200 million	2.00 meters
	14. first dinosaurs	225 million	2.25 meters
	15. first turtles and crocodile	240 million	2.40 meters
Paleozoic	16. trilobites died out	250 million	2.50 meters
	17. first reptiles	300 million	3.00 meters
	18. first amphibians	400 million	4.00 meters
	19. first land plants live on land	440 million	4.40 meters
	20. first fish	500 million	5.00 meters
	21. first trilobites	600 million	6.00 meters
Precambrian	22. first animal life (jellyfish, coral, and worms)	1.2 billion	12 meters
	23. first plant life (algae)	3.2 billion	32 meters
	24. formation of the Earth and the solar system	4.5 billion	45 meters

Make a Personal Time Line

Use the following directions to make a personal time line that tells about some of the important events in your life.

Materials:

- 8 ½" x 11" (25 cm x 28 cm) construction paper in a variety of colors
- black marker
- glue or tape
- crayons or colored markers
- hole puncher
- yarn
- photographs

Directions:

1. Obtain enough pieces of construction paper so that you will have one for every year of your life. Begin by writing the year of your birth on one piece of paper. Then write all the years until the present on the other pieces of paper.

2. On each piece of construction paper, write at least one significant event that happened in that year. Be as descriptive and specific as possible. You could tell about a new skill that you learned, a family vacation that you went on, a special event at school that you participated in, etc. You may need to rely on some oral history from family members to help you think of the events from your life.

3. Choose at least five of the years and add illustrations to the pieces of construction paper. Be sure your time line is neat and easy to read as well as colorful and interesting.

4. Use tape or glue to connect the pieces of construction paper. Start with the year of your birth on the bottom and end with the current year at the top. Punch holes at the top corners of the current year and tie a piece of yarn to them. Display your personal time line in the classroom.

5. As an alternative use one large sheet of construction paper. Fold it into as many sections as you are years old. Choose at least five of the sections to illustrate or add photos making sure to add written information to each box.

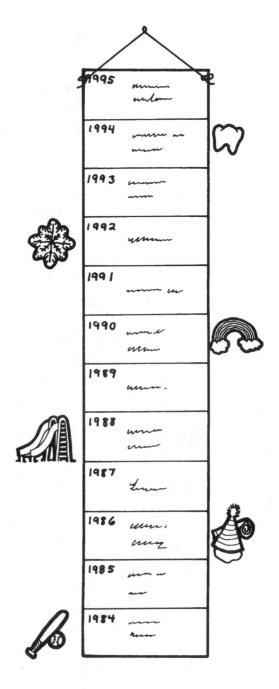

Vocabulary and Using Sources

Write the letter of the best answer.

_____1. **Prehistory** is the history of events that took place before the development of
   a. writing.
   b. stone tools.
   c. mammals.
   d. the mountains.

_____2. **Fossils** are the remains or imprints of all of the following except
   a. plant parts.
   b. animal parts.
   c. human dwellings.
   d. footprints.

_____3. **Artifacts** teach archaeologists about all of the following except
   a. the customs and beliefs of people in the past.
   b. plant and animal life in the past.
   c. where people lived and built shelters.
   d. how the people communicated and shared ideas.

_____4. A culture's **oral history** is made up of the legends, myths, and beliefs that are
   a. passed on by word of mouth.
   b. passed on through writing.
   c. discovered in fossils.
   d. discovered in the artifacts left behind.

_____5. An **archaeologist** excavates a site to look for all of the following except
   a. artifacts remaining from the past.
   b. carvings and paintings from the past.
   c. oral history from the past.
   d. fossilized remains from the past.

Write the letter of the answer that describes each type of source.

a. oral history	b. written source	c. picture source	d. artifact	e. fossil

_____ 1. a letter   _____ 4. a folktale   _____ 7. a bowl

_____ 2. a cave painting   _____ 5. petrified wood   _____ 8. a stone tablet with writing

_____ 3. a basket   _____ 6. brick with animal carved on it   _____ 9. ancient bones

You Be the Judge

Read the following statements that were made by a scientist. Write **F** if the statement is a fact, **J** if it is a reasoned judgment, or **O** if it is an opinion.

_____ 1. The radiocarbon dating on this bone tells us that this animal lived 25,000 years ago.

_____ 2. Obsidian arrowheads were found at this sight. Since there is no evidence that obsidian is found locally, we can assume these people traded for it.

_____ 3. These primitive tools were made from stone.

_____ 4. The early humans were friendly people.

_____ 5. A fire hearth was discovered inside a primitive shelter. These people must have known how to make or transport fire.

_____ 6. Grain was stored in the pottery made by the early farming communities.

_____ 7. The Neanderthal people enjoyed hunting the woolly mammoth.

_____ 8. Since early humans did not have a form of writing, they must have passed information from generation to generation by word of mouth.

_____ 9. Cave paintings were made with minerals that were ground and mixed with animal fat.

_____ 10. Since the cave paintings showed hunting scenes, we know what kinds of animals the painters probably ate.

Put the following time periods in order from that which occurred the longest ago to that which is the most recent. Then write the letter of the events that happened during that time period.

Paleozoic Era   **Cenozoic Era**   **Precambrian Era**   **Mesozoic Era**

1. _____   3. _____

2. _____   4. _____

a. The first ancient forests and swamps with primitive plants developed on land.

b. The first birds and small rodent-like mammals appeared.

c. The first ancient animals emerged from the sea and went onto the land.

d. This is the age in which the Earth first formed and the atmosphere developed.

e. Humans finally emerged and continue to dominate the Earth.

f. This was the age of the dinosaurs, such as the Tyrannosaurus Rex and Brontosaurus.

g. Bacteria and one-celled animals formed in the early seas.

h. This was the age of large mammals, such as the woolly mammoth and sabertooth tiger.

Comprehending the Past

Use complete sentences to answer the following questions. Be sure to include as many details as possible. You may use the back of this page if you need additional space for your answers.

1. Name three different artifacts that archaeologists might study to learn about early humans. What would each artifact tell the archaeologists about these people? _____

   _____

   _____

2. Why is a culture's oral history an important source of information for historians and archaeologists, especially when studying prehistoric times? _____

   _____

   _____

3. Why do archaeologists sometimes reach different conclusions about the past?_____

   _____

   _____

4. In ancient times, fewer women than men left behind written sources. How might this have affected the knowledge that historians and archaeologists have of ancient times?_____

   _____

   _____

5. How are the grids shown on modern maps similar to the grids made by archaeologists when they excavate a site?_____

   _____

   _____

6. How are archaeologists able to use stratigraphy to help them interpret what they find at excavation sites?_____

   _____

   _____

7. Why are everyday objects that belonged to common people just as valuable as artifacts that are rare and valuable treasures that might have belonged to a king? _____

   _____

   _____

Answer Key

Vocabulary and Using Sources (page 44)

Top

1. a

2. c

3. b

4. a

5. c

Bottom

1. b or d	6. c or d
2. c	7. d
3. d	8. b or d
4. a	9. e
5. e	

You Be the Judge (page 45)

Top

1. F	6. F
2. J	7. O
3. F	8. J
4. O	9. F
5. J	10. J

Bottom

1. Precambrian Era	d, g
2. Paleozoic Era	a, c
3. Mesozoic Era	b, f
4. Cenozoic Era	e, h

Comprehending the Past (page 46)

1. Accept any three reasonable answers.

2. Answers should include that during prehistoric times people did not know how to write down any information. It is only from oral history, artifacts, and pictures that we can learn about their myths, legends, and beliefs.

3. Answers should include that archaeology is not an exact science. Scientist interpret the clues to the best of their abilities.

4. Answers should include that we know less about the lifestyle of women and how they felt about their way of life than we do for men.

5. Answers should include that the grids on modern maps as well as on excavation site maps help to record and locate where specific items can be or have been found.

6. Answers should include that the different layers help to tell the age of the item, since items that are farther down are usually older than the items on the top. The layers can also tell them the different natural and human-related events that took place over time.

7. Answers should include that the everyday items help historians learn about the lifestyle of the common people which make up the majority of the population. A king's treasures may be valuable in terms of gold and jewels, but it only tells us about a small portion of the community.

Pangaea

For many years, most people thought that the Earth's continents had always been the way they are now. It was not until the twentieth century that Alfred Wegener, a German meteorologist, theorized that the Earth's land masses were once joined. His hypothesis was called the continental drift theory. Later, it was found that the Earth was made of several plates and that the plates, not just the continents, have moved and still are moving. This theory is called plate tectonics. Plate tectonics also explains how mountains are formed and why some earthquake and volcanic eruptions occur.

In this activity, students will explore the movement of land masses to understand how the Earth's plates have moved over the last 360 million years. Students will also predict where the land masses will be 100 million years in the future.

Preparing for the Lesson:

1. Reproduce the Pangaea Puzzle Pieces (page 49) for students.

2. Make overhead transparencies of Tracking the Continental Drift (pages 50-53).

3. Gather additional information regarding plate tectonics and continental drift.

4. Students will need white construction paper, crayons or markers, scissors, and glue.

5. Have a modern-day world map available for display.

Teaching the Lesson:

1. Discuss with students the theories on plate tectonics and continental drift.

2. Provide and distribute the supplies needed for this activity.

3. Distribute the Pangaea Puzzle Pieces (page 49). Have students color each land mass using different light colors so the names of each can still be read. Have them cut out the pieces.

4. Display and discuss the transparency of what the Earth was like 360 million years ago (page 50). Have students arrange the Pangaea Puzzle Pieces on their desks according to how they appear on the transparency. Point to the land masses on the transparency to help students correctly place their puzzle pieces. Provide individual assistance as necessary.

5. Display the transparency of what the Earth was like 180 million years ago (page 51). Discuss the information shown on the transparency. Have students arrange their puzzle pieces according to the transparency. Call students' attention to the direction the land masses are moving.

6. Repeat Step 5, using the transparency of what the Earth was like 120 million years ago (page 52) and then using the transparency of what the Earth was like 60 million years ago (page 53).

7. Display a modern-day world map. Have students arrange their puzzle pieces according to the map. Then ask them to predict where the land masses will be in 100 million years. Have them glue their puzzle pieces onto construction paper to show their predictions. Share these. Ask students how the climate in your area might change as the land masses continue to move.

Pangaea Puzzle Pieces

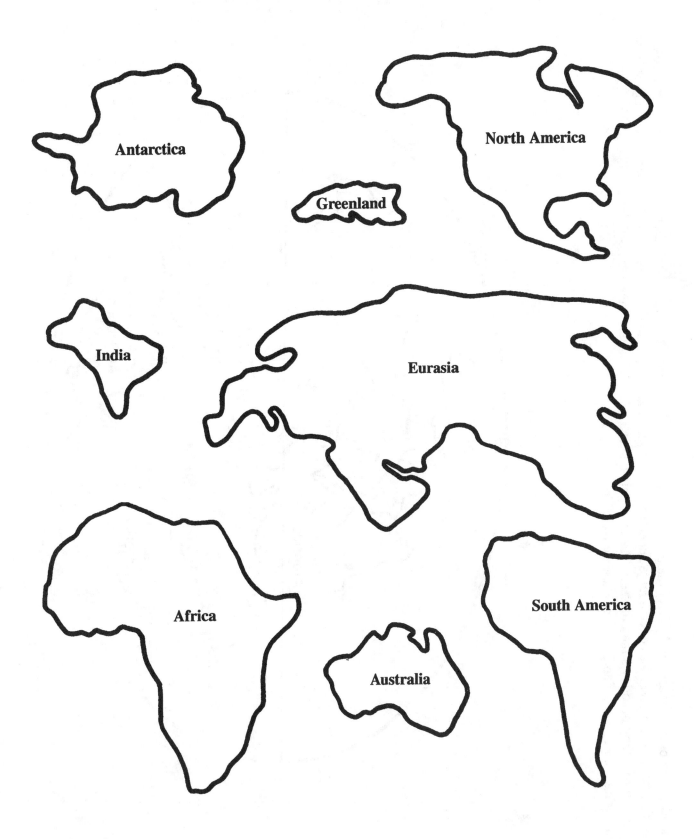

Tracking the Continental Drift

Scientists do not know very much about the position of the Earth's land masses before 200 million years ago. However, some scientists believe that there was once a huge supercontinent, which they call Pangaea. They think that over time Pangaea broke apart to form many of today's land masses. The map below shows what scientists think the Earth looked like 360 million years ago during the Mississippian Period of the Paleozoic Era.

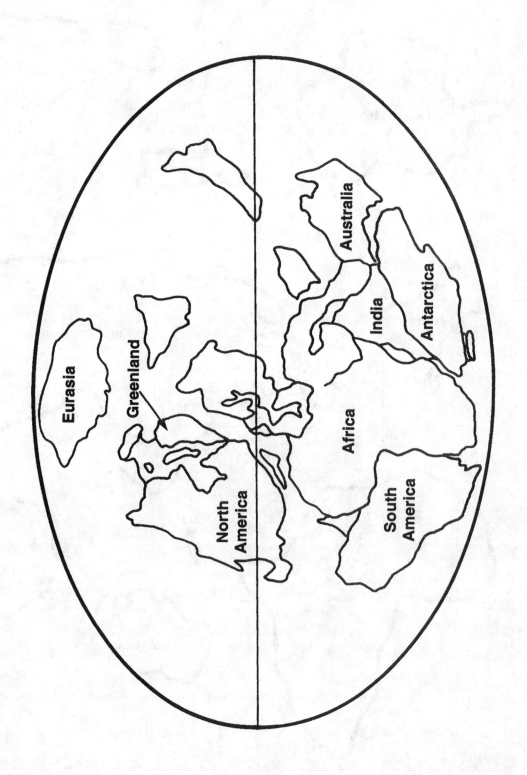

Tracking the Continental Drift *(cont.)*

Scientists believe that Pangaea started to break up about 200 million years ago. They believe it created two large land masses, which they call Laurasia and Gondwanaland. Laurasia was to the north, and Gondwanaland was to the south. A single ocean, which scientists call Panthalassa, surrounded these two land masses. The map below shows what scientists think the Earth looked like 180 million years ago during the Jurassic Period of the Mesozoic Era.

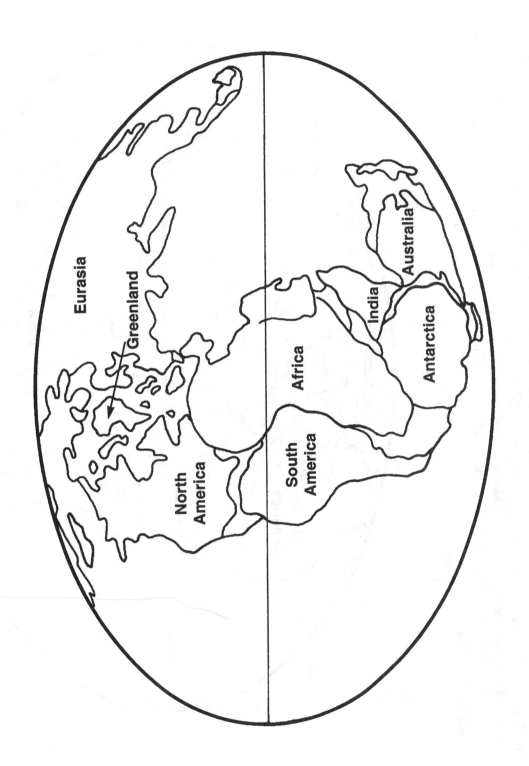

Tracking the Continental Drift *(cont.)*

Scientists theorize that Laurasia and Gondwanaland broke apart and formed the land masses that we know today. The land masses now known as Europe and Asia (Eurasia), Greenland, and North America are believed to have come from Laurasia. The land masses now known as Africa, Antarctica, Australia, India, and South America are believed to have come from Gondwanaland. The map below shows what scientists think the Earth looked like 120 million years ago during the Cretaceous Period of the Mesozoic Era.

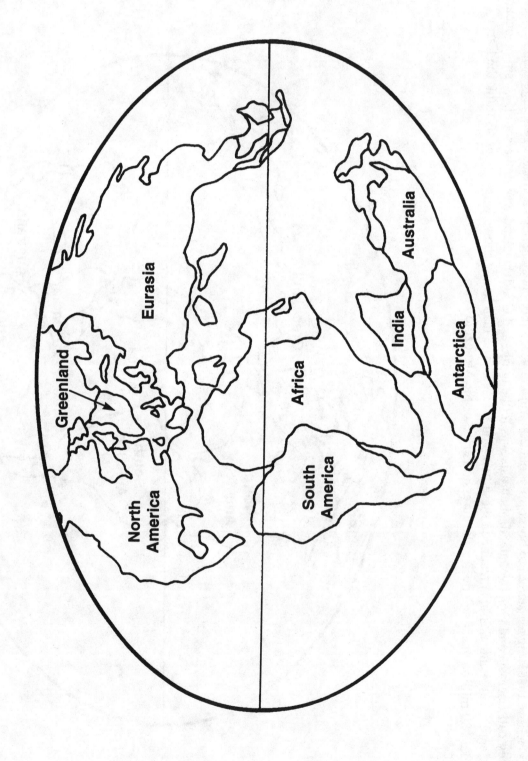

Tracking the Continental Drift *(cont.)*

Scientists believe the Earth's land masses continued to move. The map below shows what scientists think the Earth looked like about 60 million years ago during the Paleocene Epoch of the Cenozoic Era.

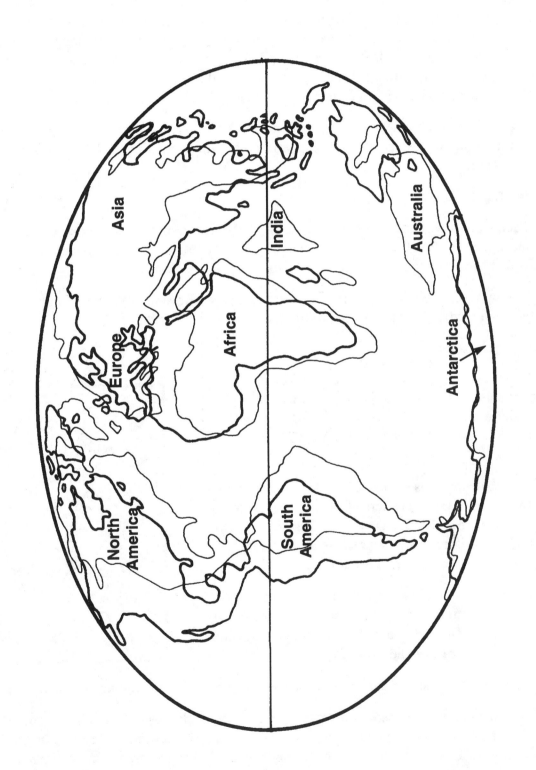

Scientists who study the Earth believe that the land masses are still moving. Look at a modern-day map to see where the land masses are today. Where do you think the land masses will be 100 million years in the future?

Sea-Floor Spreading Art

After the theory of continental drift was proposed by Wegener, scientists in the 1960's made a surprising discovery in the Atlantic Ocean. Hot liquid rock was flowing up through cracks in the sea floor. The new rock hardened, creating a new ocean floor that pushed the older floor outward. They realized that the Atlantic Ocean was becoming wider by the process of sea-floor spreading. Therefore, North and South America are drifting away from Europe and Africa just as Wegener suggested. The discovery of sea-floor spreading led scientists to propose the new theory of plate tectonics. The theory suggests that the crust of the Earth is made up of about 20 plates, or sections.

Students will recreate the process of sea-floor spreading through this simple art project. You may wish to extend this lesson with some alliteration poetry or descriptive writing about the lava flowing up through the sea floor.

Preparing for the Lesson:

1. Each student will need a piece of 12" x 18" (30 cm x 46 cm) orange construction paper and a piece of 9" x 12" (23 cm x 30 cm) blue or green construction paper. Students will also need wide black markers, fine-point black markers, glue, and scissors.

2. You may wish to create a sample for students to see. Be sure to have materials for yourself so you can model each step in the process as students work on this project.

Teaching the Lesson:

1. Discuss the process of sea-floor spreading with your students. Tell them that they are going to try to capture the essence of the lava flowing up along a crack in the ocean floor through an abstract art project.

2. Distribute the construction paper, scissors, glue, and two types of black markers. Demonstrate the steps and provide assistance as needed. Tell students that the blue or green paper represents the sea floor and the orange paper represents the lava.

   •   Make an irregular cut line that goes diagonally across (from corner to corner) the blue or green paper. This cut line will represent the crack in the Earth's crust on the ocean floor.

   •   Glue down the two parts of blue or green paper in opposite corners of the orange paper.

   •   Use a wide black marker to draw the crack diagonally down the orange paper. Make designs on both parts of the blue or green paper. The designs on the blue or green paper should look similar to each other. Students might wish to make their designs look like sea plants, sand, coral, etc.

   •   Use a fine-point marker to add more details to the designs on the blue or green paper.

Cupcake Geology

Natural forces shape the layers of the Earth's crust. By studying the layers of the Earth, geologists can determine what natural forces created those layers. One way geologists learn about the various layers of the Earth is by taking core samples in a designated region. This allows them to make a reasonable prediction about the land underneath the surface. The following hands-on activity is designed to give students the opportunity to use their critical thinking skills as they learn about taking core samples.

Preparing for the Lesson:

1. Each student will need a napkin or paper towel; five extra thick, clear plastic straws; a cupcake; a plastic knife; and a copy of Be a Cupcake Geologist (page 57).

2. Prepare 25–35 cupcakes, using the following steps:

   - Place foil cups in muffin pans. Be sure to use foil cups so students cannot see through them.

   - Prepare two boxes of white cake mix batter according to package directions.

   - Divide the batter equally into three bowls. Add a few drops of food coloring to create three contrasting colors. You may also wish to add flavor extracts, such as peppermint and orange.

   - Layer each color of batter in the foil cups that you placed in the muffin pans. Be sure each cupcake has three layers. Then bake the cupcakes according to the package.

   - Be sure that you do **NOT** frost the cupcakes or use chocolate chips, sprinkles, etc. These will get stuck in the straws when students try to take their "core samples."

Teaching the Lesson:

1. Discuss the processes that change the Earth over time. Read aloud the passage that is shown below and continues on page 56. Key vocabulary is shown in boldfaced type.

   Two major processes are continually occurring on the Earth—those that wear down the Earth's surface and those that modify and/or build up the Earth's surface. Wearing down processes include **weathering** and **erosion.** Exposed surfaces are continually changed by environmental forces, such as water, wind, temperature changes, pollution, etc. In many cases, large formations of rock are broken down into smaller materials and particles. Erosion, usually in the form of moving water, then transports these materials and particles to different areas where they accumulate as layers of **sediment.**

   Over millions of years, huge layers of sediment often accumulate. The weight of the top layers force the bottom layers to compress into rocks. Over time there are a variety of sediments moved by erosion. As a result, many types of rocks and sedimentary layers are formed. If these layers remain undisturbed, they will be found in horizontal bands with the oldest rocks on the bottom and the youngest rocks on the top. Using the ages of these layers is known as **relative dating**.

Cupcake Geology *(cont.)*

However, changes can and do occur in these layers. Forces within the Earth might push the layers upward and create hills, called **anclines**, or they might make valleys or troughs, called **synclines**. In other situations, forces within the Earth cause huge cracks in the sedimentary layers and allow large blocks of these layers to move vertically or laterally with relation to one another. These cracks are called **faults**. It is along these fault lines that **magma**, which is found deeper within the Earth, moves upward into the layers of sediment. Sometimes the magma reaches the Earth's surface and becomes the **lava** from volcanic eruptions. At other times, the magma cools within the sedimentary layers, forming large masses of **igneous rock**. Therefore, determining the age of rocks is not always as simple as labeling the bottom layer as the oldest and the top layer as the youngest.

2. Tell students to pretend that they are geologists. Explain that they will be taking "core samples" from an imaginary region to discover the geological forces that have occurred over time. Tell students that they will be using cupcakes to represent the region. Point out that students will be allowed to eat the cupcakes only after the activity has been completed. **Note:** Check for food allergies or dietary restrictions.

3. Distribute the cupcakes, napkins, straws, and the copies of Be a Cupcake Geologist (page 57). Ask students to examine the tops of the cupcakes. Have them make predictions about what cross-sections of their cupcakes will look like. Tell students to record their predictions.

4. Demonstrate how to take "core samples" by pushing the straws into the middle of a cupcake in the positions shown below. Then pull out each straw by placing your thumb over the top of the straw and gently pulling it. Point out that the "core samples" are inside the straws.

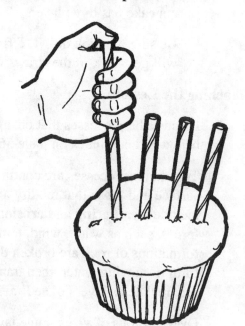

5. You may wish to guide students through the directions and questions for Be a Cupcake Geologist (page 57) or ask students to do the activity independently.

6. Before students cut open their cupcakes, be sure they make new predictions about the cross-sections based on their "core samples."

7. Allow students to cut their cupcakes in halves. Have them compare their predictions to the actual layers within the cupcakes.

8. Invite students to eat their cupcakes as you discuss the following questions. You may wish to have students use the backs of their papers to write responses to some of these questions. How is taking core samples better than just looking at the surface to predict what the layers of the Earth are like? Who might take core samples as part of their jobs? What are the limitations of using core samples as a means to predict what the layers under the Earth's surface are like? What types of geological processes might have taken place in your imaginary region to cause the layers to appear as they did?

Be a Cupcake Geologist

1. Inspect the top of your cupcake. Be sure you do not poke or peel it! Draw a cross-section to show what you think the layers inside the cupcake look like.

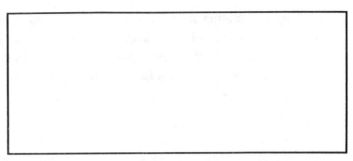

2. Use your straws to take five "core samples" from the middle of your cupcake as shown below. Color the layers as they appear in your straws.

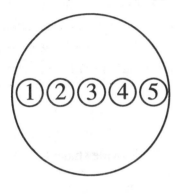   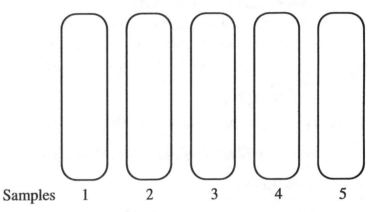

Samples   1   2   3   4   5

3. What new information did you learn from your "core samples"? _____

_____

4. Now based on your five "core samples," draw a cross-section of what you think your cupcake looks like.

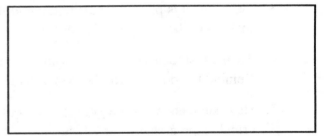

5. Use the plastic knife to cut your cupcake in half. Compare your last prediction to the actual layers inside. Now draw what the layers really look like.

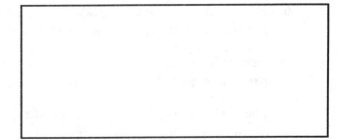

6. Were you surprised by any of your findings? Why?_____

_____

An Edible Model of the Earth

Looking at the innermost parts of the Earth may give us some clues about its beginning. Based on the theory of plate tectonics, we know that the crust is riding on a layer that consists of rocks that have melted and cooled along with molten rock called magma. This layer is called the mantle. But what is at the center, or core, of the Earth? Have students create an edible model to learn about the different layers of the Earth.

Preparing for the Lesson:

Note: Check for food allergies and dietary restrictions.

1. Have students work with a partner to create the models. You will need a measuring cup, a small rubber spatula, and a large sharp knife. The supplies shown below will make 1 model. Multiply each amount by the number of models you plan to have your students make.

    1 large round nut, such as a macadamia or hazelnut; ¼ cup (63 mL) smooth peanut butter, refrigerated to make firm; ¼ cup (63 mL) cheese spread; 2 graham crackers; 1 reclosable plastic bag

2. Provide permanent markers and plastic knives.

3. Reproduce Examining Your Edible Model (page 59) for students. Provide students with world maps.

Teaching the Lesson:

1. Review kitchen safety rules. Then have students wash their hands and pick partners. Explain each step in the process for how to make the model. Demonstrate the steps.

2. Distribute the supplies to the pairs of students.

3. Have students place the nuts in the middle of the peanut butter and roll into a ball. Tell them to make sure the nut is evenly covered.

4. Then tell students to use the plastic knives to cover the peanut butter with the cheese spread. Remind them to be sure the peanut butter is evenly covered.

5. Have students place the graham crackers in reclosable plastic bags. Tell students to carefully crumble the graham crackers until they are in small pieces.

6. Have students place their models in the bags with the graham cracker crumbs. Tell students to roll the models around in the crumbs until they are covered.

7. Ask students to seal the bags. Then tell them to write their names on the bags, using the permanent marker. Freeze the models overnight.

8. The next day, use the large, sharp knife to cut open the models. Return the models to the pairs of students. Then distribute Examining Your Edible Model (page 59) and the world maps. Have students complete the activity on page 59 and discuss their answers to the questions.

9. As an extension to this activity, you may wish to have students draw and label diagrams of the Earth's layers or create models, using colored clay.

Examining Your Edible Model

Some scientists theorize that Earth formed from a spinning cloud of dust and gasses in space. Gravity pulled the more dense iron and nickel inward to form the inner core. Lighter materials rose to form the outer core and mantle. The lightest materials formed the thin outer crust. If you think the rocks on the surface of Earth are heavy, imagine what the density of the materials in the inner core must be like.

No one has ever drilled a hole that was deep enough to reach past the Earth's crust. However, by studying the way earthquakes send shock waves through the Earth, scientists believe they have found out what lies below the crust. Study the diagram shown below and relate it to your edible model.

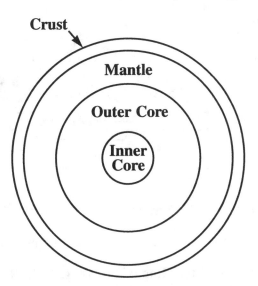

The inner core is about 1,600 miles (2,574 km) in diameter and consists of hot solid iron and nickel. The outer core is about 1,400 miles (2,252 km) thick and consists of hot liquid metals. The mantle is about 1,700 miles (2,735 km) thick and consists of solid rocks that have melted and cooled, in addition to hot liquid rock. The crust is broken down into plates that move on top of the mantle. It is about 20 miles (32 km) thick.

Use the diagram shown above to answer the following questions about your edible model.

1. What does the layer of graham cracker crumbs represent? _____

2. What does the layer of cheese spread represent? _____

3. What does the layer of peanut butter represent? _____

4. What does the nut represent? _____

5. What is the approximate depth of the crust? _____

   Use the world map to locate two cities that would be about the same distance apart as the depth of the Earth's crust. What are the names of those two cities? _____

   _____

6. Other than the vast distance, what else could prevent scientists from reaching the mantle?

   _____

7. What is the distance to the center of the Earth? _____

8. Calculate the diameter. Is this distance more or less than the circumference? _____

   _____

Ring of Fire

From previous lessons, students have learned that the Earth's crust is made up of many plates that are floating on the mantle. Earthquakes are any movement of the Earth's crust or plates. They are caused by sections of the crust slipping past each other. As a result, most earthquakes and volcanic eruptions occur in the same area, along the boundaries between plates. The following map activity gives students the opportunity to visualize the boundaries of the continental plates. You may wish to assign this activity for homework and then follow it up with an in-class discussion.

Preparing for the Lesson:

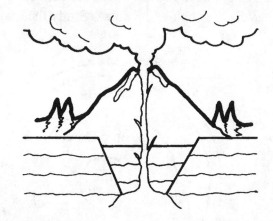

1. Reproduce the Ring of Fire Map (page 62) and Locating the Ring of Fire (page 61) for students.

2. Make an overhead transparency of the Ring of Fire Map (page 62) to show students how to locate points on the map using latitude and longitude.

Teaching the Lesson:

1. Discuss the definition of an earthquake and a volcano with students.

2. Ask students to share experiences they have had with earthquakes or volcanic eruptions.

3. Distribute the Ring of Fire Map (page 62) and Locating the Ring of Fire (page 61). Review the difference between latitude and longitude.

4. Using the overhead transparency of the Ring of Fire Map (page 62), model for students how to locate some of the points on the map.

5. Assign the maps as homework or allow time for students to complete them in class.

6. Discuss students' findings. You may wish to ask the following questions to help guide the discussion: Why do you think the term *Ring of Fire* is used? Where would you expect future earthquakes and volcanoes to occur? Where do you think the safest places would be to avoid the possibility of earthquakes and volcanoes? What can people do to protect themselves from earthquakes and/or volcanoes?

7. You may wish to have students bring in other sources of information related to earthquakes and volcanic activity. *Earthquake* by Seymour Simon (Morrow, 1991) is an excellent resource.

8. If you live close to an Imax or Omnimax Theater, you might consider going on a field trip to see the movie *Ring of Fire*.

9. Extend this activity by having students write a story about being in an earthquake or near a volcanic eruption.

Locating the Ring of Fire

Use a blue crayon to mark the following earthquake locations on the map (page 62).

Earthquake	Latitude	Longitude
1	55° S	55° W
2	50° S	75° W
3	25° S	75° W
4	10° S	105° E
5	5° S	150° E
6	0°	80° W
7	15° N	105° W
8	15° N	100° E
9	20° N	75° W
10	20° N	60° E
11	30° N	60° E
12	30° N	115° W
13	35° N	35° E
14	40° N	20° E
15	40° N	0°
16	40° N	145° E
17	45° N	125° W
18	50° N	158° E
19	60° N	135° W
20	60° N	152° W

Use a red crayon to mark the following volcano locations.

Volcano	Latitude	Longitude
1	5° S	105° E
2	5° S	155° E
3	10° S	120° E
4	15° S	60° E
5	0°	75° W
6	17° N	25° W
7	20° N	155° W
8	20° N	105° W
9	30° N	60° E
10	40° N	30° W
11	40° N	30° E
12	40° N	145° E
13	45° N	15° E
14	45° N	120° W
15	55° N	160° E
16	60° N	150° W
17	65° N	15° E

Ring of Fire Map

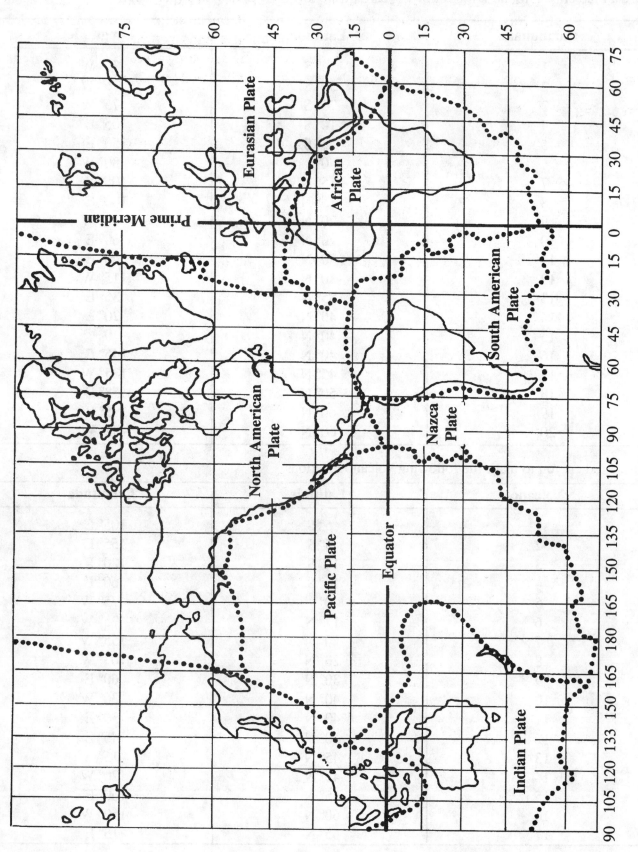

Faults

Cracks in the Earth's crust where blocks of rock have moved are called faults. Most faults lie beneath the surface of the crust, but some, such as the San Andreas Fault, can be seen. As two plates collide or slip past each other, blocks of rock along a fault may grind together, causing them to lock. If the plates continue to move, strain builds up along the fault until eventually they slip past each other, causing an earthquake. By creating the following model, students can examine the three major types of faults.

Preparing for the Lesson:

1. Reproduce the Fault Model (page 65) and Examining the Fault Model (pages 66–67) for students and yourself. Be sure to make extra copies of both pages in case students make mistakes.

2. Create a sample Fault Model (page 65) to show students.

3. Make an overhead transparency of the Types of Faults (page 64). You may wish to cut the transparency into three pieces so that you can easily show one type of fault at a time.

4. Gather scissors, markers or crayons, and transparent tape for students to make their models.

Teaching the Lesson:

1. Discuss the definition of a fault. Distribute the materials for making the models and the copies of the Fault Model (page 65) and Examining the Fault Model (pages 66–67).

2. Tell students that their models will show three different types of faults: a normal fault, a thrust fault, and a lateral fault.

3. Help students follow the steps for building their models. Ask them to show you their models before cutting along the fault lines to be sure the models are taped correctly. Show them your sample model so they will understand what their models should look like.

4. After all the models have been made, begin working on Examining the Fault Model (pages 66–67) with the class.

5. Have students use the model to form a normal fault. Ask them to make a diagram of a normal fault. After students have drawn their pictures, display only the normal fault on the Types of Faults (page 64) transparency. Allow students to check their diagrams against the transparency. Then have them complete page 66.

6. Have students follow the same procedure as described in Step 5 for the thrust fault and the lateral fault. Then have them complete page 67.

7. Discuss the students' responses to Examining the Fault Model. Ask students to compare/contrast the different types of faults.

8. As an extension activity, invite students to make other models that show the different types of faults. Display the models in the classroom. You may wish to allow students to earn extra credit for doing this extension activity.

Types of Faults

Normal Fault

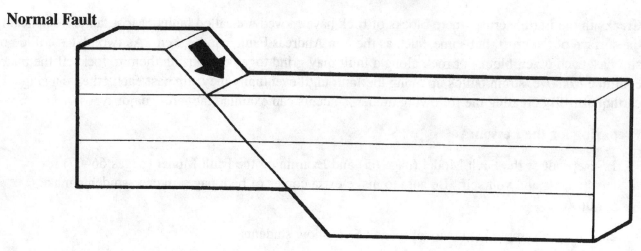

One block of rock slips down along the fault line.

Thrust Fault

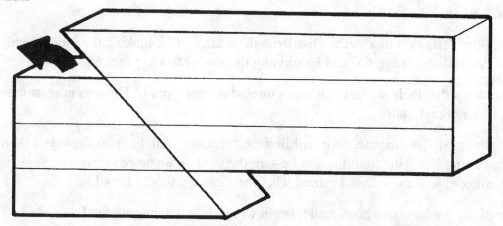

One block of rock "thrusts" upward and over the other block along the fault line.

Lateral Fault

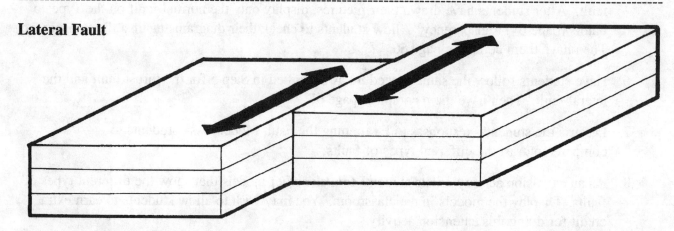

The layers do not move up or down but slide laterally next to each other, twisting the surface.

Fault Model

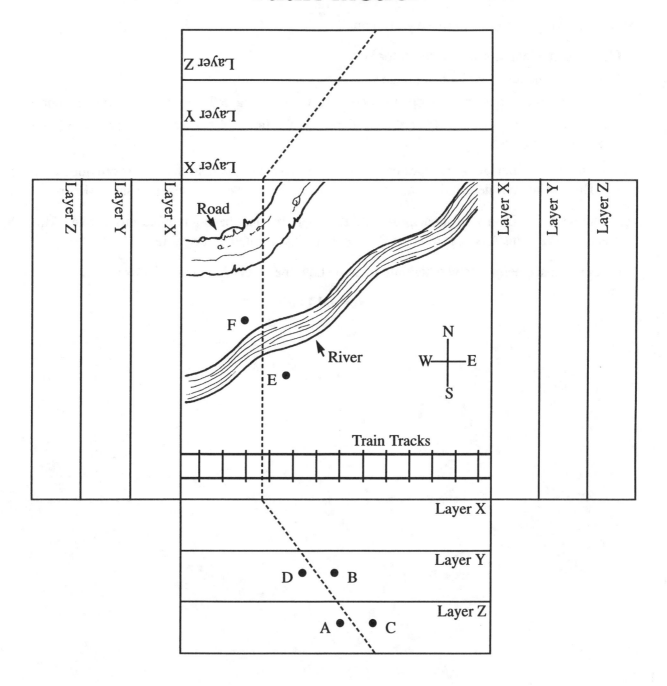

Color Key

Layer X = Purple	River = Blue
Layer Y = Yellow	Road = Brown
Layer Z = Red	Train Tracks = Black
Grass = Green	

Examining the Fault Model

Use the following directions to make your model.

- Color the model according to the color key.
- Cut out the model along its outer edge.
- Fold the flaps down to form an open-ended box. Carefully tape the corners with transparent tape.
- Carefully cut along the dotted line which represents the fault. When you are done cutting, you should end up with two pieces.

Use your model to simulate three types of faults. Draw your diagrams in the spaces provided on pages 66–67. Then write your descriptions and responses to the questions on a separate sheet of paper.

Locate points A and B on your model. Pretend that there has just been a terrible earthquake. Move the two pieces so the point A is next to point B. You have just created a normal fault.

1. In the space below, draw a diagram to show how the layers X, Y, and Z now appear.

Normal Fault

2. Describe how the Earth's surface has changed along this type of fault line.

3. Assume that the river was flowing from north to south before the earthquake. What might happen to the flow of the river now that the layers have moved?

Examining the Fault Model *(cont.)*

Now locate points C and D on your model. Pretend that there has been another tremendous earthquake. Move your model pieces so that point C is next to point D. You have created a thrust fault.

   1.   In the space below, draw a diagram to show how the layers X, Y, and Z now appear.

Thrust Fault

   2.   How has the Earth's surface changed along this type of fault?

   3.   What might happen to the river now?

Pretend that there has been one more earthquake! Locate points E and F on the top of your model. Move your pieces so that E is next to F. You have created a lateral fault.

   1.   In the space below, draw a diagram to show how the Earth's surface has changed.

Lateral Fault

   2.   Describe how layers X, Y, and Z have changed.

Create a Seismograph

Earthquake waves can be recorded by instruments called seismographs. These instruments help scientists measure the strength of earthquakes, using a special scale called the Richter scale. The strength is stated as a number between 1 and 10. The higher the number, the more powerful the earthquake. An earthquake that registers a two on the Richter scale is ten times stronger than an earthquake that registers a one. A three on the Richter scale is 10 times stronger than a two. The strength continues to increase by powers of ten. In this activity, you will build a model of a seismograph and then demonstrate how it works. Students will interpret the readings from the seismograph to determine the relative strengths of some imaginary earthquakes.

Preparing for the Lesson:

1   To build the seismograph model you will need: one paint can with a handle (should be full of paint or sand), 4-8' (1.2 m -2.4 m) of strong rope to hold the can, one broomstick without the broom, masking tape, and a marker.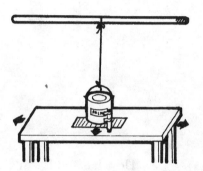

2.   Securely tie the rope onto the handle of the can. Use the masking tape to attach the marker to the can. Make sure the tip of the marker sticks out from below the bottom of the can by at least 2" (5 cm).

3.   Reproduce the Richter Scale Recording Sheet (page 69) so you will have at least five copies for your demonstration.

Teaching the Lesson:

1.   Discuss with students the uses of a seismograph and what the Richter scale is. Explain that you will be doing a demonstration to give students a rough idea of how a seismograph works during an earthquake.

2.   Place a copy of the Richter Scale Recording Sheet (page 69) on a desk.

3.   Have two tall students hold the broomstick and stand very still on their shoulders as if the class were going to play Limbo. Have them step up to the desk so that the broomstick is over the top of the desk.

4.   Tie the rope over the broomstick so that it suspends the paint can over the desk. Be sure the tip of the marker barely touches the Richter Scale Recording Sheet at the word start. Ask a student to hold the paint can still until you are ready to begin.

5.   Then allow two additional students to move the desk back and forth horizontally under the marker while you slowly pull the paper out in a motion that is perpendicular to the desk. This will cause the marker to move across the Richter Scale Recording Sheet as it records the movement of the desk.

6.   Show the paper to the class and ask a volunteer to determine the strength of the earthquake. Repeat the demonstration as many times as desired. Have students who are moving the table try to vary the intensity. Then ask students to compare the data from the different earthquakes.

Richter Scale Recording Sheet

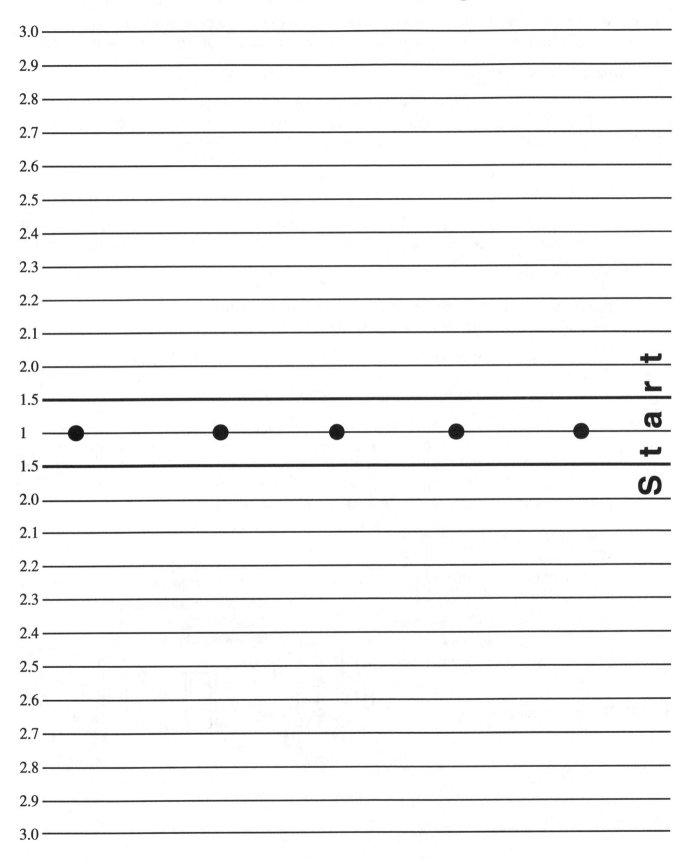

Earthquake Art

During an earthquake, the Earth shakes so violently that images may appear distorted. In this activity, students will use their creative ability to distort magazine pictures as if an earthquake is taking place.

Preparing for the Lesson:

1. Students will need large magazine pictures of single objects, such as a car, banana, or house. You may wish to tear out pictures from which students may choose or assign this task for homework rather than using class time to have students look through magazines.

2. Gather 12" x 18" (30 cm x 46 cm) pieces of construction paper that are a variety of colors, glue, scissors, and a paper cutter.

3. Make a sample, similar to the one shown at the bottom of the page, for students to examine. Be sure the color of the construction paper background contrasts with the color of the picture.

Teaching the Lesson:

1. Explain to students that they are going to create distorted picture images as if the object shown in the picture was being viewed during an earthquake.

2. Display the sample. Point out that the color of the construction paper background contrasts with the color of the picture. Allow each student to select a magazine picture and a piece of 12" x 18" (30 cm x 46 cm) construction paper for the background.

3. Distribute the scissors and glue. First, have students cut out their objects. Then have them plan how they are going to distort their pictures. Finally, have them cut their pictures according to their plans. Tell students to place the pieces of the pictures on the construction paper as they are cut. Explain that this will help keep the pieces in the correct order. Warn students that it is very difficult to reassemble the picture if they put the pieces in a pile.

4. After students have finished cutting and laying out their pictures, have them begin gluing one piece at a time. Allow the glue to dry.

5. Use a paper cutter to trim the edges of the pieces of construction paper so that the pictures are evenly framed.

6. Display the pictures on a bulletin board or on the wall.

Create Volcanic Eruptions

Students are fascinated by volcanoes and will enjoy studying them. The following demonstrations are good visual representations of why a volcano erupts and what happens during an eruption.

Preparing for the Lesson:

1. To demonstrate why a volcano erupts (page 71), you will need a large tube of toothpaste (any brand). Cover the table with butcher paper, newspaper, or a sheet of plastic for easy cleanup.

2. To demonstrate a volcanic eruption that occurs on land (page 72), you will need the following supplies: a plastic tub or pan, a small plastic bottle or beaker, vinegar mixed with red food coloring, baking soda, and a roll of toilet paper.

3. To demonstrate a volcanic eruption that occurs under the ocean floor (page 72), you will need the following supplies: a small bottle that has a narrow neck, large glass jar, paintbrush or stirrer, hot water mixed with red food coloring, cold water, string, and scissors.

4. Make an overhead transparency of the Volcano Diagrams (page 73).

Teaching the Lesson:

1. Begin with the tube of toothpaste. Unscrew the cap until it is just about ready to come off. Have a student hold the tube over the covered table and squeeze it from the end. Allow the cap to come off and the toothpaste to shoot up into the air. Ask students why the toothpaste reacted the way it did. Lead students to conclude that the toothpaste was under pressure.

    Then display the cross section of a volcano at the top of the Volcano Diagrams transparency (page 73). Explain that a volcano acts something like the tube of toothpaste. A volcano begins many miles (kilometers) below the Earth's crust. In certain places, extreme heat causes the rock located under the surface to melt. The melted pools of rock are called **magma**. Since magma is far below the crust, it bears the pressure of the many rock layers above it. Some regions of the Earth's crust are weak or cracked. If magma pushes up through cracks in the crust, it may reach the surface and spurt out in the same way that the toothpaste came out of the tube. When magma reaches the Earth's surface, it is called **lava**. Sometimes the pressure is so great that ash and rock are also blown from the volcano. This is what happened in 1980 when Mount St. Helens erupted in Washington state.

    Display the types of volcanoes shown on the Volcano Diagrams (page 73) transparency. Explain that a volcano can form in any place where there is a crack in the Earth's crust. However, the most common area for volcanoes to erupt is along plate boundaries where several kinds of movements can take place. Different types of volcanoes can be formed, depending on the plate movements. Two plates can spread apart at their boundaries, allowing volcanic activity to take place. This type of volcanic activity is common under the ocean floor. However, it usually does not produce mountain-like volcanoes, so it frequently goes undetected.

Create Volcanic Eruptions *(cont.)*

Volcanic activity can also occur if two plates collide. If two ocean plates collide with each other, one may sink under the other, forcing the melted rock to the surface. This creates **island volcanoes**. Chains of volcanic islands are formed this way. Examples include the islands of Indonesia, Japan, and Alaska.

If a continent plate collides with an ocean plate, the ocean plate will sink under the continent plate, causing magma to be pushed to the surface. This type of volcano is found along the coastline of a continent. Examples of **continent volcanoes** include Mount St. Helens and the chain of volcanoes and volcanic mountains along the west coast of North and South America.

A third type of volcano occurs in the middle of a plate where a chamber of magma has formed. Slowly, a volcano builds as magma moves toward the surface. These volcanoes are called **hot spot volcanoes**. The Hawaiian Islands were formed in this way.

2. Demonstrate how a volcano on land erupts by building a model. You may wish to wear an old shirt or apron to keep your clothes clean while doing this activity. Set a roll of toilet paper in the middle of the pan with the beaker inside. Place at least 4 tablespoons of baking soda into the beaker. Then pour in about 1–2 cups of vinegar mixed with food coloring. Once the initial foaming is over, inspect the toilet paper by cutting it apart down the length of the tube.

The layers of toilet paper represent the many layers of lava flow over geological time. The layers that are not wet would represent old layers formed during previous eruptions, the wet layers would represent newly created earth. This is one way that volcanoes grow over time.

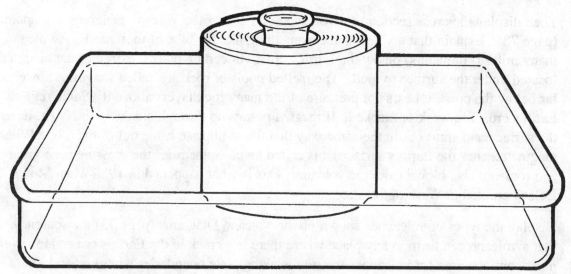

3. Now demonstrate how a volcano under the ocean floor erupts. Begin by cutting two long pieces of string. Securely tie one end of each string around the narrow neck of the small bottle. You should be able to lift the bottle by using the two pieces of string. Prepare the large jar by filling it halfway with very cold water. Pour very hot water into the small bottle until it is full. Add some drops of food coloring and mix with a paintbrush or stirrer. Continue adding food coloring until the water is bright red. Use the strings to carefully lower the small bottle in the large jar of cold water. Students should observe the hot water rising in the cold water. Explain that this looks like the smoke from an underwater volcanic eruption.

Volcano Diagrams

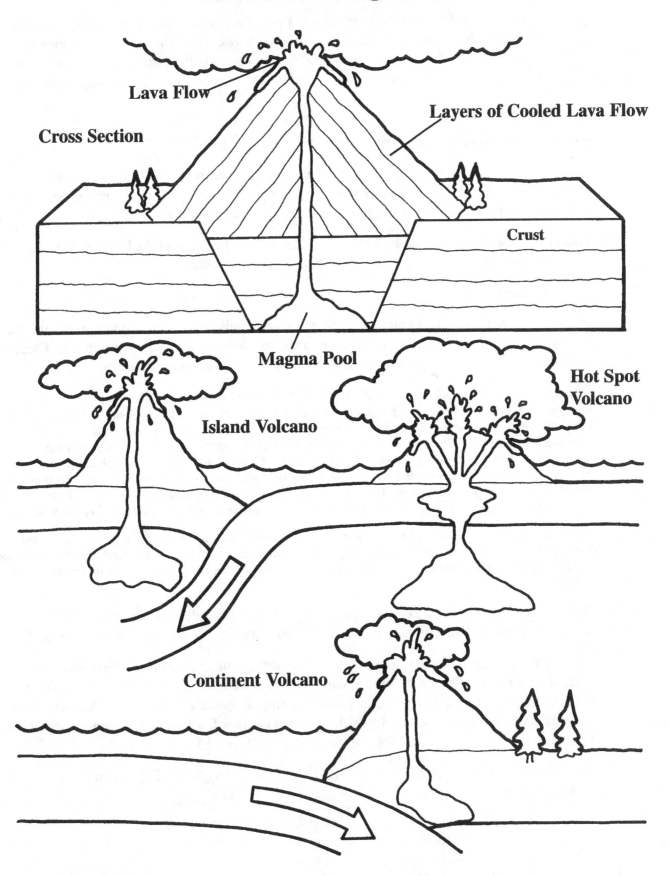

Lava Flow

Layers of Cooled Lava Flow

Cross Section

Crust

Magma Pool

Island Volcano

Hot Spot Volcano

Continent Volcano

Testing Lava Viscosity

Viscosity is a liquid's internal friction, or resistance to flow. Liquids that are easy to pour have low viscosities, whereas liquids that are difficult to pour have high viscosities. For example, honey is harder to pour than water so it has a higher viscosity. Scientists study the viscosity of lava in order to predict the type of volcano that will form and to determine the possible danger to nearby communities.

Preparing for the Lesson:

1. Reproduce the Viscosity Data Sheet (page 75) for students.

2. Gather four clear household liquids with a variety of thicknesses for your demonstration. Liquids might include cooking oil, vinegar, liquid hand soap, Karo Syrup, rubbing alcohol, or baby oil. Gather a stop watch and four marbles to conduct the demonstration.

3. Gather four identical tall clear beakers or graduated cylinders. Label the beakers A, B, C, and D. Make sure there is an equal amount of liquid in each beaker.

Teaching the Lesson:

1. Ask students to pretend that you have collected lava samples from four different volcanic sites around the world. As a class you are going to test the samples to rate their viscosity. Then, use the following passage to explain viscosity and why it is important to scientists.

   Viscosity is a liquid's internal friction. Water is a liquid that flows freely and has a low viscosity. However, both honey and maple syrup are rather thick and flow slowly. Therefore, they have high viscosities. All liquids are either thick or thin, viscous or nonviscous. The same is true for lava. The amount of silica found in lava determines its viscosity. The more silica lava contains, the thicker or more viscous it is. The thicker the lava, the slower it will flow. The viscosity of lava as it erupts form the Earth can affect the type of volcanoes that form. For example, the lava from Mount St. Helens has more silica and is thicker than some other volcanoes. Its lava flows slowly, creating a steep-sided volcano. However, the lava found in the Hawaiian Islands has less silica and is thinner than the lava at Mount St. Helens. As a result, the lava in Hawaii moves quickly, creating flat volcanoes.

   The viscosity of the lava can help scientists determine how dangerous an active volcano might be. A volcano that has swiftly flowing lava will quickly destroy surrounding communities without allowing much time for evacuation. A volcano that has slowly flowing lava is also dangerous. However, there may be more time for communities to evacuate.

2. Assign one student as the timer and another student as the marble dropper. Place the four beakers in plain view of everyone in the class. Distribute the Viscosity Data Sheet (page 75).

3. Starting with beaker A, have students describe what the sample looks like. Next, have the student drop the marble into the beaker while the other student times how long it takes to reach the bottom. Have the class record the viscosity rating in seconds on their data sheet and then determine whether it has more or less silica. Based on their findings, ask students to draw the kind of volcano that would probably be formed by this type of lava.

4. Continue these procedures with beakers B, C, and D. Discuss the findings upon completing the demonstration.

Viscosity Data Sheet

SAMPLE A	SAMPLE B

SAMPLE A

Describe the lava sample.

_____

Viscosity rating in _____ seconds.

Circle the amount of silica in this lava.

More Silica   Less Silica

Draw an illustration of the kind of volcano that might have this type of lava.

SAMPLE B

Describe the lava sample.

_____

Viscosity rating in _____ seconds.

Circle the amount of silica in this lava.

More Silica   Less Silica

Draw an illustration of the kind of volcano that might have this type of lava.

SAMPLE C

Describe the lava sample.

_____

Viscosity rating in _____ seconds.

Circle the amount of silica in this lava.

More Silica   Less Silica

Draw an illustration of the kind of volcano that might have this type of lava.

SAMPLE D

Describe the lava sample.

_____

Viscosity rating in _____ seconds.

Circle the amount of silica in this lava.

More Silica   Less Silica

Draw an illustration of the kind of volcano that might have this type of lava.

Ancient Legends About Volcanoes

Many cultures around the world live near active volcanoes. The ancient people of these regions told myths and legends about the volcanoes. In this activity, students will read or listen to two myths about volcanoes. Then they will write their own myths to share with the class.

Preparing for the Lesson:

1. Reproduce the stories Mount St. Helens (page 77), The Goddess Pele (page 78), and the Story Plot Outline (page 79) for students.

2. You may also wish to reproduce or make an overhead transparency of The Writing Process (page 13) and the Editing Checklist (page 14).

3. Make an overhead transparency of the Story Plot Outline (page 79).

4. Gather writing and illustrating materials. Decide how you plan to bind the books (construction paper and staples, shape book, binding machine, poster board tied with yarn, typed on the computer, etc.), and gather the necessary materials.

Teaching the Lesson:

1. Read the following myths about volcanoes: Mount St. Helens (page 77) and The Goddess Pele (page 78). Have students discuss or write answers to the questions at the end of the stories.

2. Discuss the elements found in these myths, such as the personification of the volcanoes as gods or goddesses and the explanation of a natural phenomenon.

3. Review The Writing Process (page 13) and the Editing Checklist (page 14).

4. Display the transparency of the Story Plot Outline (page 79). Discuss the different parts of the outline. Ask students to use the two myths to provide examples of the types of information that should go into each part of the outline. You may wish to work with students to completely fill in a copy of the outline, using information from one of the myths.

5. Tell students they will be writing their own myths to explain why volcanoes erupt.

6. Distribute the copies of the Story Plot Outline (page 79), and have students use this format to prewrite their stories.

7. Have students continue to follow the steps in the writing process. Ask them to draw illustrations and bind the books in a way that you describe. Then invite students to share their myths with students in your class or other classes.

8. As an extension to this writing activity, have students retell their stories to the class as if they were ancient storytellers sitting around the fire at a special ceremony.

Mount St. Helens

A myth from the Puyallup Indians of the Northwest

Long, long ago a terrible landslide of rocks came crashing down the hill and roared into the Columbia River near Cascade Locks. The rocks piled up and eventually created a natural bridge which came to be called Tamanawas Bridge, or "Bridge of the Gods." The bridge formed a great arch, and in the center of the arch was fire. This fire was the only fire that burned throughout the world, and so it was sacred to the people. They came from near and far to get the sacred embers.

It was believed that a wrinkled old woman, Loowitlatka, lived in the center of the arch, tending the great fire. Loowit, or "Lady of the Fire" as she was called, was diligent about her task and kind to all of the people who came to gather her fire. One day Loowit was noticed by the great chief, Tyee Sahale, for her hard work and gentle nature. He decided to give her the gift of eternal life. However, when Loowit received the gift she sadly wept.

Sahale heard Loowit crying and beckoned her to tell him of her woes. Loowit explained that she did not want to live throughout eternity as an old and wrinkled woman. Sahale told her that he could not take back his gift, but he could grant her one wish. Loowit wished to be young and beautiful again. So Sahale granted her wish, and the fame of her beauty spread throughout the lands.

One day the chief's son Wyeast came to visit the beautiful Loowit at her arch. Just as he arrived, his brother, Klickitat at came thundering down from the north. As the two young men gazed upon the beautiful Loowit, they both fell in love with her. They begged Loowit to choose one of them as her husband. Loowit thought long and hard, but could not choose. Klickitat and Wyeast began to quarrel, and then they began to fight. Each believed he was more worthy of Loowit's love than the other. As they fought, villages and whole forests disappeared in flames of anger.

The great chief Sahale was appalled to see his sons fighting. Seething with disappointment and fury, he struck Tamanawas Bridge, allowing it to fall into the river. He then turned his anger on his sons and Loowit. Where each young person once stood, the chief raised a mighty mountain. Loowit became the beautiful Mount St. Helens with its symmetrical cone of dazzling white snow. Wyeast was replaced by Mount Hood which lifts its head in eternal pride. Klickitat, for all his rough ways, had a tender heart. So in his place stands Mount Adams which bends Klickitat's head in sorrow as he weeps to see the beautiful maiden Loowit forever wrapped in a blanket of snow.

Questions:

1   What lesson do you think can be learned from this myth?

2. In addition to teaching a lesson, why do you think the Puyallup Indians told this myth?

3. Why do you think the great chief Sahale changed Loowit and his sons into mountains?

The Goddess Pele

Once, in a faraway land, there lived two sisters. The sisters were as different as could be. Pele was the goddess of fire, while her powerful sister, Namaka, was the goddess of the sea. It seemed that the two sisters were bound to quarrel from the time they were born. Eventually Pele could take the fighting no more, and she left to find a new home.

Soon she came to the island of Niihau and decided to make a home there for herself. She took her great shovel and dug a deep pit in the mountaintop. She went farther and farther until she reached the mountain's fiery core. Soon Pele was content with her volcanic cone and crater, so she relaxed by the hot fire. However, Pele did not realize that her sister had followed her. Suddenly Namaka summoned up the waters from the sea and with one mighty splash she destroyed Pele's beautiful, fiery home.

Pele was very angry with her sister, but she still did not want to have any more fights. As a result, she fled to the island of Kauai. There she used her shovel to dig another deep, fiery pit. However, Namaka tracked down Pele once again and called upon the forces of the sea to put out the fire in her sister's home. Frantically, Pele ran away again, this time to Oahu. There she dug a new home in the Diamond Head Cone, thinking she could finally escape from Namaka. Yet, once again Pele's sister followed and sent the waters flowing over her fiery home to destroy it. Fleeing angrily, Pele tried making a home on the island of Molokai and then on Maui, but still to no avail. Each time her sister followed and washed out her new home.

Pele could take this abuse no longer. She decided all that was left for her to do was to fight her sister. So Pele and Namaka fought bitterly for several days. Pele walked away with terrible injuries when at last the confrontation was over. She left some of her bones on a hill in Hana while her spirit fled to the big island of Hawaii. Namaka thought she had finally won over her stubborn sister. Yet, Pele refused to give up her fire-making. On Hawaii, Pele dug a deep, deep pit in the center of Kilauea. She was determined to make it her home. To this day the light still burns from Pele's house, and the island of Hawaii continues to grow as a result. No one knows for sure if the sea goddess, Namaka, will ever catch up with Pele again.

Questions:

1. What lesson do you think can be learned from this myth?

2. In addition to teaching a lesson, why do you think this myth was told?

3. Do you believe that Namaka will ever catch up with Pele again? Explain your answer.

Story Plot Outline

I. **Introduction**

    A. Character descriptions _____

    _____

    _____

    B. Setting descriptions _____

    _____

    _____

    C. Problems or conflicts to be resolved by the end _____

    _____

    _____

II. **Plot**—Sequence of Events

    A. Obstacales/scences leading to the climax

       1. _____

       _____

       2. _____

       _____

       3. _____

       _____

    B. Climax—the scene where the problem is solved—peak of excitement

    _____

    _____

    _____

    _____

III. Conclusion/resolution _____

    _____

    _____

    _____

Create Folded Mountains

There are three ways in which plates of the Earth's crust can interact. First, they can slide past each other laterally like the Pacific and North American plates. Second, they can move away from each other as in the sea-floor spreading of the Nazca and Pacific plates. Third, they can collide like the African and Eurasian plates. In this experiment, students will have the opportunity to see what happens when two plates collide and folded mountains are formed.

Preparing for the Lesson:

1. You will need 1 foot (0.3 m) of aluminum foil for each student with a "plate boundary" drawn down the middle, using permanent marker.

2. Reproduce Understanding Mountains (page 81) for students.

Teaching the Lesson:

1. Distribute the copies of Understanding Mountains (page 81), and review the different types of mountains, using the following passage. Ask students to fill in the information as you read aloud. Key words and phrases have been italicized for your convenience.

   Huge mountain ranges can be found all over the Earth. Have you ever stopped to wonder how they were formed millions and even billions of years ago? There are three main types of mountains, based on the way they were formed. One type of mountain is created when magma is forced up under the Earth's crust. Rather than breaking through the surface to form a volcano, the magma pushes the crust up to form a mountain with a *rounded top and a wide base*. The magma eventually hardens under the crust to form a **dome mountain.** Volcanic rock is often harder than other types of rock. Therefore, it may last long after the top layers of a dome mountain have weathered away. Stone Mountain in Georgia is an example of a dome mountain.

   Fault-block mountains are formed along faults in the Earth's crust. These mountains are created when *blocks of crust on one side of the fault move up while blocks of crust on the other side move down*. Scientists are not sure what forces the blocks to move up or down. Earthquakes are one possible explanation. The Tetons of western North America are fault-block mountains.

   The most common type of mountains is the kind that is formed when plates of crust collide. Sometimes the plates may be continent plates. When *two plates* carrying continents *collide, the crust of each plate folds, forcing the crust higher and higher* to make **folded mountains**. The Himalayas were formed when the plate carrying India collided with the plate carrying Asia. Folded mountains can also be formed when an ocean plate sinks beneath a continent plate, pushing the crust up.

2. Distribute the foil. Tell students the line represents a plate boundary. First, have students predict what they think will happen if they make the two plates collide. Then, have them put their hands on each side of the line and push together to represent the collision of the two plates.

3. Have students record their findings.

Understanding Mountains

1. Label and describe each mountain diagram based on the information given by your teacher.

_____

_____

_____

_____

_____

_____

_____

_____

_____

_____

_____

_____

2. Name an example of a dome mountain. _____

_____

3. Name an example of fault-block mountains. _____

_____

4. Name an example of folded mountains. _____

_____

5. Predict what will happen to the crust (foil) if the two plates collide. _____

_____

6. What happened to the crust (foil) when the two plates collided? _____

_____

7. Why do you think the mountains created by the collision of two plates are called folded mountains?

_____

Mountains Shaped by Water

Mountain ranges change gradually over the years. Much of this change is due to weathering and erosion by wind and water. Because of this weathering, older mountain ranges are lower and have more rounded tops than younger ranges. In this experiment, you will investigate the effects of water on mountains.

1. Fill a container, such as a juice can, with water and allow it to freeze overnight or until it is frozen solid.

2. Remove the block of ice from the container and place it on a 9" x 12" (23 cm x 30 cm) tray. Pretend that this is a newly formed mountain.

3. Draw a picture of your newly formed mountain.

4. Fill your original container with water.

5. Pour a thin trickle of water over your mountain as if it were raining. Then examine your mountain. Use the space below to write down any changes you observe.

_____

_____

6. Think about what your mountain will look like after millions of years. Draw a picture to show how weathering and erosion will have changed your mountain.

Landscape Art

Landscape art is an excellent way to reinforce students' understanding of how the Earth is made of many layers.

Preparing for the Lesson:

1. You will need some pictures of landscapes with mountains. These could be pictures torn from magazines or famous art prints. Paul Cézanne and Paul Gauguin were two Impressionist artists famous for their layered landscapes.

2. Each student will need the following supplies: a piece of 12" x 18" (30 cm x 45 cm) black construction paper; thick black crayons; tempera paint, slightly diluted with water; thin paintbrush; a plastic cup with water.

3. You may wish to have small groups of students share paint trays. Clean Styrofoam egg cartons make ideal paint trays!

4. Choose paint colors based on the desired effect for your bulletin board. Fill the cups in the tray with the different colors. There should be several empty cups left for mixing colors.

   Suggested color combinations:

   - white, green, and orange—These are earthy colors that are good for the fall or as part of a display with other earth pieces.

   - white, blue, and purple—These make cold, wintry colors.

   - white, green, and yellow—These are bright colors that are good for the spring.

5. Prepare a sample for students to examine while you are teaching the lesson.

6. You may wish to cover the tables or students' desks with butcher paper or sheets of plastic.

Teaching the Lesson:

1. Show several examples of mountain landscapes. Ask students to note the variety of layers. Point out the horizon where the mountains reach the sky. Then call students' attention to the bottom layers which are the foreground, or the part closest to the viewer.

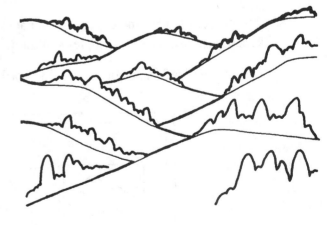

Landscape Art *(cont.)*

2. Distribute the pieces of black construction paper and thick black crayons. Have students divide their landscapes into large layers, or sections, using simple but thick lines. They should have five to eight different sections. Circulate around the classroom and check to make sure students' sections are not too detailed and that they have drawn closed lines. There should not be any trees, animals, etc., in their pictures.

3. Tell students to make their crayon lines about ¼ inch (0.6 cm) thick. Explain that this will help keep the paint in the proper sections.

4. Distribute the paintbrushes and paint trays with paints. Assign small groups of students to share the paint trays.

5. Model how to carefully mix the paint so students do not end up with a tray full of paint that is all the same color. To mix the paint, take a scoop of one color with your paintbrush and place it in an empty cup. Thoroughly rinse out the paintbrush in a cup of water. Then take a scoop of another color and mix it with the first. Warn students not to mix directly in the original cups of paint. Tell them to make sure they make plenty of any color they create so they will have enough to cover an entire section on their landscapes. Explain that sections touching each other should be painted in contrasting colors. You may wish to have volunteers give examples of what contrasting colors are.

6. Ask students to paint each section of their landscapes with a variety of colors. Tell them to paint up to the black crayon lines but not over them. Remind students that the black crayon lines create the bands that separate the different sections.

7. Allow the landscapes to dry.

8. Then carefully trim the edges with a paper cutter. Mount the landscapes on pieces of colored construction paper that complement the paintings. This frames the paintings for students.

9. Display the landscapes on a bulletin board in the classroom or on a wall in the school library.

Earth Vocabulary

Use the clues shown below to complete the puzzle and find the hidden words.

1.__ __ __   __ __ __ __ __   __ __▢__ __ __ __ __ __

2.__ __ __ __ __   __ __ __ __ __ __▢__ __ __ __

         3. __ __ __ __ __▢__ __

            4. __ __▢__ __ __

         5. __ __ __ __ __▢__ __ __ __

              6. ▢__ __ __ __

              7. ▢__ __ __ __ __

           8. __ __▢__ __

            9. __▢__ __ __

         10. __ __ __▢

1. What is it called when hot, liquid rock oozes up through a crack in the crust, causing a new ocean floor to form?

2. What is the name of the theory that states the Earth's crust is made up of several plates?

3. What is an opening in the Earth's crust through which magma, ash, and steam erupt?

4. What is the name for melted rock that forms beneath the Earth's surface?

5. What type of instrument is used to measure and record earthquake waves?

6. What is a crack in the Earth's crust where blocks of rock have moved?

7. What type of mountain forms when two plates of the Earth's crust collide?

8. What theory states the Earth's land masses are moving apart? (Continental _____)

9. What is the name of the outermost layer of the Earth?

10. What type of mountain forms when magma pushes the crust up and then hardens under the Earth's crust?

What are the hidden words in the puzzle?_____

What do those words describe? _____

_____

Inferring Cause and Effect

The statements below tell the **effect,** or what happened. Read the statements. Then use complete sentences to explain the **cause,** or the reason why, that effect occurred. Use the back of this page if you need additional space for your answers.

1.   Many volcanoes are found along the boundaries of the Pacific Ocean. _____

     _____

2.   A mountain range has high, sharp peaks. _____

     _____

3.   The Atlantic Ocean is becoming wider._____

     _____

4.   The same types of rock layers and fossils are found in Antarctica and southern Africa._____

     _____

     _____

5.   Many earthquakes occur along the boundary of northern Africa and southern Asia._____

     _____

     _____

6.   Trees are destroyed by lava and a large area is covered with ash to a depth of 450' (135 m).

     _____

     _____

7.   A range of folded mountains exists along the west coast of South America._____

     _____

     _____

8.   A mountain range is low with rounded tops._____

     _____

9.   A river that once ran straight has a large S-shaped curve along a fault line. _____

     _____

     _____

10. The Hawaiian Islands formed in the middle of a plate._____

     _____

Comprehending the Earth

In the blanks, write **T** if the statement is true and **F** if the statement is false.

_____   1. A seismograph is used to measure the strength of an earthquake.

_____   2. A crack in the Earth's crust where blocks of rock have moved is called a plate.

_____   3. Rock that is below the Earth's surface can never become magma.

_____   4. All islands are formed by volcanic eruptions in the ocean.

_____   5. A volcano can occur any place where there is a deep crack in the Earth's crust.

If a statement shown above is false, use the back of the paper, to rewrite it so that it is true.
Label and describe the following diagrams.

Faults:

1. _____

2. _____

3. _____

Mountains:

4. _____

5. _____

6. _____

Layers of the Earth:

7. _____

8. _____

9. _____

10 _____

Use the back of this page to answer the following questions. Be sure use complete sentences.
1. How do we know the continents are drifting?
2. Why do earthquakes and volcanoes often occur in the same region?
3. What is the Ring of Fire?
4. What are three types of volcanoes, and how are they formed?

Answer Key

Earth Vocabulary (page 85)

1. sea-floor spreading

2. plate tectonics

3. volcano

4. magma

5. seismograph

6. fault

7. folded

8. continental drift

9. crust

10. dome

Ring of Fire; These words describe the area along the boundaries between plates where most earthquakes and volcanic eruptions occur.

Inferring Cause and Effect (page 86)

1. The Pacific Plate could have collided with other plates causing volcanoes to form.

2. The mountain range must have recently been formed either by plates colliding to make folded mountains or blocks of rock moving along a fault line to make fault-block mountains. You can tell that it is a newer mountain range because the peaks have not been weathered or eroded.

3. Cracks in the ocean floor allow lava to seep out causing sea-floor spreading.

4. Scientists believe that at one time the continents must have been connected. However, over time the continents broke apart and drifted away from each other. This is known as the continental drift theory.

5. Based on the theory of plate tectonics, this region must be along plate boundaries which have a great deal of movement.

6. A volcano must have erupted in the region.

7. The South American Plate must have collided with the Pacific Plate causing folded mountains to be formed.

8. This must be an older mountain range because the peaks have been weathered by wind and rain over the years.

9. The river is probably along a lateral fault line, and its course changed during an earthquake.

10. There were pools of magma in the middle of the plate that forced their way to the surface, forming hot spot volcanoes.

Comprehending the Earth (page 87)

True/False:

1. T

2. F

3. F

4. F

5. T

Rewritten Statements:

2. A crack in the Earth's crust where blocks of rock have moved is called a fault.

3. Rock that is below the Earth's surface can become magma due to great amounts of heat and pressure.

4. Some islands are formed by volcanic eruptions in the oceans.

Diagrams:

1. normal fault, one side slips down past the other

2. thrust fault, one side lifts up and over the other

3. lateral fault, both sides shift side to side past each other

4. fault-block mountain, one side moves up while the other moves down along the fault

5. folded mountain, two plates collide causing the crust to lift

6. dome mountain, magma pushes up then hardens below the surface of the crust

7. outer core

8. inner core

9. crust

10. mantle

Questions:

1. Layers of identical rock and fossils were found along the coastlines of continents that are believed to have been joined millions of years ago.

2. Most earthquakes and volcanoes are found along the boundaries of the Earth's plates. They occur when the plates move.

3. Island volcanoes are formed when two ocean plates collide. Continent volcanoes are formed when ocean plates collide with continent plates. Hot spot volcanoes form when pools of magma form under the crust in the middle of a plate and eventually force their way to the surface.

88

Comparing Theories

The question of whether human existence on Earth can be attributed to evolution or creation is a very controversial topic. Every culture around the world has its own philosophy about how humans came into being. Explain that you will be presenting a variety of scientific information, as well as some beliefs from ancient peoples, to provide students with the opportunity to learn about different ideas. Be sure students and their parents clearly understand that you are not trying to tell students what to believe but rather to provide them a variety of information. You may wish to send notes to parents addressing this issue.

Preparing for the Lesson:

1. The following resources provide useful information for teaching this part of the unit:

    Keepers of the Earth, Native American Stories and Environmental Activities for Children
    Michael J. Caduto and Joseph Bruchac; Fulcrum, Inc., 1988.

    National Geographic, "1491 America Before Columbus"
    Vol. 180, No. 4; October, 1991.

    The Children's Picture Prehistory of Early Man
    Anne McCord; Usborne Publishing Ltd., 1974.

    Eyewitness Books, Early Humans
    Dorling Kindersley; Alfred A. Knopf, Inc., 1989.

2. On an overhead transparency or the chalkboard, draw a two-column chart with the headings *Creation* and *Evolution*.

3. Reproduce the Changes for Survival! booklet (pages 90–91) for students.

Teaching the Lesson:

1. Ask students to tell what they already know about the theories of evolution and creation regarding the development of humans. Record students' responses on the chart that you drew.

2. Tell students that all cultures have stories regarding human creation. Explain that in this part of the unit they will compare and contrast some of these stories.

3. Have students cut out, put together, and staple the Changes for Survival! booklets. Invite volunteers to read aloud the information from the booklets. Encourage students to take their booklets home to share with family members. Using the booklet, clarify the theory of evolution.

4. Remind students that there are still many missing pieces of information that scientists have yet to discover. The theory still does not explain where, when, how, or why the human species changed.

    Point out that the theory of evolution does not claim that the monkeys are our direct ancestors but that we have many similar characteristics, putting us in the primate group of animals. Scientists are still debating which species is considered the "first" humans. However, based on actual archaeological finds, we can tell that humans have evolved or changed physically and mentally over time. It is this evolution, or change, in the human form that the rest of the unit will focus. Where, when, how, and why the first humans came to be on Earth will continue to be a mystery.

Changes for Survival!

Homo Sapien Sapien: Modern Human
(10,000 years ago–present day)

After the Ice Age, many people still hunted and gathered their food. However, in the Middle East, the first signs of agriculture emerged. The first communities began to develop, centered around farming and the domestication of animals.

7

Changes for Survival!

Homo Sapien: Neanderthal
(100,000–40,000 years ago)

These humans lived during the Ice Age. They were named after the village in Germany where their remains were found. They were short and stocky with large muscles. Their skulls had thick brow ridges and large teeth. They hunted animals, such as the woolly mammoth, with wooden spears. They lived in caves or built simple huts. They developed language and performed burial ceremonies.

5

Homo Sapien: Cro-Magnon
(40,000–10,000 years ago)

These humans were named after a cave in France where their remains were found. They had the same skull and body structure as modern humans. They lived in caves or huts towards the end of the Ice Age. They made highly sophisticated tools and weapons. They were the first to sew more detailed clothing. They created cave paintings, and they carved small statues and figures that may have been used for religious purposes.

6

Changes for Survival! *(cont.)*

Scientists believe that one of the reasons that some species survive over time is their ability to adapt to their surroundings. Therefore, only the strongest and healthiest species that are better able to adapt will live on to produce new generations. The weaker, less capable species die out since they cannot successfully compete in their surroundings. Like other creatures that live on the Earth, humans have slowly developed and changed over the years to better adapt to the environment. This change over time is called evolution. Scientists say that humans have evolved, or changed over time, to survive. These scientists study fossils of prehistoric humans to determine both the physical and mental changes that have taken place over the last three to five million years.

1

Australopithecus
(5 million–1 million years ago)

These are the earliest relatives to humans. They stood about 47"–67" (11 cm–168 cm) tall and walked upright. They were strong with big muscles and long ape-like arms. Their brains were about half the size of modern human brains. They had large teeth and strong jaws for chewing tough plants. They ate small animals, roots that they dug up, and birds' eggs. They lived together in small groups.

2

Homo Habilis
(2 million–1 million years ago)

These humans had larger brains than their predecessors. As a result, they were more intelligent and skillful. They were the first tool makers. They created tools and weapons from stone, wood, bone, and antlers. They worked together to hunt and gather food for their group. They built simple shelters.

3

Homo Erectus
(1.5 million–250,000 years ago)

These humans were taller and walked upright without stooping. They had larger brains than did previous species. Consequently, they were able to make more sophisticated tools and weapons. They were the first to use fire. Eventually they learned how to make fire and were able to utilize it for hunting, cooking, and surviving the cold. They were hunters and gatherers who followed the herds.

4

Stories About Human Creation

All cultures have their own versions of human creation. This lesson allows students to compare and contrast the elements from various stories about human existence. Students will also make a bulletin board display based on The Navajo Story.

Preparing for the Lesson:

1. Reproduce the stories (pages 94-97) and the dramatization (pages 99-102) for students.

2. You may wish to read the *Old Testament* version of creation. Encourage students to bring to class any other versions that are told in their cultures.

3. Make a chart on the chalkboard or an overhead transparency to compare aspects from each story. The chart should include: The Tewa Story, The Northeast Woodland Story, The Navajo Story, Legend of the Miwok Tribe.

4. Reproduce the outline (page 98) for students. You will need six sheets of white butcher paper, crayons, and scissors.

Teaching the Lesson:

1. Tell students that they will be reading various stories about human creation. Remind them to respect other people's beliefs.

2. Read the stories and dramatization with students. Write important elements on the chart.

3. Discuss the similarities and differences among the stories and dramatization. Topics to compare and contrast include characters, setting, events, problems, complications, and solutions. Discuss the questions at the end of each story (pages 94-97) or have students write their answers on separate pieces of paper. Ask students to perform the dramatization (pages 99-102).

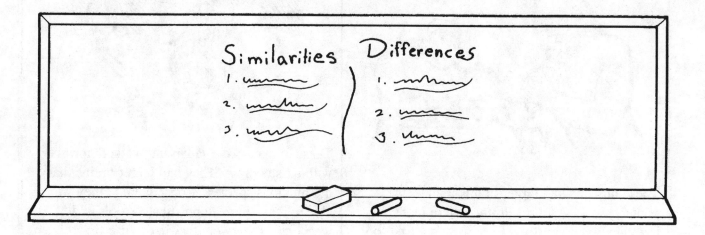

Stories About Human Creation *(cont.)*

5. Follow the directions shown below to have students make the bulletin board display.

  •   Divide the class into six cooperative learning groups.

  •   Distribute an outline for the Navajo Bulletin Board (page 98), a sheet of white butcher paper, markers, crayons, and scissors to each group.

  •   Assign each group one of the main characters from the story. First Man, First Woman, Salt Woman, Coyote, Begochiddy, Fire God.

  •   Using information from the story, have the groups fill out the top portions of their outlines to describe their characters.

  •   Then have students use their imaginations to continue to describe what they think their characters would be like.

  •   After the groups have completed their written descriptions, ask them to use the white butcher paper to draw enlarged versions of their characters.

  •   Have students cut out the pictures and display them on the bulletin board with their descriptions.

  •   Write the name of each character in large letters. Make the title "The Navajo Story of Human Creation" for the bulletin board.

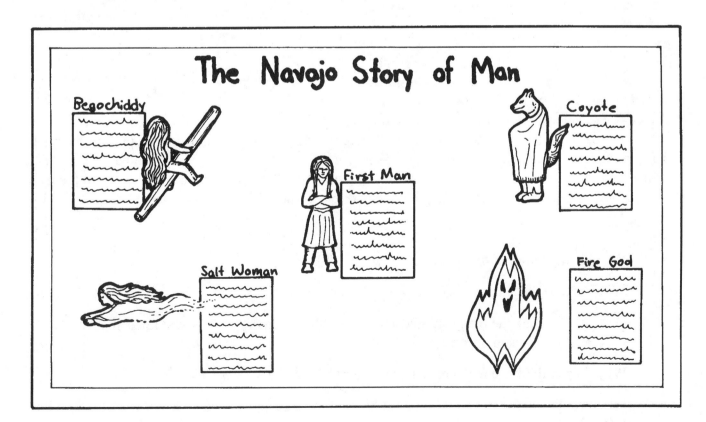

Creation Stories

Many cultures from around the world tell stories about human creation here on Earth. The Makah Indians believed mucus from a weeping mother's nose fell onto a mussel shell and became an infant. The Mississippi Choctaw tell of a great platform mound called Nanih Waiya, or "slanting hill," which they regard as the Great Mother of the tribe. At its center, the Great Spirit created the first Choctaw, and they crawled forth into the light of day. Read the stories on pages 94–97 and the dramatization on pages 99–102 to learn how some different cultures explain human existence on our planet.

The Tewa Story

In a distant time, there was a lake far to the north. Our ancestors came up out of the Earth, and they lived beneath Sandy Place Lake. The world under the lake was like this one but much darker. Spirits, people, and animals lived together. Death was unknown in this place. Deep down in the dark, within the Earth, the first mothers of all the Tewa discussed how humans might emerge onto Earth from the lake. One of the mothers was called Blue Corn Woman Near to Summer. Another mother was called Near to Ice. The two mothers decided to send one human from the underside of the lake to explore the possibilities of living on the land. They did not know what to expect, so it took great courage to send forth this human.

The chosen human was a man, and he traveled to the "above" land with no one by his side. Once on the land, he was met by predatory birds and animals. At first they attacked him, for he was different and they were afraid of him. But the man talked to the animals and birds. He convinced them that he was good. Eventually they came to trust the man and befriended him. Then they gave him gifts of weapons and clothing. The man returned to the place from which he had come. He brought back the weapons and the clothing as gifts for his people. He returned with the
call of the fox in the form of Mountain Lion. Seeing his great triumph, the people under the lake made the man the Hunt Chief. The man then in turn created a Summer Chief (blue corn) and a Winter Chief (white corn) to lead the people during the different parts of the year. The people rejoiced with the man saying, "We have been accepted." They left the dark place under the lake and emerged onto the land.

Questions:

1. What is the setting of this story?

2. Who decided that a human should be sent to live on the land?

3. How do you think the man was able to convince the predatory birds and animals that he was good and meant them no harm?

4. Why do you think the man created a Summer Chief and a Winter Chief?

5. What would you have done if you lived beneath the lake and wanted to know what life was like on the land?

The Northeast Woodland Story

In the spirit world, Tabaldak is known as the great creator, or The Owner. The Owner first created human beings in the spirit world far above the Earth. After he finished, he dusted off his hands. The dust gently fell onto the Earth. Suddenly, the dust manifested itself into a human form known as Gluscabi, the grandfather of all human beings on Earth. Gluscabi sat up from the Earth and said, "Here I am." Because of this, some of the people call Gluscabi by another name which means, "the man who made himself from something."

Now Gluscabi was not as powerful as The Owner, Tabaldak, yet he had the power to change things. Sometimes the changes he created were for the worse. When Gluscabi sat up from the Earth, The Owner was astonished. He asked, "How did it happen that you came to be?"

Gluscabi replied, "Well, it is because I formed myself out of the dust which was left over from the first humans that you made."

"You are very wonderful and clever," The Owner told Gluscabi.

Gluscabi smiled at The Owner. "I am only wonderful because you sprinkled me," he answered.

"I think we should roam around and see the wonders of your new home," said The Owner.

So it came to be that The Owner and Gluscabi roamed the Earth together. They marveled at all the beautiful sights. When they came to a tall mountain, they proceeded to climb to the very top. From there they gazed about, open-eyed with amazement. They saw the lakes, the rivers, and the trees. They saw how all the land lay. They saw the entire Earth.

Then The Owner said, "Behold here how wonderful is my work. By the wish of my mind I created all this existing world, the oceans, rivers, lakes, and land." And he and Gluscabi gazed awhile open-eyed in awe.

Questions:

1. According to this story, how was the first human created on the Earth?

2. Why do some people call Gluscabi "the man who made himself from something"?

3. Why do you think that sometimes the changes created by this human were for the worse?

4. How did The Owner react to Gluscabi's existence?

5. Why did The Owner want Gluscabi to see how wonderful the Earth was?

The Navajo Story

Before the world we know existed, there was a First World far below in the depths of the Earth. In the First World everything was black. The world was consumed by darkness, and in this darkness lived six beings. There was First Man, First Woman, Salt Woman, Fire God, Coyote, and Begochiddy. Begochiddy was both man and woman and had golden hair and blue eyes.

The First World had no mountains or plants, so Begochiddy began to make them. It made four mountains in the four directions. In the center of the First World, Begochiddy decided to form a red mountain. Then it created the ants and other insects, as well as the first plants.

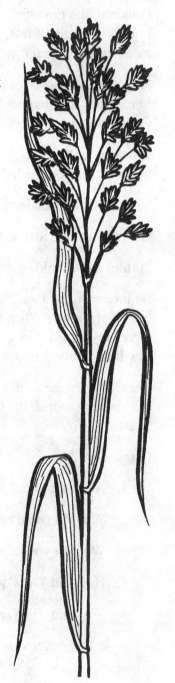

However, things were not right in this First World. Some of the beings were unhappy in this world of darkness. So it was decided that they would all leave the First World. "Gather together the many plants and other things I have created. We must take them with us to our new home," said Begochiddy to First Man.

First Man did as Begochiddy said. Then he and the other beings traveled to the red mountain. Once there, Begochiddy planted a big reed. The big reed began to grow and grow. The First Beings climbed onto it. Up and up it grew, and eventually it broke into the Second World.

Here in the Second World, Begochiddy decided to create even more things. The clouds were formed along with more plants and mountains. The Second World was blue, and other beings, such as the Swallow People and the Cat People, already lived there. For a time, everyone was happy. Yet, eventually things began to go wrong in this world as well. Once more Begochiddy planted a big reed. It grew up higher and higher carrying the Beings to the Third World.

The Third World was light and yellow. Even though there was no sun or moon, the beautiful mountains gave off light. The Beings agreed that this was the most beautiful world they had ever seen. In this world, Begochiddy created flowing rivers and springs, water animals, trees, and birds to please the Beings. Begochiddy then made lightning and all kinds of human beings. In this beautiful Third World everything communicated with one universal language. All things and beings in creation understood one another. Yet, everything was not perfect in this Third World.

Coyote roamed around freely in the Third World. Wherever he went he was curious and getting into mischief. One day Salt Woman went walking by two rivers. When she came to the place where they crossed, she noticed a baby with long black hair. Quickly she went back to tell the others. Coyote, being so curious, decided to go see for himself. When he came to the place where the rivers crossed, he saw the water baby and lifted it out of the water. Then he hid it under his blanket, telling no one what he had done.

The Navajo Story *(cont.)*

Four days passed without any consequence. Yet, on the fifth day there was a great noise. Only Begochiddy knew what it was and knew what was going to happen. Someone had obviously done wrong in this world, and now it was going to be destroyed by a flood. Once again, Begochiddy gathered all of the Beings into a big reed. However, this time was not as easy as before. Suddenly the big reed stopped growing before the Beings could enter the new world. The Spider People and the Ant People tried to get them into the new world, but they failed. Then using his hard head, the Locust pushed his way into the Fourth World. Begochiddy was the first to climb through the hole. There Begochiddy found itself on an island surrounded by water in all directions. Begochiddy went back down the big reed to get the others, and they asked how this world was.

"The new world is good," Begochiddy replied, "yet it is still fresh and has not dried. Someone must try to walk up there. Badger volunteered to go. So she stepped through the hole into the Fourth World. Her feet broke through the surface as she tried to walk, and she became covered with mud.

Begochiddy said, "This will not do. How will we dry our new land?" The winds replied that they would dry the land, and they brought cyclones and whirlwinds and even small dust devils into the Fourth World. Then all the Beings came into the Fourth World. Looking down, Begochiddy could see that the waters in the Third World were still rising.

"Who has angered the water monster?" Begochiddy asked. No one replied, but Coyote gathered his blanket more tightly around himself. Begochiddy commanded Coyote to open his blanket. And so the water baby was revealed. Begochiddy told Coyote to return the child or the Fourth World would be flooded as well. Coyote dropped the baby into the Third World, and the waters slowly receded.

Now Begochiddy was free to place the Fourth World in order. The mountains were put in their places. The sun, moon, and stars were hung in the sky. Then Begochiddy told the people the right way to live, how to give thanks, and how to take care of the plants. Begochiddy then gave the people many different languages and sent them to live throughout the world. It was now in this Fourth World that Changing Woman came to be. She became the greatest friend to the human beings by helping them in many ways. She also gave birth to the Hero Twins who traveled throughout the world, doing great deeds and destroying monsters that threatened the people. So the Fourth World came to be. Yet Begochiddy warned that this world too would be destroyed if the people do not live the right way. And that is what the Navajo say to this day.

Questions:

1. Why did the Beings move from world to world?

2. What lessons did Begochiddy teach the people?

3. Why did Begochiddy warn the people that the Fourth World could also be destroyed?

Navajo Bulletin Board

Use information from the story to describe your character.

Character's Name: _____

Physical Appearance: _____

_____

_____

Character Traits: _____

_____

_____

Things your character does or says in the story: _____

_____

_____

_____

Now use your imagination to further describe what you think your character would be like.

Physical Appearance: _____

_____

_____

Character Traits: _____

_____

_____

Things your character might do in the Fourth World: _____

_____

_____

_____

_____

Legend of the Miwok Tribe
(A Dramatization)

Characters:				
Narrator	**Coyote**	**Owl**	**Beaver**	**Bear**
Mole	**Moose**	**Rabbit**	**Big-Horned Sheep**	**Cougar**

Narrator: Long, long ago before the Earth was formed, before the sun, moon, and stars were hung in the sky, the Great Spirit wandered about the heavens. He pondered how he could finish the work of creation. Meanwhile, the universe remained dark and cold. Then, suddenly in a burst of inspiration, the Great Spirit knew exactly what to do. Snapping his great fingers he set off a spark. Half of the spark shot out into the sky and became our sun to warm and light the Earth. The other half of the spark fell swiftly to his feet and emerged as the Coyote. The Great Spirit gazed at Coyote and told him to complete the task of creation. Being a dutiful creature, Coyote set off to work and did not stop. He created the land and water, the plants and trees, and all the creatures. Then Coyote called together a council of the wisest animals.

Coyote: I have gathered you all here together in this council of the wisest animals to tell you that my labor is almost complete. I have finally reached the last stage in my creation of the world.

Bear: What do you mean? What more could there possibly be to do? Do we not already have everything that we need? Do we not have food to eat and shelter to protect us from the cold?

Owl: Yes, I agree with Bear. What more is there to do? Look around you, Coyote. Do you not marvel at the fine work you have done? There are plenty of mice and snakes in the field.

Mole: Indeed! The Earth is rich for the digging and perfect for finding roots and bugs.

Big Horned Sheep: Yes, Coyote. The mountains soar towards the heavens with a powerful majesty that cannot be matched anywhere in the universe. The rocks are steady underfoot.

Beaver: The rivers and lakes are so pure and clear, perfect for building my home.

Owl: And the skies, Coyote! Look how marvelously you have painted a soft blue background for my gentle wings to caress. Does it get any better than that? Surely your work is complete.

Coyote: All of you speak kind and good words. I am glad you are satisfied because your needs are met. Yet, one task is still left unfinished. We must make a new kind of creature. A creature that is more than just an animal. We must make a human.

Bear, Cougar, Moose, and Mole: A human?

Rabbit, Beaver, Big Horned Sheep, and Owl: A human?

Coyote: Yes, a human.

Legend of the Miwok Tribe *(cont.)*

All: Ah yes, a human!

Coyote: Now you understand. So you see you must give me your ideas since this final creation will affect us all. How shall we create this human? What special qualities shall we give it?

Cougar: I have an excellent idea! I am surprised at you, Coyote. The solution is so obvious and right before your eyes. The human should be an impressive and magnificent creature. Give the human a mighty voice, sharp claws, and fangs. Then cover it in the most splendid fur.

Bear: How ridiculous, Cougar! With a loud voice the human would only scare away the prey it wished to capture. Just the way you do, my friend! No, the human must not rely on claws and fangs. It should have great strength, amazing speed, be versatile, and walk upright or on all four.

Moose: I feel this human ought to have a great big pair of antlers for fighting. I do agree with Bear that the human ought to be fast. So I think sleek, swift legs would be ideal. The human should have fine ears, to catch any sound, and eyes like fire, sharp and piercing.

Big Horned Sheep: Oh heavens no, Moose. Antlers? Hogwash! Antlers would only get caught in the thickets and trees. The human should have protection and something with which to fight. It should have fine, rounded horns to ram through anything that gets in its way.

Beaver: All of this talk of horns and antlers is giving me a headache! You are missing the point. Don't you see? If you ate more trees you'd grow to be wiser and healthier, too. Now let us stop this flow of nonsense. The only thing that a human will really need is a strong, flat, useful tail. How else will it be able to survive and make a home near the river?

Owl: Who, whooo, whooo do you think you are mud-slapper? Tails, horns, fur? Listen, all you creatures, the answer is flapping plainly right in front of you. Wings are the answer, my friends! Finely feathered and fabulously fashioned wings! Have you ever seen anything more beautiful and graceful than a winged creature? Winds would allow this human to touch the sun and the stars, to sway into the darkness of the night and then to strike with silent invisibility.

Mole: Oh no, oh dear me. Wings will not do at all. The human would always be bumping its head on the dome of its earthen home. Dear, dear, I don't feel very good about this at all. The human needs sharp nails for digging and a strong nose for smelling, not wings for flying! Just think, with wings the human might fly too close to the sun and burn its eyes out. It's best to have no eyes at all. Yes, blind is the way the human should be.

Rabbit: No eyes? Mole, are you crazy? Of course the human will need eyes. How else will it be able to see what it is eating? Not only should the human have good eyes, but I agree with Moose and feel it should have sharp ears as well. Nice big ones that really mean business.

Legend of the Miwok Tribe *(cont.)*

Coyote: O.K., O.K., you have all had your say. And I have tried to listen carefully to each of your suggestions. Yet, I must say that I could hardly keep from laughing at such drivel. Listen to you. Each one of you wants to make the human like yourself. Are you so perfect? Why not just call yourself a human? No, no. We must make a totally new kind of creature. Now listen to me. The human must have four legs and five fingers on each leg, not unlike me. It shall not have wings. However, I think we can give it a loud voice like Cougar suggested. But the human need not roar with it at all times. The human must learn to use its voice in a wide variety of ways.

Cougar: What's that you say? No roaring?

Coyote: I do believe Bear was right that the human should move swiftly and walk upright. But I must disappoint you, Beaver. A tail will do no good at all. A tail is only good for getting fleas, and I hate fleas. So the human gets no tail.

Beaver: No tail? No tail you say? Well, well, you just wait Coyote!

Coyote: Moose's eyes and ears are pretty good. They are perhaps better than my own. The human should have good eyes and ears, but just the right size to do the job.

Moose: My eyes and ears are better than yours? That is the only sensible thing you've said so far.

Coyote: Yet, with all of this talk of fur and feathers no one has mentioned the frog.

All: Frogs? What good feature does a frog have to offer?

Rabbit: Yes, what good are frogs? They can't hop as well as me. And they don't have a nice soft fur coat to keep them warm. The thought of their nasty beady frog eyes makes me shiver.

Coyote: Yes, but frogs have no fur, and that is a blessing. Fur is a nuisance, so let's not give the human thick hair or fur. Lets give it thick skin like the frog. The human should also be able to hold things in its paws like the raccoon. But the most important gift we should give the human is a cunning wit and craftiness, the kind that has made me famous. Then it will not need horns or antlers for protection, because it can design weapons for itself.

Bear and Cougar: Coyote, you have gone too far!

Moose and Big-Horned Sheep: No horns? No antlers? What kind of weapons could the human ever make?

Legend of the Miwok Tribe *(cont.)*

Rabbit and Beaver: No sharp teeth or fangs? Unfair! We protest, Coyote!

Mole: And I thought you were wise, Coyote! I won't have any part of this human you're creating.

Owl: Honestly, Coyote! No wings either? I have never been so insulted in all my life! But wait! I have it! Here is a solution we can all live with. Let each of us use clay and make a model of what we think a human should be like. Then we can let the Great Spirit decide which is best.

All: Yes, what do you think of that, Coyote?

Narrator: Coyote said nothing. He just watched as each of the animals left to build their models of the perfect human. Oddly enough, each model resembled the very animal that molded it. Coyote was dismayed, but being the cunning creature that he was, he had a plan. That night, after all of the animals had fallen asleep, Coyote dipped the models into the river thereby ruining them. When morning came, Coyote proudly showed his model to the Great Spirit. When the other animals awoke, they were surprised at what they found!

Cougar: Look, someone has ruined our models! How could such a thing happen?

Owl: Wait everyone. Look there. What is THAT?

Moose and Big-Horned Sheep: We don't know. But it has no antlers or horns!

Bear: It does not have great size or strength.

Beaver: And look, where is its tail? How can it survive without a tail?

Cougar: Look at that creature. It has no fine, rich fur covering its body or claws and sharp fangs to kill its prey. It has a fine voice, this is true, but not nearly as loud as mine.

Owl: How silly it looks, moving about like that. Why, it can't even fly!

Coyote: But, my friends, you miss the point. That is the human. It does not need antlers, horns, or a tail in order to survive. The human has much strength in its body, but the bulk of its muscle is in its mind, heart, and spirit. The human's beautiful voice is able to make many wonderful, as well as frightening sounds. And the human will fly one day because, you see, it can dream of such things. The human has eyes not unlike my own and ears to hear a world of sounds. But the best thing about the human is that it is crafty, smart, and cunning. But come, let us go, for we have other work to do.

Narrator: And so it was that a human was created. And so it is that humans are connected to all of the living things on this Earth.

Looking Back

The next six sections include information about Australopithecus, Homo Habilis, Homo Erectus, Homo Sapien: Neanderthal, Homo Sapien: Cro-Magnon, and Homo Sapien Sapien: Modern Human.

Preparing for the Lesson:

1. Reproduce the Information Chart (pages 104-109) for students. Reproduce each page of the chart as you begin to study a different species, or reproduce all of the pages and have students staple them into folders for use as needed.

2. Reproduce the pages that tell about the different species of early humans for students.

3. Make overhead transparencies of the Information Chart.

4. Make overhead transparencies of the skulls shown for each species so that you can overlay one on top of the other. Have students note the changes.

5. Gather other resources (textbooks, encyclopedias, periodicals) about early humans.

Teaching the Lesson:

1. Distribute the pages that describe the early humans and the Information Chart. Tell students that they will be studying various human species. Ask them to pay close attention to how humans evolved over time to better adapt and compete in their environment.

2. You may wish to choose one of the following reading techniques.

   • **Round Robin Reading**—Have students orally read in groups, taking turns around the table. Work with the class to fill in the Information Chart as they read or after they have finished.

   • **Popcorn Reading**—Read orally as a class allowing students to call on other students. Have students work together or independently to fill in the Information Chart.

   • **Partner Reading**—Have students pair up and read silently or orally to each other. Then they can fill in the Information Chart together. Finally, discuss students' responses that are written on the charts.

   • **Teacher Reading**—Read aloud the information to the class and fill in the chart together.

   • **Silent Reading**—Have students read the information silently and fill in the chart as they read or when they are finished. Then discuss the charts.

3. Show the changes in skull size using overhead transparencies. After showing the last skull (page 154), have students hypothesize what human skulls might look like in a million years if the same pattern continues.

4. As each lesson is taught, compare the features of the new species to the previous one. After completing the last lesson on Homo Sapien Sapien: Modern Human, have students predict information they could write in the chart to describe humans in the next million years.

Information Chart

Australopithecus	
Dates and Place of Existence (When and where did they live?)	
Description of Physical Appearance (What did they look like? What was the average height and weight of a male? of a female?)	
Description of Shelters (What kind of shelters did they use? What materials were used to make the shelters? Were the shelters meant to be easy to move or long lasting?)	
Food (What type of food did they eat? How did they get their food?)	
Description of Daily Life (How did they live? Were they hunters and gatherers or farmers?)	
Tools (What materials were used to make tools? What purposes did the tools serve?)	
Fire (Could they make fires? What did they use to make the fires?)	
Religion and Ceremonies (What kinds of occasions were special? What did they do to worship or celebrate?)	
Development of Language (How did they communicate? Did they have written language?)	
Clothing (What did their clothing look like? What was it made from?)	
Painting and Carving (What kinds of things did they paint or carve? What materials did they use to make the paintings or carvings?)	

Early Humans   *Our Earliest Ancestors*

Information Chart *(cont.)*

Homo Habilis (Handy Man)	
Dates and Place of Existence (When and where did they live?)	
Description of Physical Appearance (What did they look like? What was the average height and weight of a male? of a female?)	
Description of Shelters (What kind of shelters did they use? What materials were used to make the shelters? Were the shelters meant to be easy to move or long-lasting?)	
Food (What type of food did they eat? How did they get their food?)	
Description of Daily Life (How did they live? Were they hunters and gatherers or farmers?)	
Tools (What materials were used to make tools? What purposes did the tools serve?)	
Fire (Could they make fires? What did they use to make the fires?)	
Religion and Ceremonies (What kinds of occasions were special? What did they do to worship or celebrate?)	
Development of Language (How did they communicate? Did they have written language?)	
Clothing (What did their clothing look like? What was it made from?)	
Painting and Carving (What kinds of things did they paint or carve? What materials did they use to make the paintings or carvings?)	

Information Chart *(cont.)*

Homo Erectus (Upright Man)	
Dates and Place of Existence (When and where did they live?)	
Description of Physical Appearance (What did they look like? What was the average height and weight of a male? of a female?)	
Description of Shelters (What kind of shelters did they use? What materials were used to make the shelters? Were the shelters meant to be easy to move or long lasting?)	
Food (What type of food did they eat? How did they get their food?)	
Description of Daily Life (How did they live? Were they hunters and gatherers or farmers?)	
Tools (What materials were used to make tools? What purposes did the tools serve?)	
Fire (Could they make fires? What did they use to make the fires?)	
Religion and Ceremonies (What kinds of occasions were special? What did they do to worship or celebrate?)	
Development of Language (How did they communicate? Did they have written language?)	
Clothing (What did their clothing look like? What was it made from?)	
Painting and Carving (What kinds of things did they paint or carve? What materials did they use to make the paintings or carvings?)	

Information Chart *(cont.)*

Homo Sapien (Wise Man): Neanderthal	
Dates and Place of Existence (When and where did they live?)	
Description of Physical Appearance (What did they look like? What was the average height and weight of a male? of a female?)	
Description of Shelters (What kind of shelters did they use? What materials were used to make the shelters? Were the shelters meant to be easy to move or long lasting?)	
Food (What type of food did they eat? How did they get their food?)	
Description of Daily Life (How did they live? Were they hunters and gatherers or farmers?)	
Tools (What materials were used to make tools? What purposes did the tools serve?)	
Fire (Could they make fires? What did they use to make the fires?)	
Religion and Ceremonies (What kinds of occasions were special? What did they do to worship or celebrate?)	
Development of Language (How did they communicate? Did they have written language?)	
Clothing (What did their clothing look like? What was it made from?)	
Painting and Carving (What kinds of things did they paint or carve? What materials did they use to make the paintings or carvings?)	

Information Chart *(cont.)*

Homo Sapien (Wise Man): Cro-Magnon	
Dates and Place of Existence (When and where did they live?)	
Description of Physical Appearance (What did they look like? What was the average height and weight of a male? of a female?)	
Description of Shelters (What kind of shelters did they use? What materials were used to make the shelters? Were the shelters meant to be easy to move or long lasting?)	
Food (What type of food did they eat? How did they get their food?)	
Description of Daily Life (How did they live? Were they hunters and gatherers or farmers?)	
Tools (What materials were used to make tools? What purposes did the tools serve?)	
Fire (Could they make fires? What did they use to make the fires?)	
Religion and Ceremonies (What kinds of occasions were special? What did they do to worship or celebrate?)	
Development of Language (How did they communicate? Did they have written language?)	
Clothing (What did their clothing look like? What was it made from?)	
Painting and Carving (What kinds of things did they paint or carve? What materials did they use to make the paintings or carvings?)	

Information Chart *(cont.)*

Homo Sapien (Wise Man) Sapien: Modern Humans	
Dates and Place of Existence (When and where did they live?)	
Description of Physical Appearance (What did they look like? What was the average height and weight of a male? of a female?)	
Description of Shelters (What kind of shelters did they use? What materials were used to make the shelters? Were the shelters meant to be easy to move or long lasting?)	
Food (What type of food did they eat? How did they get their food?)	
Description of Daily Life (How did they live? Were they hunters and gatherers or farmers?)	
Tools (What materials were used to make tools? What purposes did the tools serve?)	
Fire (Could they make fires? What did they use to make the fires?)	
Religion and Ceremonies (What kinds of occasions were special? What did they do to worship or celebrate?)	
Development of Language (How did they communicate? Did they have written language?)	
Clothing (What did their clothing look like? What was it made from?)	
Painting and Carving (What kinds of things did they paint or carve? What materials did they use to make the paintings or carvings?)	

Australopithecus

Around ten million years ago, the climate was slowly changing on the continent of Africa. In turn, the vegetation and wildlife also changed to adapt to the climate. Grassland was replacing dense forests, and a new species was evolving that was able to spend more time hunting and foraging on the land than in the trees. The members of this new species were called hominids. The hominids were different from other ape-like species because they were able to walk upright. In addition, their teeth and jaw structures looked different and their brains were larger. The first group to show these features were the australopithecines. Fossilized remains of this species date back to around 5–1 million years ago. The remains of australopithecines have been found in eastern and southern Africa. However, scientists are still not sure whether humans first evolved in this area, or whether the fossils are just best preserved there. Also, due to the lack of extensive evidence, scientists still disagree about the exact relationship between the australopithecines and modern humans. Some scientists believe this species to be our earliest direct ancestors, while others suggest they are an early relative of humans, but that they are not human themselves.

Australopithecines ranged in size from about 47"-67" (120 cm-170 cm) tall, the smallest of the species being about the size of an upright chimpanzee and the largest equaling the heights of modern humans today. By comparing bones from an Australopithecus to that of a gorilla, it was discovered that they walked upright. The spinal column on an Australopithecus, like a human, perpendicularly met the skull. This means the head was balanced on the top of the backbone. On a gorilla, the backbone meets the head at an angle, making it better suited for walking on all fours. The pelvis on an Australopithecus, also like that of a human, was short and broad, helping it to walk upright. A gorilla has a long, narrow pelvis. The feet of an Australopithecus also shows human-like tendencies. A gorilla's big toe sticks out at an angle, much like the thumb on a hand, and is used for grasping. However, the foot of an Australopithecus was more like a human's, the big toe aligned with the others.

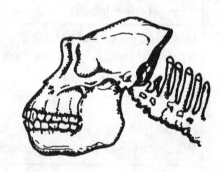

The Australopithecus' skull was similar to that of an ape because it had a low forehead, large protruding eyebrow ridge, flat nose, and jutting jaw. In contrast, its muzzle was much shorter than that of an ape's, and its teeth were arranged more like a human's, with the sides of the jaws sloping outwards. Although the Australopithecus' jaw was shaped like that of a modern human, it was far more powerful and held larger teeth which could be used for chewing tough plants.

The brains of the australopithecines ranged from 28-31 cubic inches (450-500 cc) in volume. This is less than half the size of a modern human brain, which is approximately 85 cubic inches (1400 cc) but much larger than the brain-to-body size ratio of an ape. The larger brain sizes meant that the australopithecines had greater intelligence, better communication skills, and the ability to work cooperatively. Although no evidence has been found showing that they made tools, scientists believe the australopithecines probably used branches or stones to kill their prey and defend themselves. In addition to eating animals that they hunted, these early humans, scientists believe, ate birds' eggs, insects, and such plants as berries, leaves, fruits, and roots.

Ape's Skull

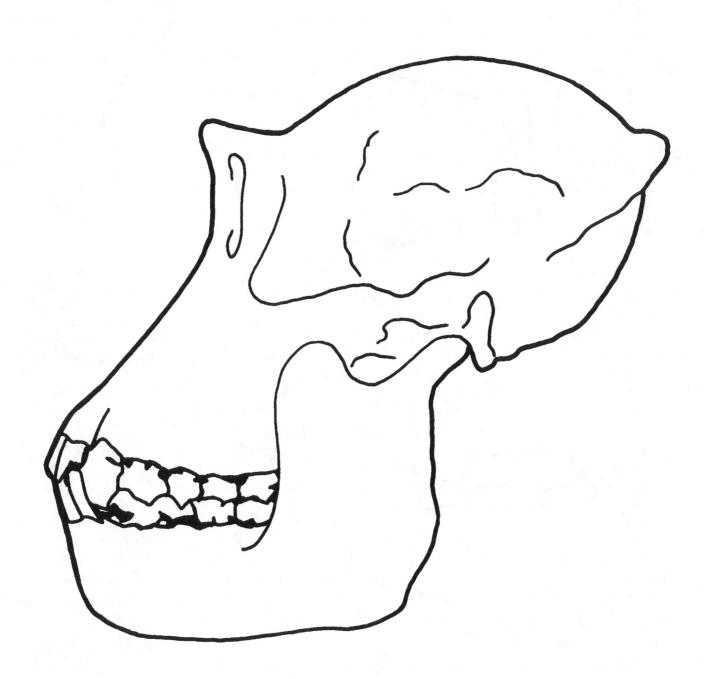

Australopithecus' Skull

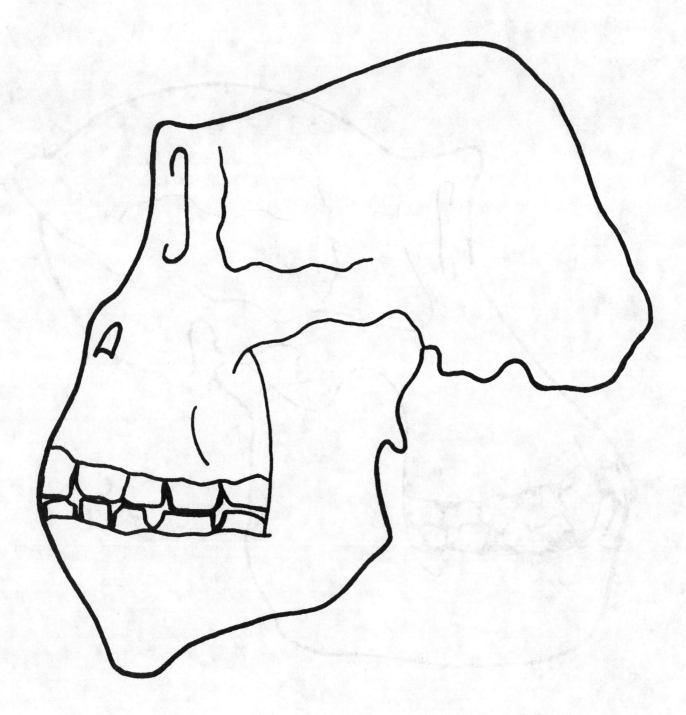

The Discovery of a Lifetime

The following article (page 114) describes anthropologists Louis and Mary Leakey's magnificent discovery of some bones belonging to an early human. After reading this information, students will create newspaper articles telling about some imaginary discoveries.

Preparing for the Lesson:

1. Reproduce The Leakey Discoveries (page 114) for students.

2. Reproduce The Ancient Times newspaper (page 115) for students.

3. You may wish to reproduce The Writing Process (page 13) for students or make an overhead transparency of this page to use for a review with the class.

4. You may also wish to reproduce the Editing Checklist (page 14) for students.

Teaching the Lesson:

1. Tell students that they are going to read an article that describes some of the major archeological discoveries by Louis and Mary Leakey. As they are reading, they should try to imagine the setting and how the Leakeys felt as they uncovered some ancient human bones.

2. Have students read the article. You may wish to use one of the reading techniques suggested on page 103, or you can create one of your own.

3. Tell students to pretend that they are archaeologists and that they have just made amazing discoveries of bones belonging to some early humans. Explain to students that you want them to write newspaper articles telling about their discoveries. Each article should include the following information: where the excavation site was located, why that location was chosen, when the dig took place, what was discovered, and how the discovery was made.

4. Show students how to plan the articles by making concept webs like the one shown below.

5. Then have students use their plans to write rough drafts of their articles. Point out that it is important for the articles to have catchy headlines in order to grab the reader's attention.

6. Ask students to draw sketches for the pictures they will include with their articles. Have them write captions for their sketches.

7. After students have edited their rough drafts, distribute the copies of The Ancient Times (page 115) for their final drafts. Tell students to draw the final versions of their illustrations and write their captions on the final drafts.

8. Display the newspaper articles on a bulletin board entitled "Early Human News" or "Extra, Extra, Read All About It!"

The Leakey Discoveries

For more than thirty years, Louis and Mary Leakey had been exploring and excavating sites in Africa. The Leakeys were both very famous anthropologists who studied past and present human cultures. On the afternoon of October 2, 1948, Louis Leakey found some fossilized bones from an extinct form of crocodile. Mary Leakey was not far away, exploring other eroded surfaces. She wanted to find the remains of some apes from the Cenozoic Era through which she hoped to better understand human evolution.

It was not long before Mary saw some interesting looking bone fragments lying on a slope. She soon saw a tooth. It had a hominid, or human, look to it. A few moments later she was shouting for Louis, and he came running with excitement. Together, they gently brushed the sediments away from around the tooth. To their amazement, not only was it a human Proconsul tooth, but it was still in a jaw. Further searching revealed that the specimen was undoubtedly warped and in many fragments, a considerable part of the face and over half of the skull were still intact. Never before had a skull this size, shape, and age been discovered. It would prove to be a vital link in evolutionary studies.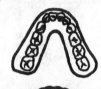

The Leakeys spent days meticulously sifting the dirt to extract every scrap of bone that belonged to their find. They enlisted the help of Heslon Mukiri for the task. Erosion over the years had forever destroyed or removed some parts of the skull. The entire eye socket seemed to be missing. However, the upper and lower jaws were complete, along with all of the teeth. The find was remarkable, but what would happen twenty years later proved to be even more extraordinary.

In 1968, Martin Pickford, a paleontologist, discovered a long ignored museum display with specimens that had been collected from the same region in Africa two years before the Leakeys' find. At first sight, the collection seemed to be tortoise scutes, which are the small bony plates that make up the bottom part of a tortoise's shell. However, Pickford's keen eye recognized a number of hominid skull fragments. These fragments proved to be the missing pieces of the Proconsul skull!

Another remarkable discovery was made in 1959. The Leakeys found themselves in a deep gorge in eastern Africa. Here, in Olduvai Gorge, Louis became ill and stayed in the camp. Mary continued their excavation work. As the sun began to set, she spotted a hunk of bone buried in a slab of ancient rock. Eagerly, Mary scraped away layers of dirt to discover that the ancient bone was actually part of a jaw that still had some upper teeth. Mary was able to tell that the jaw was human in nature. Excitedly, Mary went to get Louis and show him her remarkable discovery. After running many tests, they determined that the human bones were over two million years old. With further investigation and digging, the Leakeys recovered over 400 bone fragments at this site. By carefully sorting the fragments, they were able to reconstruct almost an entire skull. Even more exceptional was the fact that close to all of these ancient bones, the Leakeys found small stones with sharp edges. Someone had split and pounded the stones to sharpen them into primitive tools. The Leakeys had discovered and named the first Homo habilis or "handy man." As a result scientists around the world had to reconsider the dates for the beginning of the human race.

The Ancient Times

_____   _____
(headline)   (date)

by _____

_____
_____
_____
_____
_____
_____
_____
_____
_____
_____

(caption)

_____
_____
_____
_____
_____
_____
_____
_____
_____
_____
_____
_____

_____
_____
_____
_____
_____
_____
_____
_____

Reconstructing Lucy

(A Dramatization)

Characters:

Narrator   **Scientists (1-9)**   **Donald Johanson**   **Tom Gray**

Narrator: Donald Johanson and his group of scientists recount the discovery of Lucy, an australopithecine and the oldest complete ancestor of humans ever found.

Donald: *(to the audience)* On the morning of November 30, 1974, I awoke ready for the field expedition. We were camped on the edge of the Awash, a small, muddy river in Ethiopia. The site was at a place called Hadar. I was co-leader of a group of scientists.

Scientist 1: *(to the audience)* The morning was still relatively cool. We could smell smoke from the cooking fires as we awoke. Along with the group of scientists were some Afar tribesmen who worked for the expedition. Some had brought their families, so there was a small compound of dome-shaped huts about 200 yards (182 m) away from the main camp. The women of the Afar tribe had been up before dawn, tending to their camels and goats.

Scientist 2: *(to the audience)* Donald and the rest of us were here to search for fossils in a gully at Hadar, which was in the center of the Afar desert. Two million years worth of sediments had accumulated there in the bed of an ancient lake from which the water had long since evaporated. Years of rainfall had uncovered fossils that were previously buried under the surface.

Scientist 3: *(to the audience)* The morning was the favorite time of the day for most of the Americans in the camp. The many rocks and boulders surrounding the compound had cooled off during the night so that you could stand near one without feeling as though you were in an oven.

Donald: *(to the audience)* I headed for a cup of coffee. Unlike the other Americans, mornings are not my best time of the day. I am a slow starter and much prefer the evenings at Hadar. I liked to walk up to a nearby ridge just as the sun went down and turned the hillsides purple. Then, I could sit alone for awhile, thinking about the day's work and what could lie ahead. The dry, silent desert seems to intensify my thoughts and encourage me to ponder questions about human development on the Earth. As I sipped my coffee, I was joined by Tom Gray, an American graduate student who had come to Hadar to study the ancient plants and animals of the region.

Tom: *(to the audience)* I was interested in examining the fossils to reconstruct, as accurately as possible, the kinds of plants and animals that lived in this region over the many years. I also hoped to discover what the climate might have been like and how the different species interacted. Donald, on the other hand, was primarily interested in finding hominid fossils, or bones of extinct human ancestors and their close relatives, in order to uncover clues about human evolution. Yet, in order to accurately interpret any of the fossils, it was necessary to have other specialists such as myself.

Reconstructing Lucy *(cont.)*

Narrator: Over coffee, the two discussed their plans for the day.

Donald: *(to Tom)* So, what's up for today?

Tom: *(to Donald)* I'll be busy marking fossil sites on a map.

Donald: *(to Tom)* When are you going to mark Locality 162?

Tom: *(to Donald)* I'm not really sure where 162 is.

Donald: *(to Tom)* Then I guess I'll have to show you.

(to the audience) After saying this I realized that I had a lot of work to catch up on that day. We had had a lot of visitors to the camp recently. While they were here I had neglected my paperwork and cataloging. I had not written any letters or completed the detailed descriptions of any fossils. I should have stayed in camp that morning to work—but I didn't. I felt some kind of strong urge to go with Tom, so I followed it.

I know that a great deal of my work depends on luck. The fossils I study are very rare and difficult to find. This was only my third year at Hadar, and I had found several hominid fossils. That day I felt sure that I'd be lucky, that something terrific might happen!

Tom: *(to the audience)* Donald and I got into a 4-wheel-drive truck and slowly bounced our way to Locality 162, just one of several hundred sites that were being mapped in the Hadar region. Even though 162 was only about four miles (6.5 km) from the main camp, it took over 30 minutes to get there due to the rough terrain. By the time we arrived, it was already getting hot.

Scientist 4: *(to the audience)* Hadar is a wasteland of gravel and sand. Most of the fossils we found were almost completely exposed on the surface of the ground. This ancient lake bed is filled with sediments that recorded past geological events such as volcanic-ash falls and deposits of mud and silt washed down from distant mountains. The gullies are like slices of geological cake, made deeper each time it rained, exposing more and more fossils.

Donald: *(to the audience)* Tom and I parked the truck on the slope of a gully. Tom proceeded to plot the locality on the map and then we began surveying the area for exposed fossils.

Scientist 5: *(to the audience)* Some people are good at finding fossils; others are not. Finding fossils takes practice. None of us, including Donald, will ever be as good as some of the Afar people. Their lives depend on being sharp eyed. They notice things that a person unaccustomed to the desert would easily overlook.

Reconstructing Lucy *(cont.)*

Scientist 6: *(to the audience)* Tom and Donald walked around, surveying the area for a couple of hours. It was getting close to noon, and they hadn't found much: a few teeth from an extinct horse, a skull fragment from an extinct pig, some antelope molars, and part of a monkey's jaw.

Tom: *(to the audience)* I insisted on taking these things back to camp even though we already had samples of them in our collection.

Scientist 7: *(to the audience)* Each time a fossil is discovered in a new locality at Hadar, that locality must be numbered and all of the information must be recorded on a map of the area. This keeps the volumes of geological and paleontological information organized and easy to use.

Scientist 8: *(to the audience)* Donald decided to survey the bottom of a little gully. The gully had been checked twice before by other workers who had found nothing of interest.

Donald: *(to the audience)* I was aware of the "lucky" feeling that had been nagging at me and decided to make that small, final detour. We couldn't find any bones in the gully, but as we turned to leave I noticed something lying on a slope that looked like part of a hominid's arm.

Tom: *(to Donald)* It can't be hominid. It's too small. It has to be a monkey of some kind.

Narrator: They knelt to examine it.

Tom: *(to Donald)* It's much too small.

Donald: *(to Tom)* I still say its a hominid.

Tom: *(to Donald)* What makes you so sure?

Donald: *(to Tom)* That piece right next to your hand. That's a hominid's also.

Tom: *(to the audience)* As I picked up the bone, I could see that it was the back of a small skull. It was so small, the brain could be only about one-third the size of a modern human's. Then, a few feet away, we found part of a femur, or thighbone, whose size and shape clearly showed that this creature had walked upright. Later, when we further analyzed the femur, we determined that the hominid was about 25 years old at the time of death.

Donald: *(to the audience)* We stood up on the slope and saw other bits of bone from vertebrae, a pelvis, and some ribs. The shape of the pelvis revealed that this hominid had been a female. I started to wonder if all of these bone fragments would fit together to form the skeleton of a primitive person! Such a complete skeleton that was this old had never been found—anywhere! Just then Tom found ribs. I can't believe it!

Reconstructing Lucy *(cont.)*

Tom: *(to Donald)* You had better believe it. Here it is. Right here!

Donald: *(to the audience)* Tom's voice went up into a howl. I joined him, and we began jumping up and down with excitement about the small brown remains of what seemed to be a single hominid skeleton at our feet. Finally, we calmed down somewhat. I convinced Tom that we should play it cool until we could come back and make absolutely sure that the bones were from one individual and not from many individuals that were all mixed together.

Narrator: Donald and Tom collected a couple of pieces of jawbone, marked the spot, and climbed into the truck for the exceedingly hot ride back to camp. On the way, they picked up two of the expedition's geologists who were loaded down with rock samples.

Tom: *(to the geologists)* We found something BIG, I tell you. Something really BIG!

Donald: *(to Tom)* Calm down, Tom!

Narrator: Yet, Tom could not stay calm. As they neared the camp, he blasted the horn, bringing a scurry of scientists out of the river from where they were getting some relief from the sun's heat.

Tom: *(to all the scientists)* We've got it! We've got the whole thing!

Narrator: That afternoon everyone in camp was at the gully, sectioning off the site and preparing for the massive excavation. Ultimately, the collecting of the hominid's bones took three weeks.

Scientist 9: *(to the audience)* The camp was filled with excitement. On the first night of the discovery, no one slept at all. We talked all night, imagining the possibilities.

Donald: *(to the audience)* At some point during that unforgettable evening, the fossil picked up the name Lucy and has been known as such ever since. However, its official number in the Hadar collection is AL 288-1. When the excavation was finally completed, we had recovered several hundred pieces of bone representing about 40% of the skeleton of a single individual that stood about three and one-half feet (1 m) tall. Tom and I had been right. Yet, what kind of individual was it? Nothing like this had ever been discovered before.

Narrator: Lucy proved to be a species over three million years old. She remains one of the oldest skeletons ever found. By studying Lucy, archaeologists have learned valuable information regarding our earliest ancestors or near relatives, the australopithecines.

Putting Lucy Together

By examining the bone fragments of Lucy's skeleton, scientists were able to detect a number of facts about her. Use information from the Reconstructing Lucy dramatization (pages 116-119) to list each fragment and what the scientists were able to learn about Lucy from it.

Fragment	Information Learned from the Fragment

Homo Habilis

Somewhere between two and three million years ago, many changes were taking place on the Earth. A new species was evolving that was better suited to its environment. Compared to the australopithecines, this species had a larger brain, a more human-looking face, and a more human-looking pelvis. Homo, named for the Latin word meaning "man," is considered to be the first direct ancestor of humans. One of the earliest species of the genus Homo had developed techniques for making primitive tools and was therefore named Homo habilis, or "handy man."

Homo habilis probably lived between one and two million years ago. Louis and Mary Leakey were the first to find remains of a Homo habilis at the Olduvai Gorge in east Africa. More remains have shown that related groups may have also lived in the southern part of Africa and in Southeast Asia. A Homo habilis was only about 4.5 feet (1.4 m) tall. Its legs and feet seem to have been fully adapted for walking upright.

A Homo habilis had a more rounded skull than an Australopithecus did. Its face was smaller, longer, and narrower. Furthermore, the jaw was lighter and the teeth were slightly smaller than that of an Australopithecus. The jawline was curved with sloping sides, making it appear even more like that of a modern human. The brain measured 40–49 cubic inches (650–800 cc), so it was slightly larger than that of the Australopithecus. However, the brain of a Homo habilis was still only about half the size of a modern human's brain.

The increase in brain size coincided with an increase in intelligence. The Homo habilis were the first species able to use their culture to help them adapt to their environment, an ability that is unique to humans. These early humans were able to remember important information, plan ahead, and work out abstract problems in order to make tools and organize hunts. Tools that have been found indicate that the Homo habilis probably did not use weapons to hunt but would work together to creep up and pounce on their prey. Once the prey was down, the hunters would kill it with stones or branches. At the site of the kill, they would chip sharp

flakes of stone to use as knives for cutting the meat. Then they would use heavy stones to smash open the animal's bones and eat its marrow. Meat was eaten raw since fire had not yet been discovered. The Homo habilis probably got its food by hunting small animals, foraging for plants, and taking birds' eggs.

Homo habilis constructed simple huts made from branches and held in place by stones. These simple dome-shaped huts would have protected them from animals and the wind.

Scientists believe that this early species of humans was not capable of speech. Therefore, they probably communicated using some primitive gestures and simple sounds.

Homo Habilis' Skull

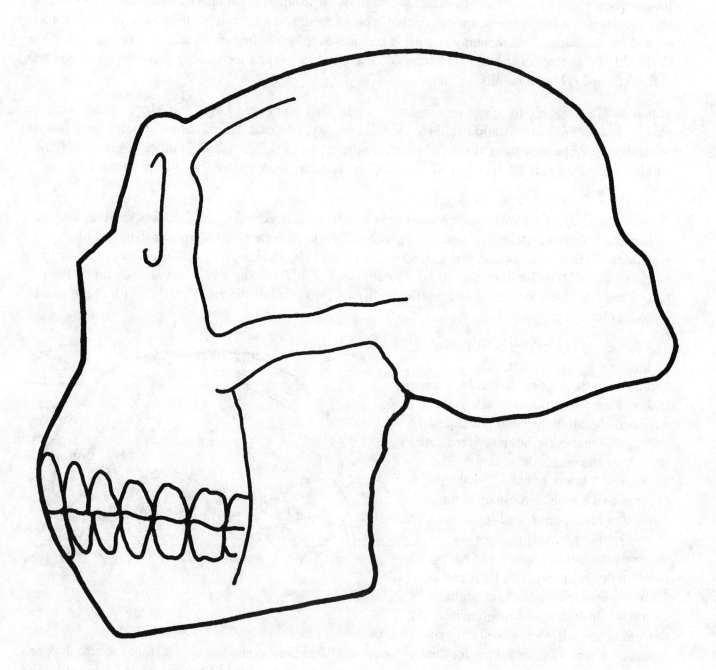

A Museum Tool Display

Homo habilis is the earliest known species to make tools. One of their tool making strategies involved flint knapping, or chipping tools out of flint or stone. Other tools were made from bones, horns, antlers, or branches, depending on their availability.

Preparing for the Lesson:

1. Reproduce the information about tools (pages 124-125).

2. You may wish to gather additional information about tool making.

3. Establish a due date and a time line for the projects. Remind students that you will be monitoring and grading both individual and group performances.

4. Divide the class into cooperative learning groups. Have the groups pick leaders, or you may wish to assign leaders. Tell students that a leader's job is to monitor on-task behavior, coordinate the efforts of the group, and resolve problems/disagreements as they arise.

5. Have students gather rocks and sticks to make tool models. Provide art materials, such as construction paper, poster board, paint, clay, Styrofoam blocks, and drinking straws.

6. Provide 9" x 12" (23 cm x 30 cm) pieces of white construction paper for students to make their display cards for the different models that they make.

Teaching the Lesson:

1. Have students work with their groups to plan their displays. Have them create general outlines of the information they would like to include and some rough sketches of the tool models they want to make. Have students do research about the different tools.

2. Review safety rules with students. Have students make the tool models, using a variety of materials. Remind them that models can be smaller than the actual tool would have been.

3. After the tools have been made, have students make display cards for their tools. Display cards are made by folding in half 9" x 12" (23 cm x 30 cm) pieces of construction paper. Ask students to draw pictures of the tools on the cards and then write brief descriptions of the tools.

4. Have students develop a format to present their information to the class. The presentation can be a tour through the museum, a trip back in time to see how early humans used the tools, a TV show about early human tools, etc. Encourage students to be creative, but give them a time limit for their class presentations.

5. Use the models and the display cards to create a classroom museum display.

6. For a final evaluation, ask students to write their responses to the following questions: What was the easiest/most difficult part about making the tools? What did you like/dislike about working in groups? The next time we work on a group project what skill would you like to improve?

7. Extend the lesson by comparing ancient tools with modern tools (pages 126-127).

Tools Used by Early Humans

Homo habilis was the first human to make tools, thus beginning the Old Stone Age or Paleolithic Age. Homo habilis made only simple tools from various types of rocks. As time went on, tools became more sophisticated and were used for specific kinds of tasks. Other materials were also utilized to make tools as humans became more skillful. Antlers, horns, and tree branches were shaped to make digging sticks and spears. Small, sharp bones were used as fish hooks and needles. Larger bones could be used as hammers for making other tools.

Flint was soon discovered to be the most suitable rock for making tools because it is easily chipped to form sharp edges. Furthermore, regular flakes come off when flint is struck, making it easy to control the size and shape of the flake. Although the earliest flint tools were very simple, making these primitive stone tools required skill and planning. The steps that an early toolmaker used to create a tool out of flint are shown below.

Flint Knapping

First, the toolmaker found an appropriate stone to use, one that was soft enough to chip, yet not so soft that it crumbled or shattered when struck with a rock or bone. Next, the toolmaker trimmed the stone to form a shape that would be the core of the tool. This was usually done by scraping the stone with another stone.

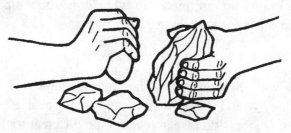

Then a stone hammer was used to repeatedly strike the core stone along the edges to remove chips from the underside. By hitting the core stone at many different angles, early toolmakers could make a variety of tools. The small flakes chipped away from the larger core stone were useful as knives, razors, and arrowheads.

Sometimes, a bone hammer was used to further trim and sharpen the edge of the tool.

Stone Tools

Hammer Stone—A pebble hammer was the simplest tool used in flint knapping. It was used to chip large flakes from the core stone of flint.

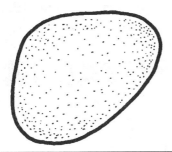

Chopper—This was an oval-shaped hand ax that was used as a cleaver but had one side sharpened for cutting. It fit easily into an early human's palm.

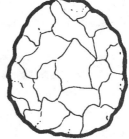

Hand Ax—This was a large, rough stone with a sharp point. It was used to dig edible roots and bulbs from the ground and to cut animal skins and plants.

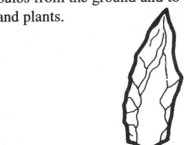

Side Scraper—This tool was similar to the chopper. It was made from an oval or rectangular-shaped flat stone. It had one straight edge for holding and one edge with tooth-like cuts for scraping animal hides and chopping meat.

Lance Head—This was a long, narrow stone that was mounted on a spear and used to thrust into animals. It had a sharp point and sharp, refined edges.

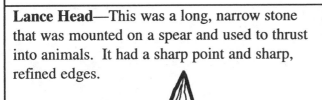

Borer—This tool was a small, pointed stone that had thin, straight edges. It was used to punch holes into animal hides that were made into clothing.

Arrowhead—This tool was made from flint flakes (small, narrow stones) chipped from a core stone. It had a sharp point and refined edges like the lance head. This stone was mounted on an arrow shaft and used for hunting animals.

Backed Flake—This was a long, narrow stone that had been chipped off of a core stone. It had one dull edge and one sharp edge. It was used as a knife or razor.

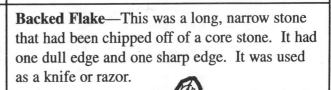

Tools We Use

The discovery of stone age tools by archaeologists unlocks some of the secrets about the daily life of the people who made these tools. Toolmaking began with Homo habilis about two million years ago when these humans first chipped a stone to form a sharp edge. It marks the beginning of the Paleolithic or Old Stone Age. Throughout the Old Stone Age humans developed their skills to make more sophisticated tools. Name and describe some modern-day tools that are improvements on the following ancient tools.

Stone Age Tools	Tools We Use Today
Lance Head—It had a sharp point and sharp, refined edges. It was mounted on a spear and used to thrust into animals.	
Side Scraper—It had one straight edge and one with tooth-like cuts. It was used to scrape animal hides and chop meat.	
Borer—It had thin, straight edges and a very sharp point. It was used to punch holes into hides that were made into clothing.	
Hand Ax—It had a sharp point and rough edges with a handle. It was used to dig edible roots and bulbs from the ground.	
Backed Flake—It was long and narrow with one dull edge and one sharp edge. This first pocket knife was probably used for cutting.	

Tools We Use *(cont.)*

We can appreciate the skill these Paleolithic people must have had in order to survive by hunting animals and gathering plants. It is impressive how they were able to make simple tools from available resources so that their daily needs could be more easily met.

Have you ever thought about the tools you use that make your work easier? Take a look at the tools you use every day at home and at school. Choose five of these tools and write their names in the chart shown below. Then use complete sentences to write detailed descriptions about how these tools make work easier and what you would have to do if you did not have them.

Name of Tool	How It Makes Work Easier	What I Would Do Without It
1.		
2.		
3.		
4.		
5.		

Homo Erectus

As thousands of years went by, humans and the environment underwent many changes. From around 1.5 million to 250,000 years ago, a new type of species existed called Homo erectus, or "upright man." Scientists believe this species of early humans lived in small groups consisting of 20 to 30 individuals. They roamed over a wide area as they hunted migrating animals and foraged for plants. Fossils have been found showing that Homo erectus probably began living in Africa, but then migrated into Europe and Asia over several generations. Fossils were discovered as far away as China and the Indonesian island of Java.

A Homo erectus was taller than previous hominids, and some may have been as tall and heavy as modern humans. It was the first species to walk completely upright without stooping, which is how it got its name. The brain of a Homo erectus ranged in size from 54–67 cubic inches (880 cc–1100 cc). This was larger than the brain of a Homo habilis. The teeth were smaller than those of a Homo habilis, but larger than a modern human's teeth. The skull was still very thick with a sloping forehead and a large eyebrow ridge. It still had a massive jaw, flat face, and no chin. The large jaw and teeth needed strong muscles to help keep the head upright. These muscles attached to a bony bump at the back of the head.

Since Homo erectus had larger brains, they were also capable of new skills in communication, toolmaking, and fire building. Earlier hominids were not capable of speech. However, Homo erectus probably grunted sounds and combined simple words with gestures in order to communicate with one another. This newly developed intelligence and language helped Homo erectus coordinate group hunting efforts. Bolas, or stones wrapped in skins tied together with leather thongs, have also been found with Home erectus' remains, providing more evidence that they possessed advanced hunting techniques. Homo erectus also made more sophisticated hand axes that could cut better than previous tools. The hand ax was used for a variety of purposes, such as cutting meat and digging.

The most outstanding achievement of Homo erectus was the ability to use, and eventually make, fire. Fossils of their remains have been found near fire-blackened hearths dating as far back as 360,000 years ago. Earlier hominids were probably frightened by natural fires in the grasslands. But Homo erectus gradually learned to take advantage of it. They used fire in hunting by catching frightened animals as they ran away from the flames. They also learned to cook with fire, most likely from noticing that animals burnt in natural fires made the meat easier to cut and chew than when it was raw. At first, they probably could not make fires on their own. Instead, they would bring to camp branches that had caught on fire in natural ways, such as lightning. They used the fire for light and warmth. Fire also enabled them to keep wild animals away and harden the tops of wooden spears. Eventually, they learned to make their own fires,  using stones struck together to form a spark or by rubbing fire sticks together to create heat through friction until a flame was produced. It is with this new development of fire that Homo erectus was able to live in a much wider range of environments and adapt to local conditions. This is how the species survived several thousands of years in Europe during the Ice Age.

Homo Erectus' Skull

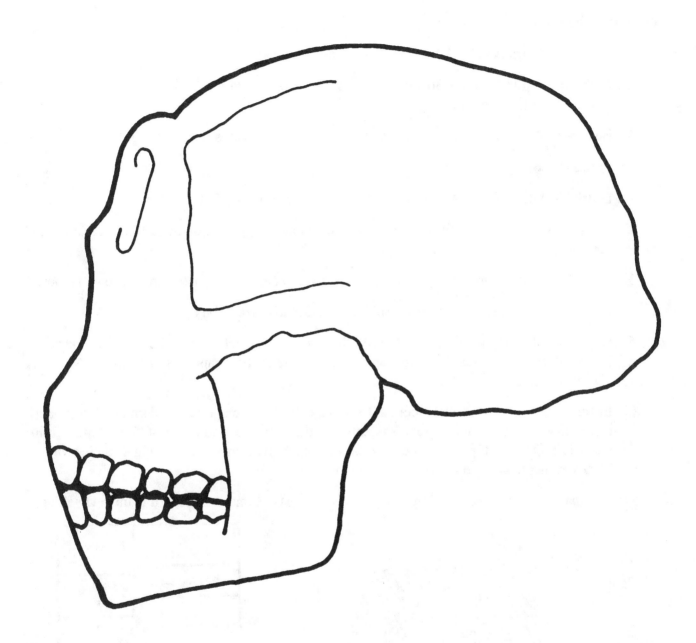

A Look at Terra Amata

Students will be amazed at the similarities between their homes and the Homo erectus camp located at Terra Amata.

Preparing for the Lesson:

1. Reproduce Terra Amata: A Homo Erectus Camp (pages 131-132) for students.

2. Gather 12" x 18" (23 cm x 30 cm) pieces of white construction paper and crayons, markers, or colored pencils for the drawings.

3. Be sure students have already been introduced to Homo erectus (pages 128-129).

Teaching the Lesson:

1. Distribute Terra Amata: A Homo Erectus Camp (pages 131-132) to students.

2. You may wish to choose one of the reading techniques suggested on page 103 or create one of your own.

3. Invite students to compare/contrast the home dwelling at Terra Amata and their own homes.

4. Distribute the pieces of white construction paper, markers, crayons, etc.

5. Have students fold the paper in half. Tell them to label the left side of their papers "Terra Amata: A Homo Erectus Dwelling" and the right side of their papers "My Home: A Modern Human Dwelling."

6. Instruct students to draw and label the floor plans for the ancient and modern dwellings. See the sample shown below. Remind students that they can use the picture of Terra Amata from the article. They will probably be better at making a blueprint-style drawing of their own homes, rather than three-dimensional drawings.

Terra Amata: A Homo Erectus Dwelling   My Home: A Modern Human Dwelling

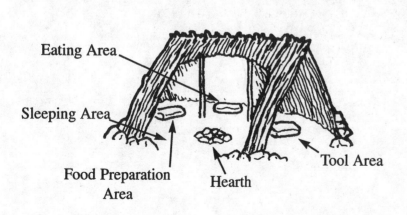

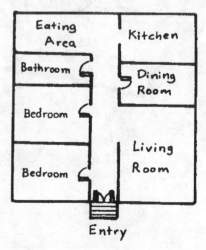

7. On the back of their drawings, ask them to use complete sentences to list at least three ways the homes are alike and at least three ways the homes are different. Share and display on a bulletin board.

Terra Amata: A Homo Erectus Camp

As you have learned, the first Homo erectus lived in Africa over a million years ago. Gradually, over thousands of years and many generations, Homo erectus migrated to parts of Europe and Asia. One of the European Homo erectus camps is now the town of Nice, a bustling city along the south coast of France. In viewing its busy streets and modern buildings it is hard to believe this was once the site of a simple campsite for a migrating band of Homo erectus. Yet, before modern buildings were built, archaeologists studied this site in detail to learn more about these primitive people. The site was named "Terra Amata" after the street in Nice where it was found.

It is believed that throughout the year, a band of hunters and gatherers moved from place to place, following the herds of animals. By studying how the layers of sand were packed down at Terra Amata, archaeologists learned that the people visited the site for only a few days or weeks at a time while they hunted animals, such as elephants and rhinos. The layers also revealed that this Homo erectus band came back to rebuild their huts year after year. The scientists were even able to determine that the people traveled to Terra Amata in the late spring, based on fossilized pollen samples from the yellow broom flower which were found in the camp.

Terra Amata was rich in resources and, therefore, a good place to hunt and gather food. The camp was located along the shore of the Mediterranean Sea near a fresh-water spring and river. Homo erectus needed a supply of fresh water for drinking, since they had no method for carrying water with them. Fresh water was also helpful in hunting since animals, such as elephants, rhinos, deer, and wild boar came to drink the fresh water, making them easy targets. The men could spear salmon in the river, while the women gathered shellfish, oysters, turtles, and driftwood for the fires. Food, such as dandelion leaves, wild wheat, almonds, figs, berries, and, quails' eggs was also gathered in this region. Archaeologists were able to determine what foods the people ate, based on the bone and food deposits that remained in the camp.

Terra Amata: A Homo Erectus Camp *(cont.)*

Another discovery at Terra Amata was the remains of a wooden hut that was large enough to sleep about twenty people. It was about 27 feet (9 m) long and 15 feet (5 m) wide. The hut was built out of branches with two wooden posts holding up the roof. Large rocks surrounded the base for support and protection from the wind. In the center of the hut, archaeologists found a circular hearth or fire pit. Pebbles were placed around the fire to shield it from the wind. The sand inside the hearth was darkened from the flames.

The people most likely slept on animal skins, huddled close to the fire for warmth as it burned throughout the night. Near the hearth was a flat stone which archaeologists believe was used for shaping tools, since stone flakes were found scattered around this area. Another flat stone was found in a different part of the hut, along with many animal bones and food deposits. The scratches on the surface led archaeologists to infer that this was a cutting block for meat and that this area of the hut was the "kitchen," or place where the food was prepared for cooking. No evidence was found at the camp to show that these people knew how to make fires. More than likely, they carried hot ashes from an old camp fire to ignite the fire at this new site.

Today the level of the sea is much lower than it was when Terra Amata existed. As a result, the area where the remains of the camp are now is farther inland than when it was inhabited by the early humans, Homo erectus.

Use a world map to locate Nice in France.

Hunters and Gatherers
Simulation Game

Homo erectus became skillful hunters and gatherers. They migrated over a wide area, searching for food. Yet, even with advanced tools and weapons, it was still difficult to find enough food to survive. This simulation game allows students to pretend that they are bands of early humans and use cooperative strategies to stay alive.

Preparing for the Lesson:

1. Each team or "band" will be made up of six to eight students. Each band will need the following supplies to play the game: 1 reclosable envelope or reclosable plastic bag, 2 copies of the recording sheet (page 140), 2 copies of the food cards (page 135) cut apart to make a total of 36 cards, 1 copy of the hunter/gatherer cards (pages 136-139) cut apart to make a total of 40 cards. It is best if you can copy the food cards on paper that is a different color from the paper used for the hunter/gatherer cards.

2. Make an overhead transparency of the recording sheet (page 140) to show how it is used.

3. Designate areas for each band to play the game. They will need enough room to sit in a circle on the floor or in chairs around tables or group of desks.

Teaching the Lesson:

1. Tell students that they are going to form bands of hunters and gatherers, much like the group of Homo erectus that hunted at Terra Amata. In their bands they will work together to try to survive. Point out that some days they will be successful at hunting and/or gathering, but on other days they will not. How they work together will determine whether they die from starvation. The band that can keep at least one member alive for the most days is the winner.

2. Review the rules for playing the game (page 134). You may wish to demonstrate a "day" or round of play with a sample band, using the overhead transparency of the recording sheet.

3. While students are playing, circulate and monitor their progress. Encourage bands to raise their hands if they have questions.

4. Since students will be "dying" during the game and unable to play or help their bands, have some activities for them to work on independently while the others finish playing. Students may use this time to write in journals to describe how they felt about being early humans during the game and to tell what they would like and dislike about living during that time period.

5. After all of the bands have "died off," use the recording sheets to see which band was able to keep one member alive the longest, thereby being the winners. Discuss the strategies the bands used to keep members alive. Use the following questions to guide the discussion: What happened once the band began dying off and your numbers got smaller? Was it harder or easier to stay alive? Why?

6. Plan other times to play the game, dividing the class into different bands or use it as a reward.

Hunters and Gatherers
Simulation Game *(cont.)*

Explain the following rules to students before they play the simulation game.

- The main goal of the game is to stay alive. You want to keep yourself healthy and at the same time prevent other members of your band from dying of starvation.

- First, you will need to assign a recorder to write down the status of your band each day.

- Your band will receive a set of playing cards and a recording sheet. There are food cards representing one day's worth of food for one person and hunting/gathering cards which tell you what happened when you went hunting and gathering that day.

- The band sits in a circle. Each member gets three food cards to begin the game. In the center of the circle, place the extra food cards and the hunting/gathering cards in separate stacks.

- The game begins with the recorder and then proceeds to the left. The recorder picks a hunting/gathering card, reads it aloud, and either takes more food cards from the center pile for being successful at hunting/gathering, does not take any food cards for being unsuccessful at hunting/gathering, or gives up food cards to the center pile for a loss of food supplies.

- The player then discards the used hunting/gathering card in a separate pile in the center. The play continues to the left until each member has had a turn. Food cards are shared during the game to keep alive as many members as possible. However, no one can be forced to give up a food card to help someone else.

- A player with only one food card is considered sickly. A sickly player cannot talk or beg. It is up to the band to share their food cards.

- When a player does not have any food cards left, she/he has died of starvation. A member will die of starvation only if no one in the band is willing to share her/his food. Remember, only members with two or more food cards are allowed to speak.

- After everyone has had a turn, the "day" is over. Each member then gives one food card to the center pile to represent the food eaten that day. If you do not have a food card to give and no one else can or is willing to give you a food card, you die of starvation.

- The recorder then uses the recording sheet to write down the status of the band for that day. The recorder must tell how many members of the band are still alive, how many members are sickly, and how many have died.

- Then the recorder draws a hunting/gathering card to begin a new day. Play continues in this manner.

- If any members of the band stay alive for an entire week, each living member receives one extra food card before beginning a new week of play.

- The game is over when the members of the band have died. If your band runs out of hunting/gathering cards during the game, reshuffle the discard pile and reuse them.

Hunters and Gatherers
Simulation Game *(cont.)*

FOOD	FOOD	FOOD
FOOD	FOOD	FOOD
FOOD	FOOD	FOOD
FOOD	FOOD	FOOD
FOOD	FOOD	FOOD
FOOD	FOOD	FOOD

Hunters and Gatherers
Simulation Game *(cont.)*

WHILE RUNNING AWAY FROM A LION, YOU TOOK REFUGE IN A PEACH TREE. TAKE ONE FOOD CARD FROM THE PILE.	YOU SHOT AT A DEER BUT MISSED. YOU SHOULD HAVE PRACTICED LIKE THE CHIEF TOLD YOU. YOU DON'T GET ANY FOOD TODAY!
WHAT A LUCKY SHOT! YOU SHOT AT A DEER AND MISSED, BUT YOU HIT A RABBIT THAT WAS RUNNING BY. TAKE ONE FOOD CARD FROM THE PILE.	WHILE YOU WERE OUT HUNTING, A WILD BOAR BROKE INTO YOUR HUT AND ATE TWO DAYS WORTH OF FOOD. PUT TWO OF YOUR FOOD CARDS BACK IN THE PILE.
WHILE YOU WERE HUNTING, A WOOLLY MAMMOTH SURPRISED YOU BY CHARGING OUT OF THE BRUSH. YOU CLIMBED UP A TREE TO ESCAPE, BUT ALL OF YOUR FOOD WAS CRUSHED. PUT ALL OF YOUR FOOD CARDS IN THE PILE.	YOU FOUND A NEST OF FURRY RODENTS. USING YOUR BOLA, YOU CLOBBERED QUITE A FEW OF THEM. SINCE THEY'RE SO SMALL, AND MOSTLY BONE AND HAIR, YOU GET ONLY ONE FOOD CARD FROM THE PILE.
YOU SPENT THE DAY FISHING WITH A BONE HOOK AND STICK, BUT THE FISH JUST WEREN'T BITING. YOU DON'T GET ANY FOOD TODAY.	USING A BOW AND ARROW, YOU SHOT A BIRD. TAKE ONE FOOD CARD FROM THE PILE.
GOOD JOB OF FORAGING! YOU FOUND A NONPOISONOUS BERRY BUSH IN SEASON. TAKE ONE FOOD CARD FROM THE PILE.	YOU MADE A BAD BUT LUCKY SHOT. WHILE AIMING AT A WILD PIG YOU SHOT A MUSKRAT IN A BUSH. TAKE ONE FOOD CARD FROM THE PILE.

Hunters and Gatherers

Simulation Game *(cont.)*

EXCELLENT SHOT! YOU KILLED A DEER WITH YOUR SPEAR. TAKE TWO FOOD CARDS FROM THE PILE.	WHILE OUT FORAGING, YOU FOUND SOME WILD WHEAT AND FIGS. TAKE ONE FOOD CARD FROM THE PILE.
YOU CAUGHT A TURTLE IN THE RIVER, USING A WOVEN SNARE. TAKE ONE FOOD CARD FROM THE PILE.	USING YOUR DIGGING STICK MADE FROM AN ANTLER, YOU GATHERED A BUNDLE OF OYSTERS. TAKE ONE FOOD CARD FROM THE PILE.
YOU KILLED A DEER, BUT IT WOUNDED YOU WITH ITS ANTLERS. BLEEDING AND WEAK, YOU WERE ABLE TO BRING BACK TO CAMP ONLY SOME OF THE MEAT. TAKE ONE FOOD CARD FROM THE PILE.	WHILE OUT HUNTING, YOU CAME UPON A QUAIL'S NEST. YOU GATHERED THE EGGS AND TOOK THEM BACK TO CAMP. TAKE ONE FOOD CARD FROM THE PILE.
YOU'VE JUST HAD THE BEST OF LUCK! YOU FOUND A WILD BOAR WITH A BROKEN LEG. YOU KILLED IT WITH YOUR CLUB. TAKE TWO FOOD CARDS FROM THE PILE.	YOU HAVE SPENT HOURS FOLLOWING THE TRACKS OF A RHINO. HOWEVER, YOU WERE NEVER ABLE TO FIND THE ANIMAL. YOU DON'T GET ANY FOOD TODAY.
YOU CHASED AN AARDVARK AND TRIED TO KILL IT WITH SOME STONES, BUT IT GOT AWAY. TIRED AND HUNGRY, YOU HIKED BACK TO CAMP. YOU DON'T GET ANY FOOD TODAY.	YOU SHOT A DEER WITH YOUR ARROW, BUT A BAND OF WILD DOGS GOT TO IT BEFORE YOU COULD. SINCE YOU WERE ALONE, YOU HAD TO LET THE WILD DOGS HAVE THE DEER. YOU DON'T GET ANY FOOD TODAY.

Hunters and Gatherers

Simulation Game *(cont.)*

GOOD JOB OF HUNTING! WORKING WITH A GROUP, YOU USED BURNING BRANCHES TO CHASE A WILD PIG INTO A TRAP. TAKE TWO FOOD CARDS FROM THE PILE.	YOU FOUND AN ELEPHANT DRINKING AT A WATER HOLE. BUT YOU STEPPED ON A BRANCH WHILE CREEPING UP ON IT, AND IT WAS SCARED AWAY. YOU DON'T GET ANY FOOD TODAY.
YOU CLUBBED TWO LARGE FISH WHILE WADING IN THE LAKE. TAKE TWO FOOD CARDS.	YOU CLIMBED A TREE AND CAUGHT A BIRD WITH YOUR BOLA. TAKE ONE FOOD CARD FROM THE PILE.
TODAY WAS SCORCHING HOT. THE ANIMALS STAYED OUT OF THE SUN, SO YOU DID NOT CATCH ANY FOOD TODAY.	USING YOUR DIGGING STICK YOU FORAGED SOME DANDELION LEAVES AND EDIBLE ROOTS. TAKE ONE FOOD CARD FROM THE PILE.
YOU GATHERED FRUITS AND NUTS TODAY AND WERE ABLE TO CARRY SOME OF THEM BACK TO CAMP. TAKE ONE FOOD CARD FROM THE PILE.	A PACK OF WILD BOARS CAME RUNNING THROUGH THE CAMP TODAY. QUICK AS LIGHTNING YOU SPEARED ONE BEFORE IT LEFT THE AREA. TAKE TWO FOOD CARDS FROM THE PILE FOR YOUR HEROIC DEED.
WHILE CLIMBING THE BLUFF ON A HUNTING EXPEDITION, YOU SQUASHED A SNAKE. YOU TOOK IT BACK TO CAMP AND COOKED IT ON A SKEWER OVER A FIRE. TAKE ONE FOOD CARD FROM THE PILE.	ON THE WAY BACK TO CAMP FROM A HUNTING TRIP YOU FELL INTO THE SWAMP, LOSING TWO DAYS' SUPPLY OF YOUR FOOD. PUT TWO FOOD CARDS BACK IN THE PILE.

Hunters and Gatherers

Simulation Game *(cont.)*

YOU DECIDED TO TAKE A SWIM INSTEAD OF GOING FISHING. YOU SCARED AWAY ALL THE WATER LIFE THAT WOULD BE GOOD TO EAT. YOU DON'T GET ANY FOOD TODAY.	WHILE OUT HUNTING DEER, YOU ACCIDENTALLY BROKE YOUR LAST ARROW. WITHOUT A USEFUL WEAPON, YOU HAD TO RETURN HOME EMPTY HANDED. YOU DIDN'T GET ANY FOOD TODAY.
YOU CAME UPON AN OLD LOG FILLED WITH TERMITES. USING A REED STRAW, YOU SUCKED UP A MEAL. TAKE ONE FOOD CARD FROM THE PILE.	ON THE WAY BACK FROM AN ELEPHANT HUNT YOU WERE CHASED BY A PACK OF WILD DOGS. TO GET RID OF THE DOGS, YOU THREW A DAY'S WORTH OF FOOD ON THE GROUND FOR THEM. PUT ONE OF YOUR FOOD CARDS BACK IN THE PILE.
WHILE OUT HUNTING RABBITS YOU SAT DOWN AND FELL ASLEEP UNDER A TREE. YOU DON'T GET ANY FOOD TODAY.	YOU CLIMBED THE CLIFFS TO HUNT FOR WILD GOATS. LUCKY FOR YOU, ONE OF THE GOATS WAS OLD AND LAME, MAKING IT AN EASY TARGET. TAKE TWO FOOD CARDS FROM THE PILE.
WHILE MIGRATING TO NEW HUNTING GROUNDS YOU MET A MEMBER OF ANOTHER BAND AND HAD A FIGHT. YOU LOST THE FIGHT AND THE OTHER PERSON STOLE YOUR FOOD. PUT ONE OF YOUR FOOD CARDS BACK IN THE PILE.	WHILE YOU WERE SLEEPING, A SNAKE CRAWLED ACROSS YOUR CHEST. YOU AWOKE JUST AS IT WAS GETTING AWAY, WHIPPED OUT YOUR HAND AX, AND CRUSHED IT WITH ONE BLOW. TAKE ONE FOOD CARD FROM THE PILE.
A LIZARD WAS SUNNING ITSELF WHEN YOU KILLED IT WITH A ROCK. ROASTED ON A STICK HE MADE A TASTY MEAL. TAKE ONE FOOD CARD FROM THE PILE.	YOU FELL OFF A CLIFF AND BROKE YOUR LEG. A WILD PIG CAME AND ATE ONE DAY'S SUPPLY OF YOUR FOOD BEFORE YOU WERE RESCUED. PUT ONE OF YOUR FOOD CARDS BACK IN THE PILE.

Hunters and Gatherers

Simulation Game *(cont.)*

How many days can your band survive? Record the status of your band each day.

Recording Sheet		SUN.	MON.	TUE.	WED.	THUR.	FRI.	SAT.	
Week 1	How many are alive?								All living members get one food card.
	How many are sickly?								
	How many have died? How did they die?								
Week 2	How many are alive?								All living members get one food card.
	How many are sickly?								
	How many have died? How did they die?								
Week 3	How many are alive?								All living members get one food card.
	How many are sickly?								
	How many have died? How did they die?								

Fire Myths

Every culture has a story to describe how humans got fire. After reading one version by the Menominee, a Northeastern Native American tribe, students well create their own myths.

Preparing for the Lesson:

1. Reproduce the story (page 142) for students.

2. Reproduce and make an overhead transparency of the Story Plot Outline (page 79).

3. Reproduce or make an overhead transparency of The Writing Process (page 13)

4. Reproduce the Editing Checklist (page 14).

5. Gather art materials such as crayons, markers, watercolor paints, and white typing paper for students to use for their final drafts.

6. Gather the following materials for students to bind their stories into books: starch; containers for the starch; thick paintbrushes; red, orange, and yellow tissue paper; 12" x 18" (30 cm x 46 cm) black construction paper; 9" x 12" (23 cm x 30 cm) white construction paper; thick, black permanent markers; glue; brass brads; hole puncher.

Teaching the Lesson:

1. Tell students that many different cultures have myths about how humans obtained fire. Explain that they will be reading a myth and then creating their own myths.

2. Read the story (page 142) with students.

3. Review The Writing Process (page 13). Distribute the copies of the Story Plot Outline (page 79) for students to use as a prewriting activity.

4. Distribute the copies of the Editing Checklist (page 14). Have students write the rough drafts.

5. When students are ready to write their final drafts, have them divide their stories into scenes to illustrate. Their books should be at least five pages or scenes. Tell students to use the top half of each page for an illustration and the bottom half of each page for the text.

6. Have students use the following directions to make the covers for their books.

   • Using the starch and colored tissue paper, make an abstract collage on a piece of white construction paper. Allow the starch to dry.

   • Fold the black construction paper in half. On the half that makes the front cover, draw a ring of flames. Cut out the center of the ring of flames, making sure there is enough room to write the title of the book inside the ring.

   • Once the tissue paper collage is dry, place it behind the black ring of flames and mark it to show where you should write the book title. Write the book title on the tissue paper collage, using a thick, black permanent marker. Then glue the tissue paper behind the black paper.

7. Punch holes and bind the books, using brass brads.

A Northeast Menominee Legend

Long, long ago, when people first came to be on Earth they had no fire. Then the cold began, and humans were soon to perish. It was then that Manabus stole fire from Old Man who lived on an island in the middle of the Big Lake.

One day Manabus asked his Grandmother, "Grandmother, the days are getting colder. Why is it we do not have fire to keep us warm?" Grandmother explained that only Old Man had fire and that he was too mean to share it with humans. Manabus declared that he would go ask Old Man for some fire. Although his Grandmother begged him not to go, Manabus would not listen and left anyway.

Fortunately, Manabus had magic within him and could change his form into anything. So he changed himself into a deer so he could run as fast as the wind. Finally, he came to the Big Lake. Manabus wondered how he could get across all of that water. Suddenly a swift breeze nudged him from behind, and Manabus changed himself into a little white feather. The wind picked him up and carried him over the Big Lake. Once on the island, Manabus changed himself into a tiny baby rabbit. Then he scurried to the water hole where Old Man's two daughters came every day. Manabus jumped into the water to get soaking wet. Then he buried himself under some leaves. Before long, the younger of the daughters approached and Manabus darted out from the leaves.

"Oh, what a pretty baby rabbit," cried the girl, "I must show him to my sister." Manabus let her catch him. "Look, Sister. Look at this pretty baby rabbit. He must have fallen in the water, for he is all wet, trembling, and cold. Can't we take him to the fire in Old Man's Lodge?" The older sister warned her not to take the baby rabbit to the fire since it would go against Old Man's wishes. But the younger sister insisted, saying that Old Man would never know since he was fast asleep.

The two sisters placed the baby rabbit near the fire, and soon Manabus was dry and warm. Just then, the girls came back to get the baby rabbit. Manabus jumped away and then called to the Wind to help him. The Wind blew some sparks from the fire onto the fur coat of the baby rabbit. Manabus ran as fast as he could, carrying the sparks out the door. The girls cried out, and Old Man woke up to see the baby rabbit running away with the sparks of fire on his fur. He knew that the rabbit had to be Manabus stealing his fire for the humans and he was angry.

When Manabus reached the edge of the Big Lake, he changed back into the little white feather, but this time the feather was on fire. Once again, the Wind blew the little white feather across the Big Lake. The Wind carried Manabus right through the door of Grandmother's lodge. As soon as the little feather drifted to the ground, Manabus changed into a rabbit with sparks on his fur.

"Grandmother, Grandmother," cried Manabus, "do you have the wood ready for the fire as I asked?" Astonished, Grandmother pointed to the hearth. Manabus shook the sparks off of his fur onto the wood in the hearth. Grandmother blew on the sparks until the wood lit. Soon the room was filled with the warmth of a blazing fire. From that day forward, humans had the gift of fire.

Neanderthal

The Homo erectus people were the first to live during the Ice Age, periods of cold and warm that lasted tens of thousands of years. Homo erectus was better suited to survive in the warm periods. Therefore, a different species was evolving and adapting so that it could survive during the cold periods. This new species was named Homo sapien, or "wise man." Remains of Homo sapiens show they existed as far back as 250,000 years ago. Around 100,000 years ago, the first distinct subspecies of modern humans can be recognized. This subspecies was named Neanderthal after the Neander Valley in Germany where the first remains were found. The Neanderthals existed from 100,000 to 40,000 years ago. Some scientists believe that these early humans migrated throughout Africa, Europe, and Asia.

Neanderthal people were short and stocky with large muscles. Some scientists suggest that this stunted body was a special adaptation to the cold climate since a more compact body was easier to keep warm. Other scientists believe the Ice Age caused a shortage in foods that would have provided the Neanderthals with the proper nutrition to grow larger. The first study of the bones led scientists to believe Neanderthals had bowed legs and poor posture. However, further studies revealed many actually suffered from arthritis, a crippling disease.

The skulls that have been excavated show Neanderthals had lower, flatter heads at the top, or crown, than modern humans. The skulls bulge at the back and sides. Neanderthals had receding chins, larger cheeks, and very prominent brow ridges. Although their brain capacity was equal to modern humans, the position of the larynx limited Neanderthals' ability to create speech.

Archaeologists who first studied the fossils from Neander Valley assumed these people were brutish and unintelligent. Further studies revealed these beliefs to be inaccurate. Scientists found the Neanderthals had a primitive form of religion and that they celebrated some ceremonies. Remains have been found which show burial ceremonies where the deceased was buried with tools and food and then covered with flowers. This shows that Neanderthals were the first to have some belief in an afterlife and that they may have pondered the question of death. Researchers have also found evidence that the Neanderthals cared for the sick or disabled. These uniquely human qualities were not found with previous species.

Neanderthal *(cont.)*

Neanderthals were also more advanced hunters, toolmakers, and home builders. These skills were important for surviving in cold surroundings. Neanderthals used group hunting strategies to hunt the woolly mammoth and other large mammals that lived during the Ice Age. Unlike Homo erectus, who made one tool for a variety of uses, the Neanderthals made several different types of tools and weapons that were used for different tasks. In addition, Neanderthals are probably the first species to make clothing rather than just draping and wrapping animal hides for warmth. As a result, special tools were needed to cure and scrape the hides, puncture holes in the leather, and tie the skins together, using animal sinew.

Neanderthals also made more advanced shelters. Remains in Russia show that these early humans stretched animal hides over mammoth bones and tusks and then weighted the skins down with more bones to protect the hut from the wind. Other discoveries show that Neanderthals lived in caves or built animal skin huts in the shelter of overhanging rocks.

However, for all of their advances, Neanderthals had limited hunting ranges and what appears to be a peculiar social life. Evidence has been found to show that Neanderthals were unable to plan into the future and make full use of the resources around them. They hunted and gathered food for immediate consumption without storing food for other times when it was not readily available. Neanderthals also did not seem to migrate to follow animal herds. They did not survive on the grasslands of the world; yet, they flourished in the margins of savannas or forests where food was continuously accessible.

Neanderthals also showed signs of a very different form of interaction than that of other humans. With the Neanderthals, there is little evidence of a tight family unit. It does not seem that they had a central sleeping or food preparation area or a system for sharing resources among small groups of men, women, and children. Different sites where Neanderthals lived show that the women stayed near the camp, gathering food for themselves, while the men went out hunting and did not return for weeks at a time. The men seemed to eat the animals they killed on the hunt while they were away from the camp. They brought back only portions that needed further preparation, such as bones for which they needed fire to get at the marrow and skulls which were the Stone Age equivalent to canned goods. It was safer and easier to work on them at the shelter than out in the open.

Neanderthals did not have long life spans. Remains show that most Neanderthals did not live past the age of 40. Scientists do not know whether these short life spans were caused by living in a harsh environment with a lack of nutritional foods or by diseases such as arthritis. Since the Neanderthals' life spans were short, they did not have grandparents to help care for the young or to pass down knowledge from generation to generation. This could be one of the factors contributing to the abrupt disappearance of Neanderthals around 40,000 years ago. Scientists continue to search for more clues about our ancestors, the Neanderthals.

Neanderthal's Skull

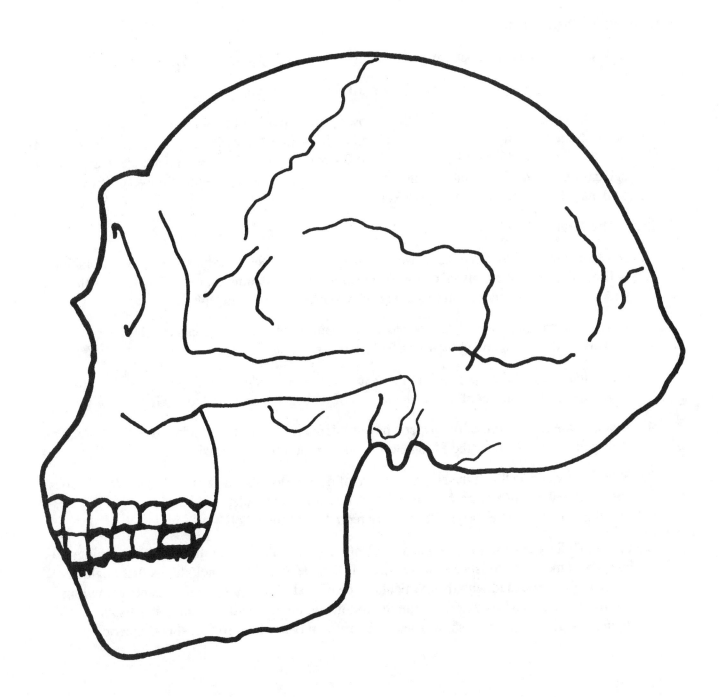

Metaphor Masks

The Homo sapiens, such as the Neanderthals, developed language and ceremonies. Their religion worshipped the many gods that they felt controlled their lives through their environment. Use the following lesson to create poems and ceremonial masks for some of the different gods that the Neanderthals might have worshipped.

Preparing for the Lesson:

1. Ask students to use notebook paper for rough drafts and typing paper for final drafts.

2. Gather books with pictures of primitive masks or use the samples shown on page 148.

3. To make the masks, you will need the following materials: white, black, and brown tempera paint, diluted slightly with water; thin paintbrushes—one per student; 9" x 12" (23 cm x 30 cm) pieces of white and brown construction paper—one of each color per student; clean Styrofoam egg cartons for mixing paint (or other similar types of containers)—one for every pair of students; thick, black permanent markers.

Teaching the Lesson: (The Poem)

1. Have students brainstorm a list of what kinds of gods the Neanderthals might have worshipped —fire, rain, sun, moon, bison, coyote, snow, deer, eagle, mammoth, etc. Tell students that they will be creating ceremonial masks along with a poem called a metaphor.

2. Have students select one of the gods to write about. Encourage students to select different gods for variety when displaying their finished products.

3. Have students fold their papers into three sections—top, middle, and bottom. At the tops of their papers, students should write the names of their gods, such as Moon God.

4. Again in the top section of the papers, have students write five to ten adjectives that describe their gods. Examples for the Moon God include: round, white, glowing, mysterious, spherical.

5. Explain to students that a metaphor is a type of description that makes a comparison but does not use the words *like* or *as* the way a simile does. For example, instead of saying, "Her lips are as red as roses" (simile), say, "Her lips are red roses." (metaphor)

6. In the middle sections of their papers, students should write at least three different "things" that have the same characteristics as their gods. Tell students to try to pick things that might not normally be associated with that particular type of god. For example, if students are telling about the Moon God they might write the following: dove—white, mysterious, distant; diamond—glowing, white, shiny, rounds; Styrofoam ball-white, round, shiny, spherical.

Metaphor Masks *(cont.)*

7. Now have students begin writing their metaphors in the bottom sections of their papers. Tell them to try to use as many of the adjectives as possible in well-elaborated sentences. Sometimes it helps to read aloud examples and have the class work together to make the metaphors longer and more vivid. Remind students that they should not use *like* or *as*.

    Example: The Moon God is a white, mysterious dove. (Poorly elaborated)

    The Moon God is a white, mysterious dove wafting in the distant heavens, trailing its midnight-blue cape behind its glow. (Well elaborated)

8. Help students keep molding and shaping the metaphors until they are satisfied. You may wish to have students work in partners or groups. Those who understand how to elaborate the metaphors may act as teaching assistants.

9. After students finish their rough drafts, have them write final drafts in neat, bold printing, or allow them to type their final drafts, using typewriters or computers.

Teaching the Lesson: (The Masks)

1. Have students examine examples of primitive masks, noting the geometric shapes, symmetry, and symbolism that are used. Tell students they will be creating ceremonial masks that the Neanderthals might have used to honor their gods.

2. Pass out the white construction paper. Have students use pencils to draw their masks as large as possible, paying special attention to making simple geometric patterns. The shapes need to be large, closed, and symbolic of the gods they have chosen from the list on the chalkboard (page 146). Ask students to let you approve their sketches before they start their final versions. Then have them trace the pencil lines, using thick, black permanent markers.

3. Pass out the paint trays with some black, brown, and white paint. Demonstrate how to make a tint by mixing a little white and brown paint in a clean cup of the tray. Tell students to make enough paint to cover an entire section of the mask. Then demonstrate how to make a shade by mixing a little black and brown paint in a clean cup of the tray. Encourage students to make as many color variations as possible for their masks. Remind them to be careful when mixing the paints so that they do not end up with an entire tray of gray paints!

4. Have students carefully paint the areas on their masks. Emphasize putting contrasting colors next to each other so that each section stands out. After the masks dry, re-outline the sections using a thick, black permanent marker.

5. Ask students to cut out their masks and glue them onto the pieces of brown construction paper. Then have them cut out the masks again, leaving a ¹/₂" (1.25 cm) border of brown around the masks.

6. You may wish to display the masks and metaphor poems on a bulletin board or glue the poems to the backs of the masks and suspend them from the classroom ceiling.

Samples of Metaphor Masks

The Moon God is a white, mysterious dove
wafting in the distant heavens, trailing its
midnight-blue cape behind its glow.

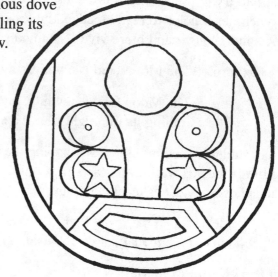

The God of Fire is a ferocious orange tiger,
greedily licking and biting its prey,
mocking it with loud, popping growls.

The Eagle God is a golden speeding bullet
descending quickly on a victim that is
unaware of its killer's name or strength.

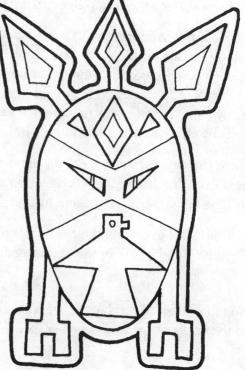

Create a Cave

Neanderthal people hunted fierce bears that lived in caves. They believed that the bear's skull and bones could make magic and keep them safe. They used the bears' caves to live in because they provided excellent shelter from the cold, bad weather and other wild animals. Have students create one or more caves in your classroom. You may wish to allow students to use the caves as special places to read, work on projects, and display the cave art that they create later in this unit.

Materials: sheets of brown butcher paper that are taller than the ceiling and crumpled up for texture, thick masking tape, push pins or T-pins

Directions:

1. Enlist the help of parent volunteers or tall students for this activity. Choose a corner of the classroom to build the cave. Be sure this area is out of the way of doors and students' desks. If space allows, you may wish to create two or more caves.

2. Measure the pieces of butcher paper so they will reach from the ceiling to the floor on both sides of the cave. Crumple the butcher paper to give it a rocky texture before hanging it up.

3. Begin on one side of the cave. Attach the top of a full-length piece of butcher paper to the ceiling and the side of a wall, using tape or pins.

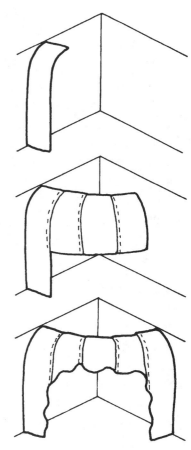

4. Depending on the size you choose to make the cave, you might need to tape additional pieces of butcher paper onto the first and join them to the ceiling, using tape or pins. Then tape shorter pieces of butcher paper together and tape them to the ceiling to create the front of the cave.

5. Then, repeat steps four and five to make the other side of the cave. Make sure all of the paper is secured to the ceiling, walls, and other pieces of butcher paper.

6. Next, tear the opening of the cave so that it is rough and irregular. You may wish to create a small opening so that the cave is dark and students need to crawl into it, or you can make a wide opening so that a table fits into the cave and students can work there.

7. After teaching the next section on the Cro-Magnon early humans, students can use chalk to carefully add cave drawings directly to the butcher paper.

Cro-Magnon

Towards the end of the Ice Age, around 40,000 years ago, Neanderthal people died out and a new type of Homo sapien with greater skills and ability to reason was evolving. Scientists named this new species Cro-Magnon after the location in France where the first remains were discovered. In 1868, workers who were widening a road cut into a roadside rock shelter known as Cro-Magnon or "big hole." There they discovered carefully buried skeletons and stone tools. These ancient cave dwellers lived under the rock overhang that was open faced and used the true cave which goes underground for special ceremonies and burials. By 30,000 years ago, Cro-Magnons had spread throughout Africa, Asia, and Europe. By 11,000 years ago, Cro-Magnons had crossed the land bridges that were in existence only during the Ice Age to occupy North and South America. Every continent but Antarctica was now populated by humans.

Cro-Magnon people were the first to have the same shaped bodies and skulls as modern humans. Their skulls had more rounded brain cases and pointed chins. Their foreheads were flat, rather than sloping, and ended in only very slight eyebrow ridges. Their noses and jaws were smaller than previous early humans and contained smaller teeth that were more crowded together. This made their faces fairly straight rather than jutting forward. In addition, based on the position of the larynx, Cro-Magnons were the first of our ancestors to be capable of producing clear speech so they could develop a more advanced language and means of communication. This enabled them to share information, work together, pass down knowledge and traditions, organize hunting and gathering trips, and speak about more complex thoughts, including planning for the future. An increased ability to use language spurred the development of a more advanced culture.

Since Cro-Magnon people lived during the end of the Ice Age, the weather was still cold and snowy. Therefore, fire was a vital part of the Cro-Magnon culture. Fire was the only source of heat in the caves or huts during the extremely cold winters. Fire was also used to chase game into traps when hunting herds or large mammals, such as the woolly rhinoceros, mammoths, or sabertooth tigers. A fire at the entrance to the cave or hut where the Cro-Magnons lived provided protection against wild animals. Fire was the only source of light at night and the only way these prehistoric people had to cook their food.

Cro-Magnon *(cont.)*

As these early humans developed, so did their tools. Cro-Magnons altered the flint-bladed hand axes into chisel-like tools called burins. These new tools could be used to split and shape stones and other materials that were softer than stone. The burins led to the invention of a series of new tools and weapons. Awls were created to make better holes in animal hides, bone needles were used to sew more refined clothes, and the first straight-backed knives were created to make cutting an even finer skill. Similarly, because hunting was the most important part of the Cro-Magnons' life, the development of new and better weapons was continually taking place. Cro-Magnons learned to carve spearheads and blades from bones and antlers, not just stone. Using bone implements, they were able to heat and straighten a crooked shaft. Discovery of the throwing stick enabled a hunter to throw spears farther and faster than before. And around 10,000 years ago the bow and arrow came into use, enabling the hunter to strike many times from a safe distance when hunting dangerous prey.

Since Cro-Magnons had not yet learned to domesticate animals or plant crops, hunting and gathering was still a daily necessity. Hunting provided food and other raw materials the Cro-Magnons needed. Animal hides were used for making clothing, robes, shelters, and bedding that were far more sophisticated than those made by the Neanderthals. After a hunt, the animal was skinned. With pegs the hide was stretched on the ground with pegs with the hair side down. Then it was scraped with special tools to remove all flesh or fat. The pegs would keep the hide from shrinking or curling as it dried. The hide was cured until it was soft and pliable. Then it was cut with stone knives into shapes that were sewn into pants, tunics, and dresses. Holes were bored, and sinew, or animal tendon, was used with a bone or antler needle to sew the clothes together. Cro-Magnon people often stitched little beads of colored rock or shells onto their clothing for decoration. They also wore necklaces made from stones, shells, fish bones, or bits of eggshell.

Cro-Magnons were very resourceful people and left nothing to waste. Sinew from animals was used to secure shelters, to braid into rope, or to form bow strings. Tusks and large bones from the leg of a mammoth were used to create shelters which were then covered with skins. Cro-Magnons stood the leg bones in mammoth skulls for support because they could not push them into frozen ground. These larger bones were also used as hammers and clubs while smaller bones were used for needles, fish hooks, and jewelry. Antlers and horns were shaped into weapons like harpoons, and antlers that had points with barbs pointing backwards were tied onto spears. Horns and antlers were also made into tools for digging.

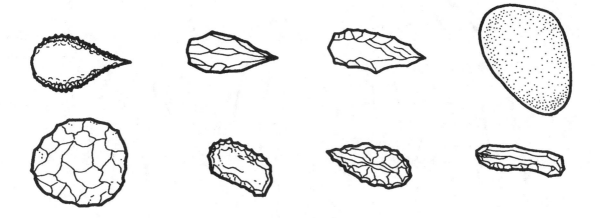

Cro-Magnon *(cont.)*

Hunting game was usually done by the men. The gathering of other types of food was a job done by the women and children of the Cro-Magnon tribes. Scientists believe that some of the plants that Cro-Magnons ate in ancient times are still popular today. The women and children might have foraged for wild carrots, beets, onions, turnips, cabbage, celery, fruits, and berries. Cro-Magnons foraged for wild wheat and other grains as well as for special plants with medicinal properties to make healing teas and poultices. Since the Cro-Magnons had no way to preserve their food, such as nuts, seeds, and fruits, it is likely that they prized food that did not spoil. These could be dried in the sun and eaten during the winter months when the ground was covered with snow. Besides plants, the women also gathered shellfish, eggs, and small animals caught in snares, nets, or nooses made of sinew.

The Cro-Magnons were a nomadic people. During the summer months they probably moved from their caves or huts to new areas, since moving from place to place enabled them to find new sources of game and plants. Summer camps also provided an opportunity for different people to get together to share stories, have celebrations, and find mates. Near Soultre, France, the bones of about 100,000 wild horses were found at the base of the cliff. Hunters used the cliff to stampede herds of horses and other animals to their death in an annual hunt. The remains of the hunters' temporary summer camp covered a large outdoor area. The size of this camp indicates that this annual "drive" was successful because many different family tribes worked together. Because of the vast quantity of bones discovered at this location, archaeologists assume this annual hunt took place for many years. Hence, summertime would have been a time of plenty. The Cro-Magnons probably even had time to relax.

Daily life for the Cro-Magnon people was very difficult. On those rare occasions when there was plenty to eat and the weather was fair, they would probably have been in a festive mood. Remains show that Cro-Magnons enjoyed many celebrations and ceremonies that revolved around a boy's transition into manhood, hunting, and the seasons. Celebrating and feasting from a good hunt probably involved gathering around the evening fire for all to hear the story about the hunt. It is possible that the story was told through dance with some members of the tribe acting out different parts and others chanting to the dance. Simple drums and percussion instruments have been discovered, showing these early humans enjoyed playing music during their celebrations.

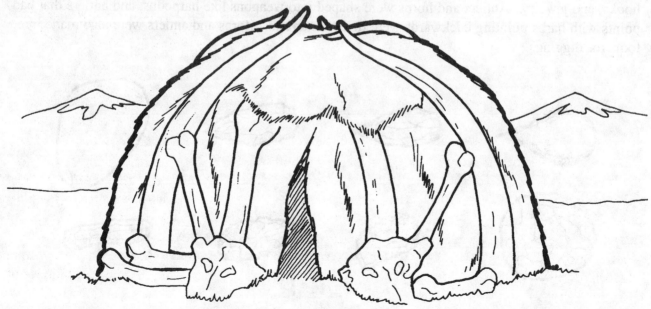

Cro-Magnon *(cont.)*

Scientists believe that Cro-Magnons showed signs of a more developed sense of religion and social structure as evidenced in their burial ceremonies. When a person died, it is possible that all members of the tribe participated in the funeral. The body was carefully placed into a shallow grave with tools, weapons, and food needed in the afterlife. The grave was then covered with dirt and stones. Most likely the Shaman, or religious leader, led the ceremony to honor the dead and request a happy afterlife.

However, the clearest sign of the Cro-Magnons' advanced culture was in their art. They were probably the first people to discover how to paint, sculpt, carve, and use color. No evidence has been found of pictures being made by earlier people. The Cro-Magnons carved designs in their tools and decorated their clothing with jewelry. They carved the first sculptures of animals and chubby female figures out of bone, ivory, antlers, and stone. Most scientists believe these figures were totems, or god figures, to ask for good fortune when hunting and gathering and to pray for more children to be born into the tribe.

These sculptures and amazing paintings were found in the deep recesses of underground caves. The earliest paintings consisted of hunting scenes and were most likely painted by men. Pictures included horses, bison, reindeer, and mammoths. These pictures have offered scientists clues about what prehistoric animals looked like. Often the Cro-Magnons painted spears in the paintings, showing that a hunt was taking place. However, few plants or people are found in the early paintings. Sometimes an artist would put his/her hand on the rock and blow paint around it with a reed. The hand symbol might have been used as magic since it was the maker of tools, or perhaps it was a prehistoric way to "sign" the picture and identify the painter. Paints were made by grinding colored rocks into powders and mixing them with animal fat. Colors included shades of red, orange, brown, black, and yellow. Paints were stored in hollow bones with lumps of fat in the ends. Brushes were made from animal hair tied to small bones. Sometimes they applied the paint with their fingers or used little pads of fur or moss.

The first cave paintings were found purely by accident. In 1879 a young girl and her father were exploring a cave in northern Spain where some stone tools had been found. Since many of the passages were narrow, only the young girl was able to reach a chamber that had never been seen in modern times. Inside, on the ceiling of the cave, she saw a herd of life-size bison. When her father saw the paintings he told others. However, they thought the paintings were a hoax, and so the cave was closed up and forgotten. Over the next 30 years other discoveries in France led archaeologists to reopen the caves in Spain. It was discovered that the paintings in the European caves were created between 12,000 and 35,000 years ago. The colors were still vivid and bright. Many other cave paintings have been found throughout the world since then, including the world famous Lascaux Caves in France. Although the original cave was closed in 1963 to preserve the paintings, a replica using the same techniques of painting can be visited today.

Cro-Magnon and Modern Human's Skull

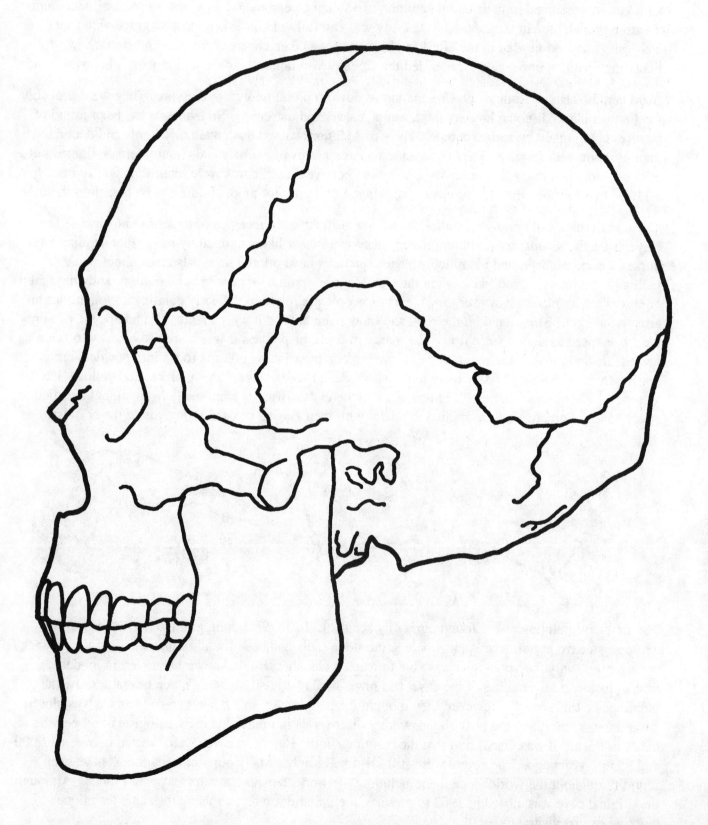

The Ice Age

During the Ice Age, huge sheets of ice and snow called glaciers covered large areas of the Earth. At this time, the glaciers advanced and retreated with the climate to extend from the North Pole southward into the middle latitudes of North America, Europe, and Asia. To this day, glaciers still exist in very cold parts of the world such as Alaska, Canada, Scandinavia, and Russia.

Glaciers from the Ice Age created new opportunities for Cro-Magnon people because the frozen water forced land bridges to surface. During the Ice Age much of the world's water was frozen into blankets of ice, thereby dropping the level of the oceans. Land that had previously been covered by water emerged, creating access to new areas. Cro-Magnons could now move from Asia to North America by crossing the Bering Straight. Land bridges also connected Australia with the islands of Southeast Asia.

The glaciers of the Ice Age also changed the land. Today, evidence can be found where glaciers have weathered the land to create depressions that eventually formed lakes or small ponds. Glaciers can also make ice-carved mountain ridges and valleys. The melting ice in front of the glacier deposits layers of sand and gravel. Rocks at the base of the glacier can scrape long grooves over the surface of rock on the valley floor.

Try the following experiment to see how glaciers change the land.

Materials: an aluminum pie pan or a shallow container, small stones and pebbles about 1 inch (2.54 cm) in height, access to a freezer, layer of potting soil or other dirt

Directions:

1. Put the stones and pebbles into the pan as shown.

2. Pour water into the pan, but let the tops of the stones stick out of the water.

3. Freeze the pan of water and stones overnight.

4. Remove your frozen glacier model from the pan and turn it over.

5. Place the glacier flat on some dirt so that the stones are in the front and on the bottom.

6. Push the model forward while pressing down. Push in a straight line for about 2 feet (0.6 m).

7. Let your model stay there to melt. After it has melted, observe everything that has been left behind. Record your observations and answer the questions below.

Observations:

1. How can you tell the direction in which the glacier has moved? _____

2. What evidence tells you how wide the glacier was? _____

3. How can you tell where the glacier melted? _____

Adapting to the Ice Age

Adapting to the glacial periods during the Ice Age was a challenge for our ancestors. Without a thick coat of fur like a woolly rhinoceros or mammoth, the people had to find other ways to stay warm and survive. The following group project allows students to create three-dimensional posters showing how humans adapted to the Ice Age.

Preparing for the Lesson:

1. Divide the class into cooperative learning groups. Assign places for the groups to work on their posters.

2. To make the 3-D posters, each group will need the following supplies: piece of white poster board; a variety of construction paper; colored markers or crayons; black markers; sugar cubes (or blocks of Styrofoam cut into cubes can be substituted); glue; 1 large index card.

3. Provide a variety of books about the different species of early humans and the Ice Age. Students can also use the handouts that you have given them for this unit.

Teaching the Lesson:

1. Point out that early humans existed and survived the Ice Age. Have students brainstorm a list of things that might have helped humans survive in this cold climate. Write the list on the chalkboard. Possible answers include: fire, advanced weapons and tools, language, clothing, building/finding more protective shelter, and migrating across land bridges.

2. Divide the class into groups. Tell students that the groups will be responsible for creating 3-D posters showing how humans used one of the ideas listed on the chalkboard to survive the Ice Age. Explain that they will also write brief descriptions to accompany their posters.

3. Explain the following steps for making the 3-D posters.
   - Use white poster board to make the background for your scene.
   - Draw and cut out people, huts, plants, etc., from pieces of construction paper.
   - Make sure your poster is clear and colorful by outlining all the pictures and using crayons or markers to color some details.
   - Glue the construction paper cutouts onto sugar cubes or Styrofoam cubes so that they will stand out.
   - Then glue the opposite sides of the sugar cubes or Styrofoam cubes to the poster board.
   - Use the index card to write a brief description of how man used that particular skill or object to survive during the Ice Age.
   - Create a title for your poster.

4. Then assign each group one of the ways early humans adapted to the Ice Age. Distribute the materials and circulate around the room while students are working.

5. Display the posters on a bulletin board entitled "Surviving the Ice Age."

Ice Man

Read the following passage about the 1991 discovery of a Paleolithic man found in the Alps. Then, write a descriptive diary entry as if you were this famous "Iceman." Describe what you were doing, how you were feeling, your hopes, and your aspirations on the fateful day when you became trapped on the mountain.

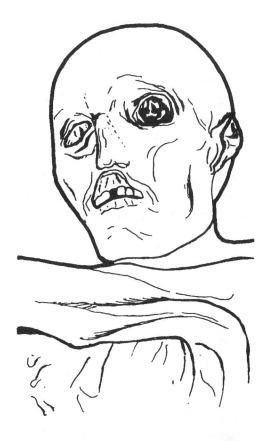

At the top of a high mountain in a rocky hollow the man stopped, possibly to rest. There in the hollow he unpacked his birchbark container. Inside were a few pieces of charcoal carefully wrapped in leaves. However, he was thousands of feet above any source of fire, so he would have to stay cold. Along with the charcoal he had a piece of ibex meat and a few berries. It looked as though he would be hungry before long, as well.

He stood 5 feet 2 inches (157 cm) tall and was in his late twenties or early thirties. He was physically fit and weighed about 110 pounds (50 g). His hair, which had recently been cut, was dark and wavy, matching that of his beard. He wore clothes made from animal skins, a cape woven from grass, a furry cap, and leather shoes stuffed with grass to help protect his feet from the cold. He clutched his ax in his hand as it was his most valuable treasure. His skin revealed tattoos or markings which might imply something about his spiritual life. The markings were sets of parallel blue lines on his back, a cross behind one knee, and stripes around an ankle. They were not done for show, but possibly designed to give him some sort of supernatural power or protection.

We may never know what brought this lonely traveler to this place where he found himself in such trouble. His body shows no signs of broken bones or disease. Perhaps he was engulfed in a sudden blizzard. He might have been weary from dehydration and lack of food or from a sickness and unable to move on. However, once he lay down his head, he never awoke. Deep snows covered the body, and for 5,000 years he lay in an icy tomb.

In September, 1991, a German couple, Helmut and Erika Simon, were hiking in the Alps between Austria and Italy when they spotted the Iceman lying face down in the snow. At first they thought they had found a discarded doll. Then, after getting help from fellow hikers, they thought it was possibly a recent accident victim. Later excavation would prove their discovery was the oldest preserved species from an Alpine glacier. The Iceman had been so quickly and naturally mummified that his brains and internal organs were undamaged. Even his eyeballs were intact!

Ice Man *(cont.)*

Unfortunately, the early excavation done by hikers and local officials was careless. Accidentally, the Iceman's backpack frame was broken while attempting to pry him loose from the ice. His six-foot bow was snapped in two, and his clothing was destroyed as hikers tugged and pulled on the body with ski poles. A gaping hole was made in the left hip with a jackhammer. Tattered and torn, the Iceman was finally airlifted to Austria for further study. On the way to a lab, his upper arm was broken while putting him into a coffin for transport, and due to the repeated flash from photographs being taken, a fungus began to grow covering his skin. Concern broke out among the scientists.

The Iceman was then quarantined to a freezer to prevent further decomposition. He was removed for only 20 minutes at a time for observation. How slender and frail he looked. His limbs were as thin as sticks. His ribs protruded against his skin, tight and leathery like beef jerky. His left arm, now broken, unnaturally crossed his body at a right angle. Possibly, he had used it as a pillow to rest his head; yet, the movement of the glacier over thousands of years had pushed it into this awkward pose. His other arm lay by his side with his hand in an open grasp as if feeling for his trusty ax. Even the shrunken skeletal head stared upward with dignity. After some political battles, it was agreed that Austria and Italy would share the Iceman and carefully study him in a way that would prevent further damage.

It is through his belongings, many archaeologists believe, that we will learn more about this Stone Age man's world. His copper ax blade revealed that he was a mummy from the Copper Age, which lasted in central Europe from around 4000 to 2200 B.C. A tool found with him was used to sharpen flint blades. In addition, he had a beautiful deerskin quiver holding 14 arrows, 12 of which were still incomplete. Some tools looked as though the Iceman had just laid them down yesterday. The bow, which was taller than himself, was unfinished and freshly cut. He carried a flint blade and a small, wooden-handled flint dagger in a carefully woven grass sheath. In addition, scientists found a bone needle, a bit of grass rope, a clod of felt-like fiber that may have served as tinder for his fire, and a four-inch (10 cm) long stick tipped with antler. Other intriguing items included a stone disk threaded with a leather thong tassel and on a leather string a piece of fungus found to have medicinal properties. Could these possibly be an amulet to ward off evil spirits and a primitive first-aid kit?

The style of his clothing and tools tell us that he was a mountaineer familiar with trekking through these ranges. The patchwork of his garment had originally been stitched together with sinew by a skilled hand. Yet, crude repairs had been made, using grass. Thus, scientists believe he must have had some ties to a community even though he was used to fending for himself. They also found spikes of primitive wheat which grew only at lower altitudes amongst his clothing. Likewise, the charcoal from his birch bag was analyzed and determined to have come from a variety of trees found throughout the Alps. Further investigation suggested that his homeland was probably in one of the valleys below the site of his death.

Perhaps he was a shepherd who had followed his flock up the mountain or he'd climbed to gather materials to make his weapons. He might have been a trader hiking towards the next village to trade flints. Perhaps his mystical tattoos meant that he was a Shaman, or medicine man, who climbed the mountain to perform rituals against evil. Maybe he was a prospector or even an outcast from his community, searching to live life on his own terms. Whoever he was, he has left his mark on this generation by allowing us an intimate glimpse into the life of a Stone Age man.

Living History Day

Cro-Magnon man marks the end of the prehistoric period, the time before recorded history. It is only with bits and pieces of clues that we can draw conclusions about their culture. Before heading into the dawn of modern humans, treat students to a Day in the Life of a Cro-Magnon! On this special day allow students to dress like they did, eat like they did, paint like they did, and celebrate like they did by dancing a ritual with instruments and face painting.

The Living History Day can take part of or an entire day. Reproduce the following for descriptions of the kinds of activities you can plan for the Living History Day.

Suggested schedule:

1. Have students arrive at school wearing appropriate Cro-Magnon attire. Encourage them to bring in foods to share (page 161) and materials to make instruments (page 162).

2. Divide the class into six groups or "clans" so they can work together to make instruments and create ceremonies.

3. Have students fashion their instruments to the best of their abilities, marking them with special patterns and designs that symbolize their clans.

4. Have students create cave paintings (pages 163-165).

5. Students prepare a Cro-Magnon feast (page 161) to eat at a picnic style lunch.

6. Introduce the different ceremonies (page 168) for the day. Have students practice appropriate movements, gestures, and sounds for each ceremony.

7. Have the clans practice and rehearse their presentations of different ceremonies.

8. Have the clans paint appropriate designs on their faces (pages 166-167) for their rituals. Then students can perform for the class while other clans try to guess which ceremony they are performing.

Other activities throughout the day include:

- presentations of any research projects assigned throughout this unit
- storytelling by groups of students
- walking a geological time line (page 42)
- sharing fire myth stories (page 141)
- playing the Hunters and Gatherers Simulation Game (pages 133-140)
- completing the 3-D posters about ways to adapt during the Ice Age (page 156)
- sharing diary entries from the Iceman (pages 157-158)

Living History Day *(cont.)*

Dear Parents,

Please join our class for a day in the life of the Cro-Magnon Stone Age cave dwellers. Our Living History Day will be celebrated on _____.

Below is a schedule of activities planned for that day.

Time	Activities

Please read the attached pages describing food, costumes, and materials for making instruments. Students should arrive at school already dressed in their costumes and bring in materials to make their instruments. Please sign up at the bottom of this form if you are able to bring a food item for our feast. Any help that you can provide will be greatly appreciated. We are really excited about our Living History Day activities and hope that you can join us.

Sincerely,

_____
Clan Leader

- -

We are looking forward to the Living History Day on _____.

My child, _____ , will bring _____ for the feast.

I will/will not (circle one) be able to join the class.

_____
Parent Signature

Living History Day *(cont.)*

Cro-Magnon Feast Menu

- water or herbal iced tea to drink
- almonds, walnuts, pine nuts, and pecans
- a variety of cold cuts torn into strips to represent wild pig (ham), wild pheasant (turkey), and bison (beef)

- carrot and celery sticks
- a variety of berries
- sunflower and pumpkin seeds

Cave Man Clothing

Look in books to get ideas for costumes.

Hair—Use a wig or tease the hair, using a fine-toothed comb and lots of hair spray.

Face and Skin—Rub charcoal or dark face make-up all over to give that dirty foraging look.

Tunic—Any kind of fur or fake fur draped over the shoulder or cut to make a tunic works. Students can use old shredded bath towels, furry bath mats, fuzzy blankets, a car chamois, a cut up T-shirt, pieces of leather or suede, burlap, an old poncho, etc.

Shoes—Anything that looks like it was made from an animal skin works well. Try boots, suede slippers, fuzzy slippers, leather sandals, etc.

Cave Man Accessories—These can include bones tied in the hair, bone and shell necklaces, bracelets, grass skirts used as capes, any other natural item formed into jewelry, etc.

Students should come dressed in a costume for the day. The parents are also invited to dress up also if they would enjoy doing so.

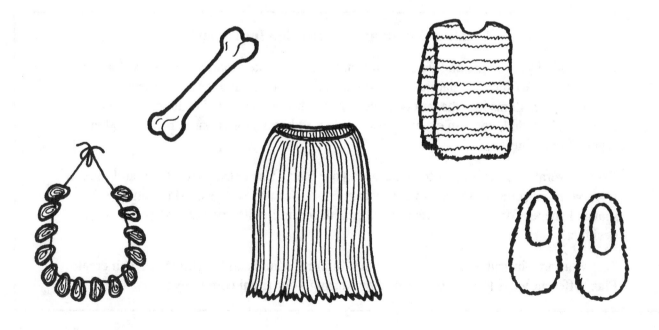

Cro-Magnon Music

Scientists have found evidence that makes them believe that early humans used music before they had the ability to speak. Speaking is actually a more complex skill than chanting. Based on studies of early human skeletal remains, the use of the voice to produce speech goes back only 80,000 years. However, chanting possibly began half a million years ago.

In prehistoric times, music was not to provide pleasure or enjoyment. Rather, it was used to help people in their struggle against nature. To prehistoric humans, music was mysterious and magical. It was intended to evoke fear in humans and in evil spirits. Music was played at ceremonies to prepare for a hunt, christen a birth, send a boy into manhood, mourn the dead, and worship the many gods that controlled the lives of these people. Primitive musical instruments can be grouped into three categories: percussion, wind, and stringed.

Percussion instruments were associated with bodily movements of ritualistic dance as well as with communication. Different percussion instruments included rattles made from dried seeds, seychelles, seed pods, gourds, and twigs; scrapers made from bone, horns, and gourds notched and scraped with a stick; xylophones made from stalks of dried bamboo, stones, or a hollow tree trunk; and drums made from a wide variety of materials ranging from a hole in the ground to rocks banged together to skins wrapped tightly over wooden bases.

Wind instruments could be found in the form of bone or reed flutes. One bone flute that dates back to 32,000 B.C. was found in the Siberian ice. Trumpets made from conch shells and horns were both associated with magical or religious functions and signaling.

While stringed instruments were rare among primitive people, zithers, harps, and lyres are thought to have descended from the hunting bow. There is a cave painting in France, dating from about 15,000 B.C., in which a man is apparently "playing" a bow as he holds it to his face.

Create a Cro-Magnon Percussion Instrument

Look around your home and yard to find materials to make a rattle, scraper, xylophone, or drum. Try to stick to "natural" materials, such as sticks, shells, rocks, seeds, nuts, etc. Use large items like the wooden stick off the broom and smaller items like wooden spoons. If needed, you can even use use cardboard boxes, toilet paper rolls, or other types of containers.

Bring several items to school to share with your clan. Use extra paper, tape, and glue to form your instrument. Perhaps your instrument rattles and scrapes. Make unique and unusual shapes for your instrument, and then decorate it with special clan patterns and designs.

Test your new instrument to hear all of the different sounds and rhythms you can create. Plan different ways to use your instrument during your ritual ceremony!

Cave Painting

Archaeologists have discovered paintings and sculptures from the time of the Ice Age in more than 150 sites throughout Western Europe. The American Southwest and the central Sahara Desert of Africa also contain several well-preserved samples of these early artists' masterful works.

Have students create their own cave art, using paper and chalk (pages 163–164) or plaster and paints (page 165).

Preparing for the Lesson:

1. Gather books that show several examples of cave art for students to examine. The paintings should not contain people since these came much later. For your convenience a few examples are provided at the bottom of this page. You may wish to reproduce these for students.

2. If possible, find some primitive drum or chanting music to play while students are drawing. African or Native American music often works well. If you have a music specialist at your school, she/he might have some suggestions.

3. You may wish to turn off the lights and allow students to work by candlelight to simulate what it was like inside of the caves. **Warning:** Be sure to check your school's fire safety codes to see whether this is allowed. In addition, discuss safety rules with students before lighting any candles. If it is against school code to use real candles use electric or batttery operated candles, or a flashlight rigged up to look like a torch.

4. Arrange the desks so that two to four students can share art materials.

5. Gather the following materials to create the cave art:

   - 12" x 18" (30 cm x 46 cm) pieces of manila colored paper, one per student
   - scratch paper for students to practice drawing shapes
   - colored chalk (**NOT** pastels) that is any shade of brown, black, red, yellow, and orange
   - 12" x 18" (30 cm x 46 cm) pieces of red, brown, and black construction paper
   - inexpensive aerosol hair spray

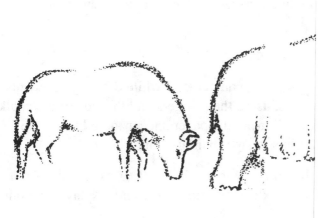

"What archaeologists look for

Cave Painting *(cont.)*

Teaching the Lesson:

1. Set the stage by reading the following passage:

   Close your eyes and imagine this scene. You enter a cave; walking deeper and deeper, you move almost instantly into complete darkness. Lighting a torch soaked in animal fat, you gingerly make your way through a passageway with a low ceiling. Clinging to the cool, damp wall for support, you stumble over loose stones. As the passageway takes a sharp turn, your smoky torch suddenly reveals two great bison lunging straight for you with their horns lowered! Fur flying, jaws agape, the eight-feet (2.4 m) long beasts seem to be airborne. You freeze, poised to flee. Then you realize that you have been tricked by a masterful illusion. A clever artist has used the natural contours of the cave wall to create a three-dimensional picture that seems to leap from the rock.

   Stone Age artists created these works of art thousands of years ago without any modern conveniences, such as latex paints or machine-fashioned paintbrushes. These prehistoric artists applied their paint to the walls and ceilings of caves by the flickering light of animal fat torches, taking advantage of bumps and cracks in the rock walls to form the animal figures. For paints, they used ground-up minerals—red ochre or iron oxide for red, manganese for brown, charcoal for black, and clay ochre for yellow. They mixed the mineral powders with animal fat, honey, blood, or the whites of eggs and stored them in hollowed bones. According to a recent theory, these painters also used the calcium water of the limestone caves, resulting in the first enduring watercolor paintings.

   Cave dwellers used some techniques and tools that we recognize today. They made brushes from animal hair, feathers, or chewed twigs and reeds. They even made painting pads out of wads of dried bison hide or moss. Painters usually outlined their animals first and then painted or used moss pads to fill in the colors. Sometimes, flint chisels were used to chip a bas-relief sculpture or incise a line. Many paintings were "signed" by the artist. Powered pigment was placed in a hollowed bone and blown over a hand placed against the cave wall.

2. Allow students to examine examples of cave art. Distribute scratch paper and practice drawing flowing lines. Remind them that they are attempting to duplicate a Stone Age painting.

3. Distribute the manila paper. Have students crinkle the paper to give it contours and tear the edges to give it a unique shape.

4. Distribute the chalks and paper towels for wiping hands.

5. Play the music. If using candles, light them. Discourage any talking while drawing. Students should draw the outlines first, rubbing in the colors, using their fingers and the side of the chalk. Rubbing different colors across the background will make the paper appear more like a cave wall. Encourage students to make chalk hand prints to sign their art works.

6. In a well ventilated area pray the drawings with hair spray to set the chalk and prevent it from smearing. Mount the cave art on red, brown, or black construction paper and display it in your classroom cave (page 149).

Alternative Cave Art Project

Use the directions shown on this page to have students make plaster cave wall reliefs.

Materials: Plaster of Paris or white tile grout; deep Styrofoam meat trays or aluminum trays; plastic wrap; mixing tub or bowl; watercolor paints; paintbrushes; fine-point, black permanent markers.

Directions:

1. You may wish to have students work in pairs or in groups.

2. Cover the tables or desks with butcher paper or newspaper.

3. Have students wear old shirts or smocks to keep their clothes clean.

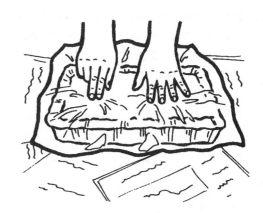

4. Mix the Plaster of Paris or tile grout according to the directions on the package. Pour the mixture into the Styrofoam or aluminum trays. Each tray should have a layer of plaster that is about one inch (2.5 cm) deep.

5. As the plaster begins to solidify, have students press the plastic wrap on the surface to create dents and ridges such as those found on a cave wall.

6. Then tell students to remove the plastic and allow the plaster to dry completely.

7. After the plaster has dried, help students carefully take it out of the trays. Then have them paint the entire surface with a wash of brown watercolor paint. (A wash is paint mixed with plenty of water.) It will dry unevenly, making the cracks appear darker just like a real cave.

8. Once the brown wash is completely dry, have students use pencils to lightly sketch their cave drawings. Tell them to use fine-point, black permanent markers to outline their drawings.

9. Tell students to use the red, yellow, brown, and black watercolors to paint in their pictures.

10. Show students how to use paper towels to blot up any excess paint or water. Allow the paints to dry before displaying students' projects.

Clan Dancing and Face Painting

Cro-Magnons were the first to have a well-defined social life and sense of religion. They held ceremonies in hopes of bettering their lives. By studying primitive tribes that exist today, anthropologists can generalize what the ceremonies and rituals of our ancestors might have been like.

Preparing for the Lesson:

1. Reproduce the information about different types of ceremonies so that you will have one copy to cut apart and make into assignment cards. You may wish to post an additional copy of this on the chalkboard in case students lose their assignment cards.

2. Make a large poster showing the names of the different types of ceremonies.

3. Obtain six clean Styrofoam egg cartons or similar types of containers to use as paint trays. Pour small amounts of black, brown, white, red, and yellow tempera paint into separate cups in each tray. The face painting requires very little paint so you do not need to fill the paint tray cups.

4. You may wish to have students create their own instruments (page 162) or gather percussion instruments for students to use. The primary grades or music specialist at your school might have drums, sand blocks, rattles, and scrapers.

5. Arrange for students to have a large area in which to practice and perform the ceremonies. An outside field, a stage, or a classroom with the furniture pushed aside will be suitable.

6. Invite parent volunteers to help monitor on-task behavior while students practice their dances.

7. If possible obtain a video that shows primitive dancers. Videos on African or Native American tribes often show dancing and rituals.

Teaching the Lesson:

1. Begin by going to the dance area if you are using an outside field or the stage, or have students help push aside your classroom furniture.

2. Place the poster with the names of the different ceremonies in a place where it can be easily seen. Have students gather in a circle and sit down. Tell students that the circle is called "the communal circle" and that it signifies the unity of the clan. Point out that it represents a never-ending union with nature.

3. Discuss the importance of sounds and gestures to these primitive people. Point out that they did not have a well-developed language, so they needed to rely on different vocalizations and chants to relay messages. Work with students to practice making sounds that might indicate emotions, such as joy, sadness, excitement, anger, and fear. Lead the discussion, using the following questions: What does it mean if you make... loud sounds? high-pitched sounds? low-pitched sounds? fast, repetitious sounds? slow, languid sounds?

Clan Dancing and Face Painting *(cont.)*

4. Then have students practice making body movements and facial expressions that might help convey different emotions and ideas. Tell students to make their gestures and expressions repetitive and use large sweeping movements with their arms rather than small hand movements which can be difficult to see.

5. Finally, have students practice some different dance steps or movements that primitive humans might have used. Emphasize repetition, rhythm, and the use of the communal circle. The dance steps can be broken into three main categories: stomping, walking, and twirling.

    Show students how to stand in the communal circle and beat a rhythm with your feet. Encourage students to try stomping their feet. Invite volunteers to create different rhythms for repeating.

    Demonstrate how to incorporate walking with the stomps. Have everyone walk in rhythm into the center of the circle. Then have one or more volunteers walk in rhythm around the circle. Form simple routines using stomping and walking.

    Show students how to add simple twirls that consist of turning around in circles. Invite volunteers to make short, simple routines that include stomping, walking, and twirling.

6. Discuss the importance of creating dances with clear beginnings, middles, and ends. Remind students that the dances should incorporate sounds, gestures, and movements in ways that convey the meanings of the different types of ceremonies. Tell students to consider the following questions as they create their dances: How will we begin—by entering in a rhythmic walk, by starting in a circle with our faces toward the ground? How does the dance climax (reach a point of excitement)? How will the audience know when our dance is over?

7. Divide the class into clans (groups). Distribute the ceremony assignment cards (page 168).

8. Allow time for students to plan their dances. Be sure students decide what their routine will be and what instruments they will use before they begin practicing. Sometimes a lack of sound or movement in a "pause" is also an effective way to communicate a message or change to a new message.

9. Then allow time for students to practice their dances. Remind students that school and classroom rules are still in effect. Have parent volunteers help you monitor on-task behavior while students are practicing their dances.

10. On the date of your Living History Day (page 159-161), allow students to paint each other's faces, using cotton swabs and small amounts of tempera paint. Remind students that they do not need to use a great deal of paint when making designs.

11. Take students to the dance area if you are using an outside field or the stage, or push aside your classroom furniture. Display the poster with the names of the ceremonies. Then invite the clans to perform their ceremonial dances as the culminating activity for the Living History Day. You may wish to announce the names of the ceremonies before the dances are performed or invite the audience to guess the names, based on the actions in the dances.

Ceremonies

Mammoth Hunt Ceremony

Winter is approaching, and the days are getting shorter. The large mammoth migration has already occurred, leaving only those that are old or sick and cannot make the journey. The meat supply of your clan will not last the winter. Tomorrow the hunters of your clan must be very brave when trying to kill a mighty mammoth. Create an appropriate ceremony asking the gods for courage and a successful hunt.

Birth Ceremony

You are very proud of your family clan. The woman of your group just gave birth to a boy. With the gods' blessings, this child will survive to become an adult. Some day this child might grow up to be a strong and skillful hunter. Create an appropriate ceremony for asking the gods to bless this new birth and to help this new baby survive.

Medicine and Healing Ceremony

Today your clan is collecting plants to make special medicinal mixtures. Many of the plants will be stored and used during the cold harsh winter. Many illnesses can be eased through the proper mixture and application of these plants. Hot mustard leaves relieve chest pain, and boiled chamomile leaves ease an aching head. Plan an appropriate ceremony to thank Mother Earth for her healing gifts.

Rain Ceremony

The waters from above have not come in a long time. The elders of your clan say that Mother Earth must be angry. The land is barren, and the animals are leaving your valley. The leaders of the different clans in the valley have met to discuss the situation. They have decided to hold a ceremony to honor Mother Earth and ask her to send some life-giving rain. Plan an appropriate ceremony.

Funeral Ceremony

Your clan has plenty of food, thanks to yesterday's successful hunt. But your clan is upset over the loss of the most able-bodied hunter. The hunter whose life was lost had a plan to isolate one rhinoceros from a giant herd. The plan was well-developed, but it was still dangerous to try to kill a rhinoceros. This hunter died while killing the rhinoceros so that the clan would have food. Plan an appropriate funeral and burial ceremony for this brave hunter.

Toolmaking Ceremony

Sabertooth tiger tracks have been spotted near your clan's cave. It has already eaten some of your food supplies. Your hunters are preparing to track down and kill the tiger. This will ensure the safety of the group and provide meat and valuable fur. New weapons that are strong and sharp are needed in order to strike and kill this beast. The master toolmaker tells the clan to have a special ceremony to ask the gods for skillful hands, hard but pliable rocks, and sharp weapons.

Modern Human

The Ice Age ended about 10,000 years ago. As the weather became warmer, trees and other plants grew again. Animals such as the woolly rhinoceros and mammoth, best suited to the climate during the Ice Age, died out and were replaced by forest-dwelling mammals. The people living at this time were called Homo sapien sapiens. They were the first Modern Humans and looked very much like people do today. Modern Humans had made many advances in hunting and gathering. Axes with wooden handles were made to chop trees. Fish traps and dams were built to catch larger quantities of fish, and the first bows and arrows were used to hunt deer. Boats were carved from hollowed tree trunks to transport the people to new areas for hunting and trade. Modern Humans even learned to tame dogs by bringing back wolf pups to the camp. Wolves live in packs and follow the strongest leader. As a result, when a pup was raised among humans it learned to be obedient to its master. Modern Humans trained these pups to help them when they were hunting wild game. Modern Humans also made advances in culture. For the first time humans were portrayed as the subjects of rock paintings. People were beginning to record their involvement with the world around them.

During this time, many advances were also taking place that caused some humans to settle down in one location and raise their own sources of food, rather than wander to hunt and gather. This transition towards settling down marked the end of the Paleolithic Age, or Old Stone Age, which began when Homo habilis made the first tool. Now a new way of life emerged, a life centered around agriculture and the community. Hence, the discovery of agriculture marks the beginning of the Neolithic Age, or New Stone Age. However, the move toward using agriculture as a way of life did not occur overnight. A gradual trend toward settling down happened at different times in different places. For example, 10,000 years ago the people in Europe were still foraging for food, but the first farmers were emerging in the Middle East.

Modern Human hunters and gatherers searched for areas where there was plenty of game, as well as wild grains, berries, nuts, and tasty plants and roots. The region in the Middle East from the Mediterranean Sea to the Tigris and Euphrates rivers was such a place. This strip of crescent shaped land had good soil and was named "The Fertile Crescent." Surrounded by plenty of food, these people were able to stay in one place for months at a time. This meant that they could build longer-lasting homes. In the Fertile Crescent, wheat grew wild on the hills. People collected the grains, fruits, and nuts, they found there. As they carried the grains back to their camps, some probably fell on the ground and grew naturally. Once the people learned that the wheat plants grew from fallen seeds, they tried scattering seeds on cleared land near their camps and waited for plants to grow.

Modern Human *(cont.)*

They collected the ripened wheat, storing the surplus grain in special storage bins for times when food was scarce. Using a stone mortar and pestle the wheat was ground into a coarse brown flour, and then mixed with water. Then it was shaped into flat, round loaves and baked in mud ovens to make a thin, hard bread. Scientists believe the early farmers' teeth were ground flat due to eating bread that contained the grit from the stone mortar and pestle.

As the hunters and gatherers began to settle down, they learned more about their environment. They observed the wild grains in different stages of growth and noticed the conditions that helped them thrive. At harvest time, they did not gather all of the grain but left some of the plants so that their seeds could be used the next season. They also learned more about the habits of the animals they hunted, such as wild sheep and goats. Scientists believe Modern Humans may have first protected these herds by driving away predators. This in turn helped the herds increase in size. Eventually, the people probably captured some of the young from herds of wild pig, goat, sheep, and cattle. The young animals were tamed once taken back to the camp. After these animals grew up and had babies, they too, were tame. Soon the village had herds of animals. The people protected and cared for their herds, making the animals dependent on the humans for survival. Modern Humans domesticated plants and animals by controlling their growth and behavior. The cows and goats provided the people with plenty of milk, and all of the animals could be killed when meat or skins were needed. In addition, wool from the sheep was used to make clothing. Modern Humans no longer needed to hunt wild animals in order to survive.

Obviously, the transition into farming and herding was a slow and difficult process. Early producers and raisers faced such problems as crop-killing insects, bad weather, and plant and animal diseases. Even after agriculture had begun, many farmers still continued to hunt and gather to supplement their food supplies. Furthermore, many tribes never adopted the agricultural lifestyle even though farming did have many advantages. With farming, not everyone was needed in the fields to raise food for the group. This allowed people to explore and specialize in other occupations, creating a division of daily labors and advances in such new technology as building, craft making, and toolmaking. This also allowed more time for religion and government.

Builders were needed to make new, longer-lasting types of shelter. Homes were built out of bricks made from mud and straw that had dried and hardened in the sun. Roofs were sometimes thatched with straw and covered with mud. Some of the houses had many rooms with floors covered by woven mats made from rushes. Shrines were built for worshipping, and a granary, or store house, was used to protect surplus food supplies. In the courtyards of the houses, there were usually large, dried-mud ovens. Pottery was invented, using mud baked in the ovens. Pottery was an excellent place to store food and water. Herdsmen built looms and learned to weave using sheep's wool.

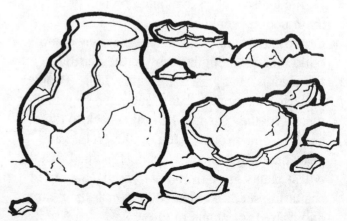

Modern Human *(cont.)*

The cloth was dyed and made into clothing that was better for use in the warm climate than animal hides. Straw mats and baskets were woven, using the grasses and rushes from near the water. Wooden boxes with lids and wooden bowls were carved and decorated.

Agriculture also required specialized tools and organization. One early farming tool was the sickle. It was made out of flakes of flint fixed into handles made from antlers, animal jawbones, or wood. The sickle was used to cut the stalks of wheat. Toward the end of the Neolithic Era, villagers began working with metals to make plowshares, crafts, jewelry, and weapons.

Leaders were needed to help organize the work in the farming village and help the growing population get along. The earliest leaders were the priests, who unified the group through more complex religious ceremonies, rituals, and daily worshipping at shrines. In time, the power shifted to governmental leaders, such as kings, who made the laws and offered protection for the village with the development of a military.

By 3,500 B.C. the small farming communities in the Fertile Crescent area of the Middle East were developing into cities, marking the rise of civilization. These complex societies shared the following characteristics:

They had a stable food supply from domesticated plants and animals, and they were able to store surplus food to use during the lean months. They had some form of an irrigation system for the crops, using water from a nearby river or lake in case there was not enough rain.

They had a specialization of labor so that different people learned different trades. People depended on each other to make the community work. Trading, or bartering, with other members of the community was necessary to provide for the family.

There was some system of government that helped organize the community and form laws. Leadership was needed to organize work and enforce the rules.

The community was divided into social levels, or classes. Some people were considered wealthy, while others were considered poor. Although "coins" used as money came much later, wealth depended on what a person owned, his/her occupation, and his/her relation to the religious or governmental leaders.

They had a highly developed culture that included art, architecture, music, religion, and law. Many civilizations also developed advanced language and writing systems.

Thousands of years have passed since the first Neolithic farmers built their villages in the Middle East. The very gradual change in their lives shows us that it takes many generations to mold and create a civilization.

Brick-Making Challenge

The first people to settle in the Fertile Crescent of the Middle East, along the Tigris and Euphrates rivers, built shelters made from mud bricks mixed with water and straw. See whether you can make a brick that is strong and durable enough that it could have been used for building a shelter 10,000 years ago. If your brick can pass the series of tests, you will be considered a Master Brick Maker!

The following list tells some of the things that made the Modern Humans' bricks special.

1. The bricks were piled and rolled to building sites, without crumbling or falling apart.

2. The bricks withstood the weight of other bricks when they were piled on top of each other to make a building. They also held up a doorway without breaking in two.

3. The bricks were well dried so that they would not wash away when it rained. Although some of the brick would "melt" in the rain, the bricks had to be strong enough to keep the buildings from collapsing and injuring the occupants.

Classroom Simulation

1. Your brick will be set on the cement and flipped over five times. If it can be flipped without crumbling and breaking apart, you will have passed the first test of strength and durability.

2. Your brick will be placed on two books to create something that looks like a small doorway. Choose one small student to lightly step up on the brick. If your brick does not break in two, you have passed the second test of strength and durability.

3. Finally, your brick will be submerged in a bucket of water for 30 seconds. If you can not snap it in two with your hands when you remove it from the water, you have passed the final test of strength and durability. This entitles you to become a Master Brick Maker!

Making the Brick

Use the following directions to make your bricks. You may want to experiment with different materials. Be sure to allow your bricks to dry over several days.

1. Use a box, such as a shoebox, to make your mold.

2. Try mixing different combinations of dirt, soil, sand, grass, weeds, straw, clay, flour, cereal, etc., with a little water. You may **NOT** use any cement, plaster, or tile grout.

3. Tightly pack the mixture into the box. If you make the mixture too wet, it will take too long to dry. If you make it too dry, the brick will crumble when you remove it from the box. You will probably want to make a few bricks and bring the best one to class.

4. Allow the mixture to dry in a warm place for several days. Remove the dried brick from the box. If you find that your brick is still damp, you may wish to ask your parents' permission to put it in the oven on a low temperature. Make sure you set it on a rack and turn it over periodically so that both sides dry.

MY FINISHED BRICK IS DUE AT SCHOOL ON _____.

Brick Maker Award

has earned the

grand honor of becoming a

Master Brick Maker!

May your dwellings never crumble!

Hunters and Gatherers vs. Producers and Raisers

The development of agriculture began a new way of life for early humans. Have students compare and contrast the Paleolithic hunters and gatherers to the Neolithic producers and raisers.

Preparing for the Lesson:

1. Make an overhead transparency of The Writing Process (page 13).

2. Reproduce the Editing Checklist (page 14), the Compare/Contrast Chart (page 175) and the Early Human Outlines for students to do their illustrations.

3. Make an overhead transparency of the Compare/Contrast Chart (page 175) to model the prewriting activity for students.

4. Write the compare/contrast words (page 176) on the chalkboard or on a chart.

5. Gather 12" x 18" (30 cm x 46 cm) pieces of colored construction paper to display the writing and illustration.

6. Have students take out the articles that they have been given relating to Paleolithic and Neolithic early humans. You may need to reproduce additional copies of these if some students no longer have their copies.

Teaching the Lesson:

1. Review The Writing Process (page 13) and Editing Checklist (page 14).

2. Distribute the copies of the Compare/Contrast Chart (page 175). Tell students that they will be using these forms for a prewriting activity.

3. On the transparency of the Compare/Contrast Chart, write *Hunters and Gatherers—Paleolithic Humans* for Subject #1 and *Producers and Raisers—Neolithic Humans* for Subject #2.

4. Next, have the class brainstorm a list of categories to consider when comparing/contrasting the two subjects. Possible categories include: physical appearance, where they lived, what they ate, how they got their food, what type of tools they had, what type of art they made, and what type of ceremonies they had. Write the categories on the transparency in the middle column.

5 Divide the class into small groups. Have students use any information they have collected during this part of the unit to fill in the details about the different categories for the two subjects. Allow time for groups to work on filling in this information.

6. Then have students share the information they wrote on their charts. Encourage students to add information to their charts as facts are being shared.

7. Explain to students how to use the Compare/Contrast Chart that you made in the prewriting activity to write a composition that compares and contrasts the Paleolithic early humans to the Neolithic early humans (page 176).

Compare/Contrast Chart

Introduction:		
Subject #1:		**Subject #2:**
Supporting Details	**Categories**	**Supporting Details**
Conclusion:		

Writing a Compare/Contrast Composition

Discuss the following steps to help students learn how to use the Compare/Contrast Chart that they made to write a composition that compares and contrasts the Paleolithic early humans to the Neolithic early humans.

1. Display the transparency of the Compare/Contrast Chart (page 175). Start by calling students' attention to the introduction. Point out that the introduction should give the reader some interesting background that will make her/him want to read the rest of the composition. Tell students that the introduction should also let the reader know the name of the two subjects (Paleolithic early humans to the Neolithic early humans) that are going to be compared and contrasted in the composition.

2. Tell students to begin new paragraphs to tell the first category.

3. Show students how to provide specific supporting details for each subject based on that category. Review the compare/contrast words shown at the bottom of this page to help students use a variety of words. You may wish to have students brainstorm additional words.

4. Then tell students that they should begin new paragraphs for two to three more categories. Be sure students understand that they should provide specific supporting details for each subject based on those categories. Students may have categories written on their charts that they do not use for their compositions. Explain that they will want to write their compositions using the categories for which they have the most information. This will make the composition much easier to write.

5. Call attention to the conclusion at the bottom of the Compare/Contrast Chart. Explain that conclusions should restate the names of the two subjects (the Paleolithic early humans and the Neolithic early humans), give a short summary that describes what the composition was about, and provide any closing remarks.

6. Have students follow The Writing Process (page 13) as they have done for other assignments. Remind students to use the Editing Checklist (page 14) to improve their rough drafts before making their final drafts.

7. You may wish to have students staple their final drafts inside, on the right, of the colored construction paper and make illustrations inside, on the left, of the paper.

8. Allow time for students to share their compositions with the class. Then display the compositions in the classroom for parents to see or in the library for other classes to enjoy.

Words that Compare	
same	too
similar	much alike
also	as well as
alike	similarly
in common	likewise
each	both

Words that Contrast	
different	
however	but
yet	unlike
on the other hand	differences
hand	differ
although	differently

Early Human Outlines

Complete the drawings of these early humans. Add some objects, tools, weapons, instruments, or pottery that these early humans might have used in their daily lives. Then color your picture. Finally, label the clothing and the objects you have drawn.

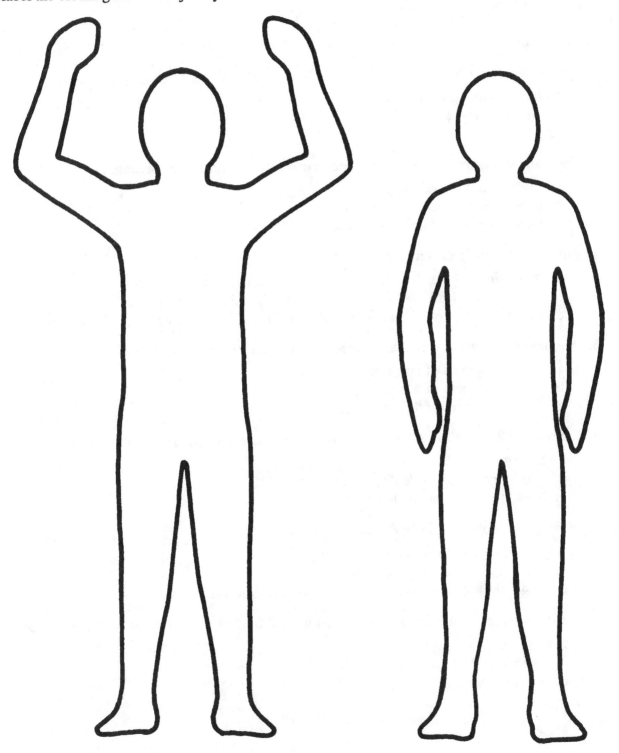

A Paleolithic Early Human

A Neolithic Early Human

Multiple Choice

Write the letter of the best answer on the line.

_____ 1. The oldest fossils of any human ancestors were found in

      a. Europe.

      b. Africa.

      c. Antarctica.

_____ 2. By studying human bones, archaeologists can tell all of the following except

      a. how tall the species was.

      b. whether the species walked upright.

      c. how the species made tools.

_____ 3. Evidence shows that as the human species evolved over time, they became more

      a. likely to live alone, independent of any group.

      b. dependent on hunting for survival.

      c. likely to care for those who are old or sick.

_____ 4. Early hunters and gatherers survived by

      a. harvesting crops and raising domesticated animals, such as sheep and goat.

      b. burying their dead in shallow graves with possessions for their afterlife.

      c. following the herds of migrating animals and searching for edible plants and roots.

_____ 5. An important development that enabled early humans to work together was

      a. the development of language.

      b. the development of boats.

      c. the development of the hand axe.

_____ 6. From about 250,000 to 12,000 years ago, glaciers advanced and retreated during the

      a. Ice Age.

      b. Old Stone Age, or Paleolithic Age.

      c. New Stone Age, or Neolithic Age.

_____ 7. Which of the following in **NOT** true of the Ice Age?

      a. The climate was colder than it is today.

      b. The oceans were higher than they are now.

      c. Huge sheets of ice and snow covered areas in North America.

_____ 8. The development of agriculture by humans in the Middle East marks the beginning of the

      a. Ice Age.

      b. Paleolithic Age.

      c. Neolithic Age.

Match the Humans

Read the statements shown below. Then write the letters for the groups of early humans that are being described by the statements.

a. Australopithecus	**d. Homo sapien: Neanderthal**
b. Homo habilis	**e. Homo sapien: Cro-Magnon**
c. Homo erectus	**f. Homo sapien sapien: Modern Human**

_____ 1. These humans were the first of the species to use fire for capturing prey, keeping warm, lighting shelters, scaring away wild animals, and cooking food.

_____ 2. These humans were short and stocky with heavy eyebrow ridges. They lived during the Ice Age and hunted the woolly mammoth.

_____ 3. These humans are thought to be the very first early humans. "Lucy" is the fossilized remains of someone from this primitive group.

_____ 4. These humans made the first tools which marks the beginning of the Paleolithic Age, or Old Stone Age.

_____ 5. These humans made clothing out of woven wool from domesticated sheep.

_____ 6. These humans made sophisticated clothing from animal skins sewn with bone needles and animal sinew.

_____ 7. These humans were the earliest Homo sapiens to have a ritual burial for their dead.

_____ 8. These humans were the first farmers in the Middle East, marking the beginning of an agricultural way of life and the Neolithic Age.

_____ 9. These humans were the first to paint pictures on cave walls using ground minerals mixed with animal fat. They also made small sculptures of animals and female figures.

_____ 10. These humans were the first to use boats. They hunted deer with bows and arrows in the forests of Europe after the Ice Age.

_____ 11. The name for this group of humans means "handy man."

_____ 12. These early Ice Age hunters and gatherers migrated to Terra Amata each spring to follow the herds of animals. They built shelters out of branches supported with stones. They had areas inside their shelters for making tools and preparing the food.

Comprehending Early Humans

A. Answer the following questions on a separate piece of paper. Be sure to use complete and well-elaborated sentences.

1. Why do scientists believe the Ice Age encouraged early humans to migrate and spread throughout the Earth?

2. How did the development of tools allow early humans to take advantage of a wider range of food sources?

3. Why was the development of fire important to early humans? Give at least three examples.

4. How did the development of domesticated plants and animals make life easier for early humans? Give at least two examples.

B. Examine the picture of an archaeological site that is shown below. Write a paragraph stating the name of the group of early humans you believe lived here. Then give plenty of details that describe the evidence shown in the picture that supports your conclusion.

C. Select a species of early humans. On another piece of paper, write a description that tells what a typical day might be like for a group of them. Be sure to include details about their type of shelters, what they ate, how they obtained their food, their tools, their religious beliefs, their clothing, their art or culture, and any other achievements.

Answer Key

Suggested answers for the Information Chart (pages 104-109) are below and on pages 182-183.

	Australopithecus (page 104)	Homo Habilis (page 105)
Dates and Place of Existence (When and where did they live?)	5 million–1 million years ago in Africa	beginning Paleolithic Age 2 million–1 million years ago in Africa, Asia
Description of Physical Appearance (What did they look like? What was their average height and weight?)	120 cm–170 cm tall, walked upright, human foot, ape-like skull, large teeth, brain less than half the size of modern human	4 1/2 feet tall; walked upright; rounded skull with smaller face and teeth; brain half the size of modern human
Description of Shelters (What kind of shelters did they use? What materials were used to make the shelters? Were the shelters meant to be easy to move?)		simple huts made from branches and stones; dome-shaped
Food (What type of food did they eat? How did they get their food?)	used branches or stones to kill prey; foraged for berries, leaves, fruit, roots, eggs, and insects	didn't use weapons; organized hunt to catch animals; used tools to cut meat and smash bones for marrow; ate plants also
Description of Daily Life (How did they live? Were they hunters and gatherers or farmers?)	nomadic lifestyle; hunters and gatherers	nomadic lifestyle; hunters and gatherers
Tools (What materials were used to make tools? What purposes did the tools serve?)	used branches or stones to kill prey;	simple tools from stone; a hand axe with sharp sides
Fire (Could they make fires? What did they use to make the fires?)		
Religion and Ceremonies (What kinds of occasions were special? What did they do to worship or celebrate?)		
Development of Language (How did they communicate? Did they have written language?)		primitive form of communication, using gestures and sounds
Clothing (What did their clothing look like? What was it made from?)		none
Painting and Carving (What kinds of things did they paint or carve? What materials did they use to make the paintings or carvings?)		

Answer Key *(cont.)*

	Homo Erectus (page 106)	**Neanderthal** (page 107)
Dates and Place of Existence (When and where did they live?)	1,500,000–250,000 years ago, Europe, Asia, Africa Ice Age	100,000–40,000 years ago during Ice Age in Africa, Europe (Neanderthal Valley-Germany), Asia
Description of Physical Appearance (What did they look like? What was their average height and weight?)	taller than habilis; walked upright without stooping; larger brain; sloping forehead; big jaw; bony bump on back of skull	short and stocky with large muscles; some had arthritis; low, flat head with bulges at the sides and prominent brow ridge
Description of Shelters (What kind of shelters did they use? What materials were used? Were they meant to be easy to move?)	lived with 20-30 members in a group; made huts with fire hearths	more advanced huts using skins and bones; some lived in caves
Food (What type of food did they eat? How did they get their food?)	foraged over wide area, following migrating animals; used group hunting to kill elephants, rhinos, and oxen	used group hunting strategies for woolly mammoth; did not store food or migrate to follow herds; men hunted, ate the meat; women and children gathered their own food
Description of Daily Life (How did they live? Were they hunters and gatherers or farmers?)	nomadic lifestyle; hunters and gatherers	didn't migrate to follow herds; hunters and gatherers; sexes seemed to live separate lives; women and children stayed in the camp; men went hunting for a long time
Tools (What materials were used to make tools? What purposes did the tools serve?)	made bolas for hunting; hand axes for purposes such as cutting and digging roots	tool making–Used fire to help during Ice Age. Made different tools for different purposes.
Fire (Could they make fires? What did they use to make the fires?)	first to use fire to hunt, cook, keep wild animals away, harden tools	made fire with stones or sticks probably for the same purposes as Homo erectus
Religion and Ceremonies (What kinds of occasions were special? What did they do to worship or celebrate?)	traveled to Terra Amata each spring, following herds of animals; feasted there with other Homo erectus clans	first to show evidence of ceremony to bury dead and signs that they cared for the old and sick
Development of Language (How did they communicate? Did they have written language?)	grunted sounds and simple words combined with gestures	limited range of speech because of larynx position
Clothing (What did their clothing look like? What was it made from?)	use draped animal skins to keep them warm during cold periods	first to make clothing by curing hides, punching holes, and tying with leather
Painting and Carving (What kinds of things did they paint or carve? What materials did they use to make the paintings or carvings?)		

182

Answer Key *(cont.)*

	Cro-Magnon (page 108)	Modern Human (page 109)
Dates and Place of Existence (When and where did they live?)	40,000 - 10,000 years ago during Ice Age; migrated to Americas across land bridges	began Neolithic Age; 10,000 years ago to present day
Description of Physical Appearance (What did they look like? What was their average height and weight?)	same-shaped bodies and skulls as people today	same-shaped bodies and skulls as people today
Description of Shelters (What kind of shelters did they use? What materials were used? Were they meant to be easy to move?)	cave dwellers; also made animal skin shelters inside caves	built homes and shrines from mud bricks; built special rooms for storing surplus grain
Food (What type of food did they eat? How did they get their food?)	migrated to hunt and gather; used harpoons, fish hooks, spears; gathered plants: such as carrots, beets, onions, cabbage, celery; drove wild horses over cliffs	first farmers; domesticated plants and animals; ate wheat, meat from sheep, pigs, goats, cattle; drank milk
Description of Daily Life (How did they live? Were they hunters and gatherers or farmers?)	nomadic lifestyle; hunters and gatherers	farmed in one place (still some groups of hunters and gatherers); domesticated wolf pups; priests were first leaders
Tools (What materials were used to make tools? What purposes did the tools serve?)	burin chisel tool was created to make other tools: awl, bone needle, straight-backed knife, spearheads, throwing stick, and later, the bow and arrow	advanced hunting tools like boat, bow and arrow; made farming tools like sickle; eventually used metal
Fire (Could they make fires? What did they use to make the fires?)	fire important during Ice Age for heating, hunting, protection, cooking, light	used fire for heating, protection, light; baked bread and made pottery in mud ovens
Religion and Ceremonies (What kinds of occasions were special? What did they do to worship or celebrate?)	used totems, medicinal plants; gathered with other clans for festivals; held manhood rituals, funerals, and ceremonies	priests were the first leaders; built shrines for organized worship
Development of Language (How did they communicate? Did they have written language?)	first to be capable of clear speech because of larynx position	fully developed language; eventually developed writing
Clothing (What did their clothing look like? What was it made from?)	pants, tunics, dresses made with awl and bone needles: decorate clothes with stones and shells, jewelry	used wool to weave clothing on looms; wore jewelry and decorated clothing
Painting and Carving (What kinds of things did they paint or carve? What materials did they use to make the paintings or carvings?)	painted animals on cave walls, using ground minerals; carved figures and totems for worship	made decorated pottery, baskets, wooden boxes, and bowls; first to paint people in pictures

Answer Key *(cont.)*

Putting Lucy Together (page 120)

Suggested answers:

Fragment	Information Learned from the Fragment
skull	brain about 1/3 size of modern human
femur	walked upright; was about 25 years old
pelvis	female of the species
whole skeleton	3½ feet tall

Compare/Contrast Chart (page 175)

Introductions and conclusions may vary. Accept all reasonable responses.

Subject #1: Paleolithic Hunters and Gatherers	Categories	Subject #2: Neolithic Producers and Raisers
migrated to follow animal herd; caves or huts made from branches, animal hides, or bones; 20-30 people in a clan; lived mostly in Africa, Asia, and Europe, mostly; some moved to North and South America	Where they live	earliest farmers; lived in the Fertile Crescent of the Middle East; built mud bricks homes with thatched roofs; villages had hundreds of people; stayed in one place
wild game, plants, rabbit, deer, fish, woolly mammoth, woolly rhino, birds, shellfish, roots, berries, fruit, nuts, seeds, eggs	What they ate	domesticated plants and animals; wheat, barley, vegetables, sheep, pigs, goats, milk; harvested crops, stored surplus for later use
hunted, gathered, and fished. migrated each year to follow the herds of animals; relied on nature to provide food; small storage of dried fruits and nuts for use later; spear, bow and arrow, digging stick	How they obtained food; tools	domesticated plants and animals; used the sickle to harvest crops; protected herds and killed some of the animals when needed food; controlled nature to get food; surplus allowed for different jobs to be done; made pottery, cloth and baskets from weaving, and metal tools
cave paintings of animals, burial ceremonies, music and dancing, developed language, simple religion tied to animals, superstitious, simple leadership in family clan	Aspects of culture	surplus allowed for different jobs to be done; had better organized religion (priests and shrines) and beginnings of government; began painting people; developed writing

184

Answer Key *(cont.)*

Multiple Choice (page 178)

1. b

2. c

3. c

4. b

5. c

6. a

7. a

8. c

Match the Humans (page 179)

1. c

2. d

3. a

4. b

5. f

6. e

7. d

8. f

9. e

10. f

11. b

12. c

Comprehending Early Humans (page 180)

A. Short Answers

1. Answers should include information about the land bridges and migrating to find animals.

2. Answers should include the fact that they could kill larger animals than they could kill with their bare hands and that tools gave them access to plants that were under hard ground.

3. Answers can include warmth, light, cooking, scaring away wild animals, helping to make weapons and tools, and using them to hunt.

4. Answers can include the fact that they could now stay in one place, they could gather a surplus and store it for other times, they no longer needed to hunt and depend on available animals, and they no longer needed to gather plants and depend on just what they could forage.

B. Answers should describe a Cro-Magnon group since they were the first to live in caves and paint. Details should also be given to point out the other items and how they are indicative of a Cro-Magnon group.

C. Accept all reasonable responses.

Literature Planning Guide

Using Literature

The literature lessons are arranged so that they correspond to sections in the book. Below is a suggested format for each section of the book.

- **Prereading Activity**—discuss past chapters, predict future events, connect the story to other classroom activities

- **Read the Section**—choose a reading strategy (page 103)

- **Vocabulary Activity**—see the lists for each section (pages 192, 195, 200, 206, 211) and suggestions for activities (page 189)

- **Comprehension Activity**—see the questions for each section (pages 192, 195, 200, 206, 211) and suggestions for activities (page 190)

- **Written Language Activities**

- **Hands-On Activities**

Preparing for Teaching the Literature Lessons

1. Students can make a literature journal by stapling writing paper into construction paper covers before starting the lessons. This allows them to keep a record of their responses to comprehension questions, definitions for vocabulary words, and thoughts and feelings about the story as they read it. Have students decorate the front covers with the title of the book, their names, and appropriate illustrations.

2. You may wish to have students trace the map that is shown in the book and staple it inside their literature journals.

3. Preview the story and make notes in your copy of the book. This allows you to easily find vocabulary words, descriptions, figurative language, and sections covered by the comprehension questions.

4. Review the different activities for the literature unit. Plan to gather the materials you need ahead of time. Decide how much time you want to schedule for each of the activities.

5. Make overhead transparencies of the vocabulary lists and comprehension questions (pages 192, 195, 200, 206, 211) and reproduce them for students as you begin each section. Discuss the vocabulary with students. Ask them whether they already know the meanings to any of the words. Ask students to pay close attention while reading to see whether they can use context clues to determine the meanings of unfamiliar words. Then, discuss the comprehension questions with students. Ask volunteers to help you determine key words in the questions. Underline the key words on the transparencies.

6. Make an overhead transparency of the outline (page 79) to use as students are reading the book. You may wish to reproduce this outline for students to fill in their own copies.

Background Information

About the Author

Ann Turnbull was born and raised in England where she grew up loving adventure books, such as *The Chronicles of Narnia* by C.S. Lewis and *The Jungle Book* by Rudyard Kipling. She has been writing since she was about six years old.

Ms. Turnbull was inspired to write *Maroo of the Winter Caves* after viewing picture books about cave paintings in Europe. She was in awe of these primitive people's ability to create such sensitive and beautiful art. Ms. Turnbull has attempted to use archaeological data to reconstruct a more personal and human view of these primitive people encountering a difficult way of life.

Ms. Turnbull now resides in England with her husband and two children.

Book Summary

The story takes place during prehistoric times at the end of the last Ice Age, about 25,000 years ago. Maroo and her people live in an area that would be considered part of present-day France. Her people are a band of hunters and gatherers who live in caves during the winter months and travel to other sites during the summer. Each year the family makes a long journey, following the herds of wild animals.

The story opens in early spring with the children anxiously awaiting the summer journey. A group of hunters return from a successful hunt and are welcomed by the clan. The people feast on bison and sing and clap to the rhythm of a drum. The next day they leave on their long journey for summer hunting by climbing the White Mountain which they believe to be the home of unfriendly spirits and cave lions. Otak and Maroo find a wild puppy which they name Rivo and are allowed to keep. The band eventually arrives at the Mediterranean Sea.

Autumn arrives and other groups head for the winter caves. Maroo's family is delayed by her mother's pregnancy. After her mother gives birth, the winter snows begin to fall. Maroo's family must struggle through the blizzards to make it back to White Mountain. At the base of the mountain, they must stop to build a snow house for protection. The threat of starvation is ever present.

Out of desperation to save the rest of her family, Maroo and Otak leave to cross the dreaded White Mountain and get help from the Winter Camp. There Maroo slips in a glacial crevasse and is rescued by Otak. They believe the mountain's spirits are angry as blizzards force them to stop and make shelter. When Maroo kills a rabbit with her brother's spear, the two siblings argue. Angrily, Otak leaves the next morning to hunt, taking Rivo along. When he does not return, Maroo is forced to search for him and then continue her journey alone. Bravely, she fights off a mountain lion before finally reaching the camp. The others help rescue the rest of the family at the base of the mountain. As they return to camp all hope is lost for Otak and Rivo. Yet, in the end, they, too, return to the warm embrace of their family.

Vocabulary Activities

You can help your students learn and retain the vocabulary suggested for each section of the story by providing them with interesting vocabulary activities. Here are some ideas to try.

1. Have students write each word in their journals. Then have them find the word in the story and look up the definitions in dictionaries. Have students write in their journals the definitions that match the uses of the words in the book.

2. Have students work in groups to make vocabulary flashcards by writing the sentences from the book that contain the vocabulary words on one side of some index cards and the meaning of the words on the other side. Have students quiz each other about the definitions of the words. Cards can also be used by individual students to test themselves.

3. Have individuals make illustrated vocabulary dictionaries by writing the words and definitions on large index cards along with illustrations. As words are added while reading the book, keep rearranging the cards so that the words are in alphabetical order. After students have read the book, bind the cards together, using a hole puncher and yarn.

4. Have students make a synonym/antonym chart in their journals. As they write down their vocabulary words and the sentences from the book, have them also write synonyms that could be substituted in the sentences without changing the meanings. Then have them write antonyms that change the meanings of the sentences when they are substituted for the vocabulary words.

5. Tell students to make parts of speech charts in the journals. The headings should include *Noun, Verb, Adjective,* and *Adverb.* Ask students to write the sentence from the book with the vocabulary word highlighted under the appropriate heading.

6. Have students use the vocabulary words to write poems or summaries about the chapters in that section. Highlight the vocabulary words and display some of the best poems or summaries.

7. Challenge students to work in pairs and use graph paper to make vocabulary crossword puzzles. Reproduce some of the best puzzles to distribute to the class.

8. Have a vocabulary bee that is similar to a spelling bee in your class. Students can play individually or in teams. Students should spell the words and give the correct definitions after you read aloud the sentences from the book that contain the appropriate vocabulary words.

9. Play vocabulary hide-and-seek by having students work in groups to write the sentences from the book that contain the vocabulary words on one set of index cards and the definitions of the vocabulary words on another set of index cards. Give one group a designated area to hide their cards and have another group try to find the cards, matching the words with their definitions.

10. Have students play vocabulary charades by acting out each vocabulary word.

11. Write a vocabulary word on the chalkboard before students enter the classroom. When students arrive tell them that the word for the day is written on the chalkboard. Discuss the meaning of the word. Ask students to correctly use the word a frequently as possible throughout the day. Make a tally mark next to the word each time students use it.

Comprehension Activities

You can help your students better understand the story by using the comprehension questions suggested for each section and one or more of the comprehension activities suggested below.

1. Have students answer some or all of the questions, using complete sentences, in their literature journals. Invite students to discuss their answers.

2. Play comprehension "hot seat." Have one student come to the front of the class to portray one of the characters from the book. Have the rest of the students ask appropriate questions from the list along with questions of their own. The student in the hot seat should respond to the questions as if they were that character. Tell students to think carefully about how the character would talk, feel, move, etc. Evaluate students' ability to respond correctly, based on their assumed identity. Have students take turns being in the hot seat and pretending to be other characters.

3. Have students make comprehension comic strips that show scenes from the story that answer one or more of the questions.

4. Have students make illustrated posters or dioramas to answer one or more questions.

5. Play comprehension hide-and-seek by writing the questions on one set of index cards and the answers on another set. Hide the cards and have students find them, matching the questions with the correct answers.

6. Divide the class into groups. Ask each group to dramatize the answer to one of the questions.

7. Have students write dialogues between characters from the story, answering one or all of the questions. Invite volunteers to read their dialogues to the class.

8. Play comprehension Jeopardy by dividing the class into two teams. Have each team write questions for that section of the book or any previous sections. Write the student-created questions (worth 5 points) and the comprehension questions (worth 10 points) on strips of paper. Put the strips in a container to be drawn. Have each team take turns drawing out a question, discussing, and then answering a question. (Do not let them know ahead of time who will be called on to answer for the team; that way everyone on the team must participate.) The team with the most points wins.

9. Play cooperative group comprehension battle by dividing the class into groups of four. Assign each person in the group a number from 1-4. Give each group pieces of scratch paper to write their answers. Have them write their group's "name" at the top of each piece of paper. Using the questions from the list, assign each question a point value based on its difficulty. To play the game, read a question aloud and how much the answer is worth. Allow the groups to quietly discuss their answer for about one minute. Call "time" and then tell the class which person in the group is to write the answer (person 1,2,3, or 4). There is to be no talking while the person is writing. Allow them 1-2 minutes to write their answer and WALK it up to you. The paper must be in your hands before the time is up or the team receives no points. Read the answers and give all or partial points for their responses. Continue until all questions have been answered. Assign writers in a random order so that all students must participate on each question.

Before the Book

Before you begin reading *Maroo of the Winter Caves* with your students, do some pre-reading activities to stimulate their interest and enhance their comprehension. Here are some activities that might work for your class.

1. Ask students to examine the front cover of the book. Point out the title and the illustration on the front cover. Have them predict what the story might be about based on the title and cover illustration.

2. Discuss the Ice Age with students. *Maroo of the Winter Caves* takes place during the end of the last Ice Age, more than 25,000 years ago, in prehistoric Europe. The people inhabiting this area at the time were bands of hunters and gatherers who migrated to different hunting grounds at different times of the year. That means these people did not know how to farm and raise animals. They had to rely on nature to provide them with all of their food. Therefore, when food was scarce due to bad weather, they had to move on to find new food sources.

   On the chalkboard write *Food, Clothing, Shelter,* and *Dangers.* Have students predict what kind of information the story will provide that will fit in these categories. Have students speculate on how people protected themselves from the dangers that existed during prehistoric times.

   Tell students they will read to find out how their ideas about prehistoric hunters and gatherers match what happens to the characters in the book.

3. Show students the route map that is shown in the book. Although the story is fictional, it is based on real archaeological evidence found in the European area. The map shows the setting of the story and the wide area this band of hunters and gatherers had to cover in order to obtain food. The landforms on the fictional map correspond roughly to landforms in southern France. The sea is the Mediterranean, the Summer Mountains are the southern Alps, and the Winter Caves are in the Central Highlands of France. Have students make simplified copies of the map. As students read the story, they should note the important events that happen and mark the route from start to finish on their copies of the map.

4. Begin a class Story Plot Outline (page 79) for the book, using an overhead transparency. As you read each section, refer to the story outline to fill in the characters, setting, problem, etc. This is a good way to review the section that students have just read.

5. Ask students what bravery is. Have them share experiences about times when they had to be brave. Ask them to tell why an early human might need to be brave.

6. Ask students what they think would be exciting about living during the Ice Age.

7. Read aloud the information on the back of the book. Ask students to describe what they would do if their family was trapped in a blizzard.

8. Have students read books or newspaper/magazine articles about blizzards. Ask them to give oral reports about the books or articles.

Vocabulary

Chapter 1	**Chapter 3**
recess	ibex
hemmed	**Chapter 4**
spirit	tentatively
Chapter 2	submissive
feigned	battered
flaying	

Comprehension Questions

1. Why are the children excited about summer? (Chapter 1) _____

   _____

   _____

2. What are all of Maroo's treasures? (Chapter 2) _____

   _____

   _____

3. Why does Maroo fear the spirits? (Chapter 2)_____

   _____

   _____

4. Maroo's clan eats a variety of food. Describe five of their different and unique foods that we do not eat today. (Chapter 3) _____

   _____

   _____

5. What steps are taken to build the clan a hut? Give specific, well-elaborated details. (Chapters 3 and 4) _____

   _____

   _____

Figurative Language

Metaphor: used to make a comparison between two things
Example: Her long, straight hair was the black night, deep, dark, and mysterious.

Simile: used to make a comparison between two things using the words LIKE or AS
Examples: Her long, straight hair was like the black night, deep, dark, and mysterious.
OR
Her hair was as dark as the black night.

Personification: used to give human characteristics to objects or animals
Example: The puppy smiled and did a little jig while it waited to be fed.

Ann Turnbull uses a variety of techniques to paint a vivid picture of Maroo's life for the reader. Look on the pages listed below to find examples of similes and personification.

1. Similes on pages 8 and 27 _____

   _____

2. Personification on pages 2 and 3 _____

   _____

Now use your writing skills to write descriptions using these techniques.

3. Use similes to describe the following:

   Maroo _____

   _____

   Nimai _____

   _____

4. Use personification to describe the following:

   the fire _____

   the wind _____

5. Use metaphors to describe the following:

   the puppy_____

   the ibex _____

Making a Treasure Chest

In Chapter 2, Maroo gathered her "treasures" together in order to leave for the summer hunting. Have students imagine what possessions they would take if they needed to suddenly leave their homes.

Preparing for the Lesson:

1. Each student will need a shoebox. Gather colored construction paper, scissors, glue, tape, crayons, and markers.

2. Gather writing paper and highlighters.

Teaching the Lesson:

1. Tell students to list the ten most important possessions they own with an explanation as to why those items are so important to them.

2. Have students look at their lists. Tell them to pretend that they are going to have to leave their homes tomorrow. Explain that they can only bring items that they can carry in a shoebox. Have students highlight the items on their lists that they will be allowed to bring. Discuss the items that will have to be left behind. Ask students how they feel about leaving behind some of their possessions. Have students compare their prized possessions to Maroo's.

3. Have students update their lists by writing only those items that will fit in the box. You may also wish to have students write down what they will wear, since they will not be able to pack any clothes in suitcases.

4. Using the shoeboxes, construction paper, scissors, markers, etc., have students construct a treasure chest to hold their prized possessions. They can make models or draw pictures to represent the real possessions. Then have students put the models or pictures in the treasure chests. Ask students to compare/contrast the items in the boxes.

The Dog Debate

In Chapter 4, Otak and Maroo find a dog. When they bring it back to the camp, there is a discussion as to whether or not to keep the dog. Divide the class into two teams. Ask one group to be for and the other group to be against keeping the dog. Lead a debate, flipping a coin to determine which team goes first.

Tell students that they must respectfully listen to others. They should be sure everyone on their team gets a chance to speak.

Remind students to begin the debate by stating their positions. Then students should give specific reasons to support their positions, using supporting information from the story. Tell them to be sure their reasons make sense. Students may respond to the other team's comments. However, they must point out faulty logic in the ideas rather than making personal attacks on members of the other team.

The debate ends when neither team has any additional reasons to support its position.

Vocabulary

Chapter 5	Chapter 6	Chapter 7
snarled	timidly	draggled
intricacies	expanse	
plait	bask	

Comprehension Questions

1. Who is the new friend? What difficulties or benefits does this bring to the clan? (Chapter 5)

   _____

2. Why does the clan not have to work hard during the spring season? (Chapter 5) _____

   _____

3. How would joining with Sovi's group increase the chance for being successful? (Chapter 5)

   _____

4. How do they know that other people had lived in the cave by the sea before? (Chapter 6) _____

   _____

5. How is Areg's clan able to follow Sovi's group? (Chapter 7) _____

   _____

6. What is the "rock spirit" that clapped back to the clan? (Chapter 7) _____

   _____

7. In Chapter 7, the author uses foreshadowing to let us know that something bad is going to happen. List sentences from the book that would be considered foreshadowing. _____

   _____

   _____

   _____

   _____

A First Sight

In Chapter 6, the children view the sea for the first time. The author vividly describes the colors, smells, and sounds of the beach. Have students write descriptive paragraphs describing the first time they experienced something. You may wish to extend the lesson by having students give oral presentations about their experiences.

Preparing for the Lesson:

1. Draw the following Descriptive Writing Web on the chalkboard or an overhead transparency.

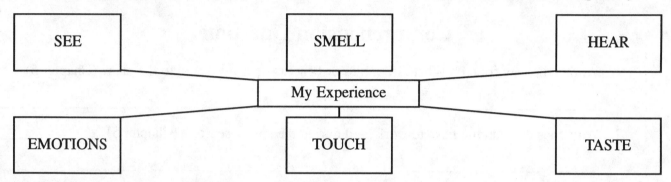

2. Reproduce the Editing Checklist (page 14) for students.

3. Make an overhead transparency of The Writing Process (page 13).

4. Have students reread pages 36-37 in *Maroo of the Winter Caves.*

Teaching the Lesson:

1. Review The Writing Process (page 13) with students.

2. Have students think of a time when they first experienced something. It could be a certain type of food, a sport, a place, etc.

3. Call students' attention to the Descriptive Writing Web. Have volunteers provide you with some sample words and phrases that could fit under the different headings of the web.

4. Have students each draw a Descriptive Writing Web on a piece of paper. Then ask them to think about their first-time experiences and fill in the webs. Allow time for students to write words and phrases on their webs.

5. Encourage students to use thesauruses to select a variety of words and use the words and phrases on their webs to make similes, metaphors, and personifications.

6. Then have students write their descriptive paragraphs.

7. Distribute the copies of the Editing Checklist (page 14). Remind students to make changes in their rough drafts before attempting to write their final drafts.

8. Allow time for students to read each other's descriptive paragraphs, or you may wish to have students present the information in speeches (pages 16–17).

Preparing for the Hunt

In Chapter 7, the men prepare to leave for the ibex hunt. Use the pages shown below to create a minibook. Then use the minibook to describe the steps the men took to prepare for the hunt. (The first step is found on page 50.) Be sure to use complete sentences that are well elaborated. Then draw colorful pictures to illustrate the steps.

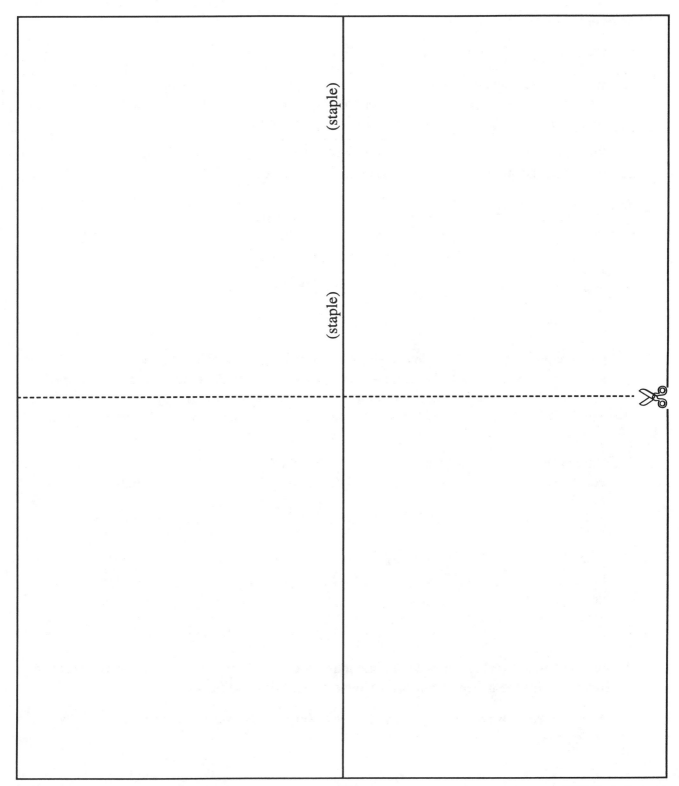

Concentration Clapping Patterns

In Chapter 5, Areg and Sovi's groups joined together to head toward the sea. One evening they celebrated by singing and clapping rhythms. Have your students simulate the intricate clapping patterns by playing a game called Concentration. This game is different from the one by the same name with which you might already be familiar.

Directions:

1. Have students sit cross-legged in a circle on the floor.

2. Explain to students that they will be creating a rhythm pattern by using the following movements: (1) slapping both hands on the thighs, (2) clapping the hands together, (3) snapping fingers on the right, and (4) snapping fingers on the left.

3. Point out that the words will follow the same pattern. Chant the following words to a four-beat pattern: Concentration, now begin, keep the rhythm, keep all beats.

1	2	3	4
(thigh slap)	(clap)	(snap right)	(snap left)
con-	cen-	tra-	tion
now	we	be-	gin
keep	the	rhy-	thm
keep	all	four	beats

4. Play begins with the first student saying his/her own name when the fingers are being snapped, and then that student says the name of another student when the other fingers are snapped. Then the second student named must take a turn. That student must say her/his name and the name of a third student in the class. This continues on the beat until someone makes a mistake.

1	2	3	4
(thigh slap)	(clap)	(snap right)	(snap left)
con-	cen-	tra-	tion
now	we	be-	gin
keep	the	rhy-	thm
keep	all	four	beats
(silent)	(silent)	Ann	Billy
(silent)	(silent)	Billy	John
(silent)	(silent)	John	Susan
etc.			

5. When someone makes a mistake, he/she must sit out. The last person who correctly said the names begins the pattern again with "Concentration, now we begin...."

6. As fewer students remain playing, you may wish to speed up the beat until there is only one person left.

Owl Pellet Dissection

On page 50 of *Maroo of the Winter Caves*, the men search the area for signs of wildlife. They find "a crevice in the rock where owls were nesting, betrayed by regurgitated balls of fur and feathers nearby. Areg picked one up and showed the children that the owl had eaten voles and a hare." Have your students dissect owl pellets to discover their diets.

Preparing for the Lesson:

1. You will need to order the pellets at least two weeks prior to doing this activity. Students can work individually, in pairs, or in small groups.

Pellets, Inc.

3004 Pinewood

Bellingham, WA 98225

1-206-733-3012

2. Gather tweezers, picks, brushes, and rubber gloves, large index cards, and glue. You will also need a plastic tub or similar type of container to soak the pellets in water so they will be easier to dissect.

3. Reproduce the bone chart shown at the bottom of this page for students.

Teaching the Lesson:

1. Distribute the dissecting materials to students. As they find pieces, have them match the pieces to the bone chart. If they do not match the bone chart, have students analyze the bones and tell what they think the animal might have been. Students may wish to look at pictures of skeletons to help them identify the animals. Point out that they may have more than one skeleton in their pellets. Be sure students save even the tiniest pieces of vertebrae.

2. Once students have completed the dissection, have them clean up their work areas and distribute the index cards and glue. Have students carefully glue down their skeletons and label the different parts.

3. Display the skeletons on a bulletin board.

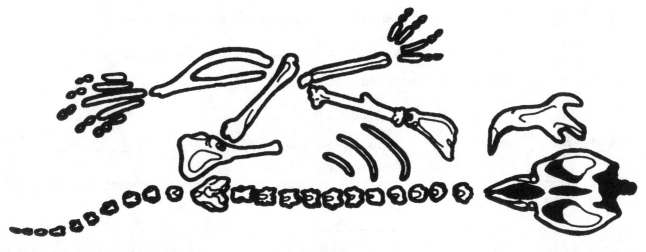

Vocabulary

Chapter 8	**Chapter 9**
slack	clambered
instinctively	sodden
contorted	**Chapter 10**
reluctantly	ravenously
	brandishing

Comprehension Questions

1. Why do Old Mother and Tikek paint their faces? (Chapter 8) _____

   _____

2. What does Vorka mean when he says "It will not speak to me." (Chapter 8) _____

   _____

3. Describe the burial ceremony. (Chapter 8)_____

   _____

4. What foreshadowing does the author use in Chapter 8 to suggest another obstacle the family
   must overcome on their journey?_____

   _____

5. What does the author mean by "...the trail grew colder every day"? (Chapter 9)_____

   _____

6. What is the significance and symbolism in finding the ptarmigan? (Chapter 9)_____

   _____

7. List the steps for building a snow house. (Chapter 10) _____

   _____

8. How do Maroo and Otak save the family? (Chapter 10) _____

   _____

Descriptive Verbs

Ann Turnbull writes with descriptive verbs and phrases. Her sentences show action and give specific details. First, find the sentences in the book. Then write the verbs in the sentences. Finally, on the lines next to the numbers, tell whether each sentence is a **simile** (S), **metaphor** (M), or uses **personification** (P).

_____ 1. Page 59 "...she _____ herself _____ like a spider upside-down."

_____ 2. Page 68 "Sometimes, _____ on a high point of rock, they could _____ water _____ down the mountainside, from rock to rock in a turmoil of white foam, to the Winding River on the plain below."

_____ 3. Page 68 "So the knowledge that they were late _____ at the back of the adults' minds."

_____ 4. Page 69 "It was as if winter were a giant _____ behind them, his shadow already _____."

_____ 5. Page 73 "The stone _____."

_____ 6. Page 74 "...when they _____ the wind ___ past their shelter and the _____ icy sting of the air."

_____ 7. Page 74 "All night the shelter _____ and _____ at its anchorages as if it _____ to join the wild _____ of the wind."

_____ 8. Page 86 "Tikek _____ on her son like a wild animal, tears _____ down her face."

Now you try it. Read the following sentences. Change the verbs and add phrases to make the sentences more descriptive, as well as more exciting. Try to include each of the following at least once: simile, metaphor, and personification. Use your thesaurus to find more descriptive verbs.

1. The snow fell hard. _____

_____

2. The family became hungry. _____

_____

3. Maroo went down the cliff. _____

_____

4. Maroo and Otak got food for the family. _____

_____

5. Vorka felt sad when Areg died. _____

_____

6. Rivo left the ice house. _____

_____

Eulogy for Areg

In Chapter 8, the family prepares a burial for Areg. Reread the passage about Areg's burial. Then write a eulogy that could have been read at the ceremony. A eulogy usually describes the person and his/her special talents or achievements. Use the space below to write your eulogy. Then share your eulogy with the class.

Designing a Burial

Have students make a class pop-up book describing a burial. Bring in examples of obituaries from the newspaper and read them to students. Ask students to note the style of the writing and the information that is included. Have students write an obituary for a fictitious person. Ask them to describe things they think should be buried with that person. Ask students to explain why they selected those items.

Use the following directions to make the class pop-up book.

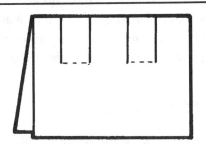

1. Use 9" x 12" (23 cm x 30 cm) construction paper folded in half. Cut slits.

5. Glue pictures onto the tabs. Glue in the description.

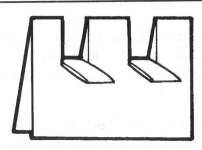

2. Fold over the paper at the slits to make tabs.

6. Use glue to mount the piece of 9" x 12" (23 cm x 30 cm) paper onto a piece of 12" x 18" (30 cm x 46 cm) paper.

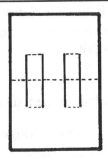

3. Reopen the paper.

7. Staple together students' pages to form the book.

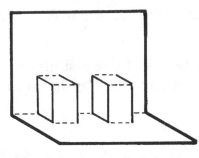

4. Gently push the tabs so they will stand out.

8. Glue a piece of 9" x 12" (23 cm x 30 cm) paper as shown to bind the book.

Ceremonial Masks

In this section of the book, Areg dies and the family performs a burial ceremony. Have students create masks for a variety of ceremonies that could be performed by early humans.

Preparing for the Lesson:

1. Cover the work area with butcher paper or plastic.

2. To make the masks, students will need: scratch paper; a large balloon (1 balloon for every 2 students); strips of newspaper; white glue mixed with water (1 part glue to 1 part water); pie tin or tray for glue mixture; masking tape; Styrofoam trays, rolled newspaper, or paper plates; scissors; tempera paint, paintbrushes, and paint trays; feathers, yarn, shells, bones, glitter, and other decorative materials.

3. Reproduce the examples of ceremonial masks (page 205) for students to use.

4. Gather index cards for students to write their descriptions for their masks and explanations for the ceremonies.

Teaching the Lesson:

1. Have students brainstorm a list of different ceremonies the early humans might have performed. Ceremonies might include: burial, transition into manhood/womanhood, bravery, preparing for a hunt, rain, birth, healing, preparing to battle a rival tribe, making special tools or weapons, the coming of spring, and meeting another tribe.

2. Distribute the scratch paper and have students plan their masks based on their chosen ceremonies. Tell students that the masks should be symmetrical and use shapes and symbols to help convey the meaning of the ceremonies they have chosen.

3. Have pairs of students work together to cover an entire large balloon with two layers of newspaper strips dipped in the glue mixture. Allow the balloons to dry overnight. The next day, have students cover the balloon with two additional layers of newspaper and glue. Allow the balloons dry overnight.

4. The next day, use scissors to cut the balloon in half. Each student in the pair gets half.

5. Have students add facial features to their masks, such as noses, eyebrow ridges, chins, etc., by taping on rolled up newspaper, cut Styrofoam trays, or paper plates. Have students cover the features with two layers of newspaper strips and the glue mixture. Allow the masks to dry.

6. After the masks are completely dry, help students cut eye holes. Then have them paint the masks with tempera paint.

7. After the paint is dry, have students add decorative touches with feathers, shells, etc. Have students describe their masks and ceremonies on the index cards. Display the masks with the cards.

Ceremonial Masks *(cont.)*

Vocabulary

Chapter 11 trudging ascent banish **Chapter 12** prodding exertion	**Chapter 13** desolate contemptuously pretense

Comprehension Questions

1. According to Old Mother, why is the clan's oral tradition important? (Chapter 11)_____

_____

2. Give at least two examples from Chapter 11 of hard decisions that might have to be made by the family in order to survive. _____

_____

3. Describe how Maroo and Otak feel about their first night alone in camp. (Chapter 11) _____

_____

4. What is the obstacle Maroo faced in Chapter 12? How does she overcome this obstacle?_____

_____

5. Why does Otak bring the ibex horns even though they are heavy and take up space? (Chapter 13) _____

_____

6. Give at least two examples from Chapters 12 and 13 that seem to indicate that the mountain spirits are against Maroo and Otak. _____

_____

Plurals and Possessives

Singular Noun: a noun that describes one person, place, or thing
    Examples: dog   child   Chris

Singular Possessive Noun: a singular noun that shows possession by always adding 's
    Examples: the dog's bone   the child's doll   Chris's boat

Plural Noun: a noun which describes more than one person, place, or thing
    Examples: dogs   children   mice   the Smiths

Plural Possessive Noun: a plural noun which shows possession by adding 's if the word does **NOT** end in s or by just adding ' at the end if the word **DOES** end in s
    Examples: the children's doll   the mice's cheese
    Examples: the dogs' bones   the Smiths' house

The following words can be found in *Maroo of the Winter Caves*. Fill in the blanks by writing the proper spelling for each word. Use the information at the top of the page to help you.

SINGULAR NOUNS	SINGULAR POSSESSIVES	PLURAL NOUNS	PLURAL POSSESSIVES
1. group	1. _____	1. _____	1. _____
2. _____	2. ibex's	2. _____	2. _____
3. _____	3. _____	3. ice houses	3. _____
4. _____	4. _____	4. _____	4. mountain lions'
5. hide dress	5. _____	5. _____	5. _____
6. _____	6. drum's	6. _____	6. _____
7. _____	7. _____	7. children	7. _____
8. _____	8. _____	8. _____	8. geese's
9. wolf	9. _____	9. _____	9. _____
10. _____	10. rescuer's	10. _____	10. _____
11. _____	11. _____	11. feet	11. _____
12. _____	12. _____	12. _____	12. spirits'
13. glacier	13. _____	13. _____	13. _____
14. _____	14. crevasse's	14. _____	14. _____
15. _____	15. _____	15. blizzards	15. _____
16. _____	16. _____	16. _____	16. bruises'

Cross-Age Storytelling

In this section of the book, Old Mother reminds the children of the importance of storytelling to keep their spirits up. Have students write a story that they can share with younger children. After writing have them practice telling it with expression and gestures. They may wish to include some simple props for story. After they feel comfortable telling the story, have them present it to a class of younger students.

Ceremonies

At the end of Chapter 11, Maroo thinks about the different ceremonies performed by her clan. Have students name some of the ceremonies that are listed in the book. Write these on the chalkboard. Then encourage students to add the names of other ceremonies that might also be performed. You may wish to refer to the information in this unit about ceremonies (page 168) and ceremonial masks (pages 204 and 205). Divide the class into groups and have students create some of the ceremonies. After allowing students to practice, have the groups perform their ceremonies while other students try to guess what type of ceremony they are performing.

A Night Away

After reading Chapter 13 have students choose one of the following two options for writing. Have them complete this assignment as if it were an entry in a diary.

Option 1:

Maroo and Otak have to spend time away from their family. Think about a time that you spent the night away from your family. This could be with friends or another family member such as an aunt. How did you feel when you were away from your own home, your room, and your parents? Were you excited or scared or a little of both? Describe the visit in detail, including the age you were when it took place. How did it differ from staying at home with your family? What did you learn from being away?

Option 2:

Both Maroo and Otak spend the night away from their family for the first time. What feelings do you think they felt? Did they enjoy the experience? Was it easy to fall asleep? Write a diary entry as if you were either Maroo or Otak, and it is the next morning. Reflect about how you feel after having just spent the night away from your family for the first time. How are you different? How are you the same? What have you learned about your experience? Take this into account as you write.

A Hard Decision

In the beginning of this section of *Maroo and the Winter Caves*, Maroo and Otak are given advice from Old Mother about their journey. They may face some very difficult decisions. Have students find and list the difficult decisions mentioned in Chapters 10 and 11. Then have them list difficult decisions that they might face in the next five or ten years. Point out some examples of the kinds of things students might have to make decisions about, such as using drugs, alcohol, or cigarettes; joining a gang; staying in school; going to college and getting a job while going to school. Write the list on the chalkboard or an overhead transparency.

Have each student select one of these difficult decisions as the topic of a persuasive composition. Tell students that they are trying to persuade friends to make the right decision about a particular choice. They are to try to persuade them to make the right decision as convincingly as possible. Reproduce the Persuasive Organizer (page 210) for students to use in a prewriting activity. Make a transparency of the organizer to use as a model.

Explain the different parts of the Persuasive Organizer, using the transparency and the following information.

- **Introduction:** The introduction should give some background to get the reader interested. It should then tell what the writer is trying to persuade the friend to do.

- **Reasons and Supporting Details:** There should be three clearly stated reasons telling why the writer believes the way she/he does. For each reason, there should be three or more supporting details. The supporting details can be examples. There should be enough information for each reason to be a separate paragraph.

- **Conclusion:** The conclusion should briefly restate what the writer is trying to persuade the friend to do. It should also include a strong closing statement.

Have students use The Writing Process (page 13) and the Editing Checklist (page 14) to write their persuasive compositions.

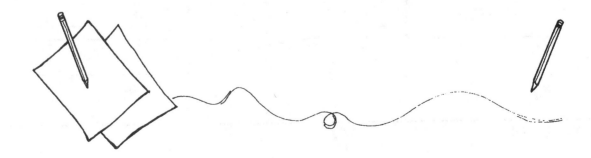

Persuasive Organizer

INTRODUCTION:

SUPPORING DETAILS:

REASON:

SUPPORING DETAILS:

REASON:

SUPPORING DETAILS:

REASON:

CONCLUSION:

Vocabulary

Chapter 14	Chapter 15
merged	monotony
hoisted	mercilessly
ebbing	vague
subsided	eclipsing
sulkily	

Comprehension Questions

1. What is Old Mother's proverb, and what does it mean? (Chapter 14) _____
_____

2. Name the personification in Chapter 14 that is used to describe the mountain. What descriptions does the author use to describe Maroo's, Otak's, and Rivo's feelings? _____
_____

3. Why is Otak angry at Maroo for killing the hare? (Chapter 14) _____
_____

4. Why does Maroo decide to travel alone? Describe her feelings about having to make this decision. (Chapter 15) _____
_____

5. Give at least two examples of how Old Mother's wisdom helps the children in these chapters.
_____
_____

6. How does Maroo overcome the mountain spirit? (Chapter 15) _____
_____

7. How does Rivo save Otak? (Chapter 16) _____
_____

Goals

In the final chapters of the book, Maroo is able to save the rest of the family by making it to the autumn camp. Think of a time in your life when you had a goal to achieve despite any obstacles that might have been in your path. It could have been learning a new skill, competing in an athletic competition, passing a test, or being given a new privilege at home. Use the space below to tell about your goal.

GOAL (What was your goal? What were you trying to accomplish?): _____

_____

_____

OBSTACLES (What kinds of things got in your way? What might have prevented you from achieving your goal?): _____

_____

_____

DEGREE OF SUCCESS (Were you able to accomplish your goal? If not, why not?): _____

_____

Now use the space below to set a new goal for yourself. Remember to be realistic when setting your goal. Do not try to do something that is not humanly possible.

NEW GOAL (What is your new goal?): _____

_____

WAYS TO ACHIEVE YOUR GOAL (What can you do to help yourself be successful?):

_____

_____

POSSIBLE OBSTACLES (What might interfere with you achieving your goal?):_____

_____

_____

EXPECTED DATE FOR MEETING YOUR GOAL (By when do you expect to have this goal accomplished? How long do you expect to have to work to achieve this goal?): _____

_____

Environmental Poem and Picture

After completing *Maroo of the Winter Caves*, have students use their knowledge of figurative language to describe the different settings of the story.

Preparing for the Lesson:

1. Gather the following materials to make the art project:
   8 ½" x11" (22 cm x 28 cm) pieces of white typing or ditto paper
   9" x 12" (23 cm x 30 cm) pieces of construction paper in assorted colors
   12" x 18" (30 cm x 46 cm) pieces of black construction paper
   black permanent markers
   markers in assorted colors

2. Draw a Descriptive Writing Web (page 196) on the chalkboard and have students copy it onto pieces of paper.

3. Gather writing paper for rough drafts. You may wish to have students use typewriters or computers for their final drafts.

Teaching the Lesson: (The Art Project)

1. The art project needs to be completed before students can write their poems because the description will be about their pictured environments.

2. Have students brainstorm a list of the different settings Maroo and her family were in throughout the book. Write these on the board. The environments should include: mountains, plains, river, ocean, beach, blizzard, winter cave, cave with a roaring fire, autumn camp, summer camp, cliffs, snow house, glacier, etc.

3. Tell the students that they will be creating abstract images of one of these settings and then describing their settings, or environments, with poems. Point out that the object is **NOT** to draw a landscape, but rather a series of patterns, shapes, and designs that give the feeling of a certain type of environment.

4. Distribute the white typing paper. Have students select an environment to depict. Using pencils, have them lightly divide the paper into sections. Then tell students to add shapes, lines, patterns, etc. Explain to students that stiff, angular lines might represent ice, mountains, or cliffs while soft, flowing lines might represent the ocean or spring flowers. Have students experiment with overlapping shapes and designs to help suggest depth.

5. After students have finished their pencil drawings, ask them to use black permanenet markers to trace over their lines.

6. Next, ask students to decide on a color scheme that helps the viewer have an understanding of their settings, or environments. Explain that they should have only three to four colors. Discuss the difference between warm and cool colors. Ask students to tell which colors might create a "happy" tone or mood for the picture and which ones might create a more "foreboding" tone or mood. Have students carefully color their pictures.

Environmental Poem and Picture *(cont.)*

7. To mount the pictures, use pieces of 9" x 12" (23 cm x 30 cm) construction paper that have compatible colors. Use only a little glue around the edges to mount the pictures.

8. Have students use the pictures to write poems as described below.

Teaching the Lesson: (The Poetry)

1. Redistribute students' pictures if you have collected them. Ask students to draw a Descriptive Writing Web. Have students brainstorm words and phrases to describe what would be noticed by their different senses if they were standing in their environments. Encourage students to use thesauruses to find more descriptive words. Remind them that they can include metaphors, similes, and personification!

2. Distribute the writing paper. Have students write at least one elaborated sentence or phrase for each of the senses. Read the sample poem shown below and have students share their ideas aloud to help others get ideas. Then allow students to write their rough drafts.

3. After students are satisfied with their rough drafts, have them neatly write or type the final drafts of their poems. Tell students that their poems cannot be more than four inches (10 cm) tall if the poems are going to fit on the papers with the art projects.

4. Mount the pictures and poems on black construction paper and display.

Sample poem for a picture of the sea:

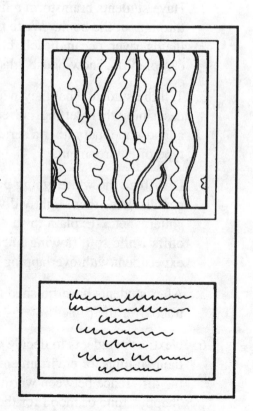

As I dive carelessly into the cool, blue sea,
The smooth sultry seaweed meanders softly through my wet feet.
It reaches up to the crystal sky, anticipating a sip of fresh sea air.
Slowly it wraps around my legs, playfully tugging and pulling at my free limbs.

The soft, rippling water echoes of dancing porpoises,
Singing their songs of joy like mermaids with high pitched voices.
Gulls soar into the air, squawking to join the chorus,
As they dip and dive over the splashing waves.

I emerge from the sapphire abyss.
The salty water tingles along my face like the flow of a cool silk scarf.
Below, the sandy floor squishes between my toes,
As I trudge to shore one soggy step after another.

I glance back at the vast blue sea as it shimmers in the afternoon sun,
Reflecting dimples of gray, green, and violet.
Contentment fills me along the shore of this calm, beautiful water.

Vocabulary

Write the word from the box that correctly completes the sentences.

1. Nimai's small, smiling _____ form was looking up at her from the lake. Maroo's reflection came up and stood beside it.

2. The women helped to lower the animal onto the flat ground, and began _____ it with sharp stone knives to cut the meat and hide.

3. "Now leave him, and let his wounds mend," said Old Mother firmly as all three crouched beside the puppy and Nimai _____ stroked his head.

4. Maroo wondered how long it would take to tame the puppy. He still _____ savagely whenever she put out a hand.

5. Nearly every morning of her life she had watched Old Mother coil her hair _____ into a cone shape on top of her head.

6. The children _____ about the hillside, searching out grassy patches where mushrooms sprang up in clusters overnight.

7. "Go! Go!" Maroo shouted at the wild dogs, _____ the burning torch at the nearest dog.

8. An ibex fell, but Areg missed his footing and fell too, and so did Vorka who had sprung forward _____ to try and save his brother as he went down.

9. The place where they found themselves was bare and _____ . The deadly cold breath of the glacier blew upon them, and Maroo felt the bones of her face stiffen.

10. Flat, snow-covered tracks wound between the rocks. They _____ aimlessly, linking and doubling back on each other.

11. Tears came quickly, and she turned so that Otak would not see. He might start crying again too, and then their _____ of courage would be over.

12. Maroo watched until the hare's fur blended and _____ with the color of the bluish snow and it hurt her eyes to look.

13. There was no sun to mark the shape of the day and nothing to break the repetitious _____ of wind and snow day after day.

14. It was not yet dark, and Maroo was feeling better. She could feel her fear _____ away little by little as she took off her pack and leaned against a rock.

recess	spirit	flaying	ibex
tentatively	snarled	draggled	plait
expanse	slack	instinctively	brandishing
prodding	desolate	meandered	exertion
pretense	banish	ebbing	merged
monotony	mercilessly	clambered	vague

Plot Problems

Pick three characters from the story. Describe them, and tell one important action each character did in the story.

_____

_____

_____

_____

_____

_____

Answer the following questions, using complete and well-elaborated sentences.

1. What was the main problem of the story? _____

_____

2. What were three obstacles the family had to overcome during the story? _____

_____

3. Who do you think was the main person to keep the family going? Give details to support your reasoning. _____

_____

4. Who would you consider the "hero" of the story? Give details to support your reasoning.

_____

5. What scene would be considered the "climax" of the story? _____

_____

_____

6. How would the plot of the story be different if it took place during modern times? Give at least three examples. _____

_____

7. What have you learned about early humans by reading this book? Name at least two things.

_____

8. What was your favorite scene from the story? Why? _____

_____

Answer Key

Section 1 (Chapters 1-4): Comprehension (page 192)

1. The children are excited for summer because it brought a change to their life. They are tired of being hemmed in the cave, and looked forward to seeing the sea for the first time.

2. Maroo's treasures consist of necklaces, a skin bag full of shells and bone beads, a reed whistle, stone knives, bone needles, and a bow-drill.

3. Maroo fears the spirits because she does not know what it is, and she gets the feeling that they are something fierce based on the reactions of the adults.

4. They eat dried roots, berries, blood, herb-flavored water, liver of bison, beetles, grubs, sweet leaves, insects, ibex, salmon, and deer meat.

5. First the men look for a good place to build the hut. Then they begin digging the base of the hut close under the rock overhang. The men cut willow branches which they set into the base, bending them over and crisscrossing them to make a low domed building. Smaller branches had been woven in and out between the main stems.

Figurative Language (page 193)

Similes:
Page 8—Otak and Maroo are off like spring hares. Page 27—Old Mother was very old, her skin like soft creased leather... Only her eyes are still young, not filmy like some of the old men's, but dark, and bright as a knife.
Personification:
Page 2—Old Mother brought small pieces of the precious wood from her store and fed the hungry flames. Page 3—The flames were leaping up brightly now,...

Section 2 (Chapters 5-7): Comprehension (page 195)

1. Rivo the wild puppy is the new friend. The difficulties might be trying to tame the dog, feeding it food they need, and fearing that it might attack the people. Benefits might include companionship, protection from other animals, and helping the people to hunt.

2. In the spring and summer food is plentiful, so the group does not need to work hard.

3. Joining Sovi's group would mean more people to work together to hunt and other women to help with the birth of Tikek's baby.

4. They find bones and a broken shell necklace in the cave which tells them other people had camped there before.

5. Areg's clan is able to follow Sovi's group by watching for the smoke from their fire and also by following the signs left by Sovi, such as patterns of sticks and stones or a drawing scratched into a stone.

6. The "rock spirit" that clapped back to the clan is an echo.

7. Sentences that foreshadow that something bad is going to happen include page 51, "But when they returned to the campfire, Old Mother was uneasy. 'Two men were not enough to hunt ibex,' she said, and Sovi was too far ahead now to be called." Page 52, "At dusk the men had not returned. Old Mother said, 'It is nothing. They will sleep out and hunt again in the morning,' but Maroo sensed her anxiety." Page 55, "'You must search for the men,' Nimai said importantly. Maroo felt cold inside. She looked at Old Mother. Old Mother turned around, and Maroo saw that she was afraid."

Preparing for the Hunt (page 197)

First the men made a circuit of the camp by wandering around looking for signs of animals. Next, they began to talk and plan the hunt. They also sharpened their spears. They brought out two horns filled with red and black minerals mixed with fat. They painted their faces with a pattern of stripes and diamonds to look like the ibex. Finally, the men took up their spears and began climbing higher up the mountain until they were out of sight.

Answer Key *(cont.)*

Section 3 (Chapters 8-10): Comprehension (page 200)

1. Old Mother and Tikek paint their faces for the burial ceremony of Areg. The paint is to make magic signs that will help Areg make his way in the spirit world.

2. Vorka does not want the drum that belongs to his brother because it is special to Areg. Areg has the musical talent to make it "speak," and Vorka does not have that special quality. That is why he says, "It will not speak to me."

3. First the women paint their faces with the magic paint from the horns. Then they clean Areg's face and paint special symbols to guide him into the spirit world. The women then dig a shallow grave beside the stream. They put Areg's body into the grave and then cover it with soft hides. In the grave they also place his spear, harpoon, and drum. Next, the women place heavy stones on top of Areg's chest and legs to keep his spirit from walking away. Since there is no soft dirt, they continue to cover his body with stones. The women make a wailing repetitive sound, part crying and part singing as they work. They do not stop until the body is completely covered and safe from predators.

4. The foreshadowing on page 67 is, "If the snows overtake us, we will not survive." This means they will probably run into bad weather and more difficulties due to snow.

5. "…The trail grew colder every day" means that Sovi's group is getting further and further ahead of the family. His signals are getting more difficult to follow, and they are feeling very alone.

6. The ptarmigan bird is special to Maroo because it is her name. Sighting the flock of birds is a symbol of hope.

7. First Old Mother and the children cut and shape blocks of snow. Tikek and Vorka build them up and seal their joints. Gradually they curve the walls inward to make a low-domed house similar in shape to the huts of the summer. Then they build an entrance tunnel with a bend in it to keep out drafts. Inside they make a new fire.

8. Otak and Maroo save the family by getting deer meat from a pack of wild dogs. They chase away the dogs by using torches of fire and then drag the carcass back to the snow house.

Descriptive Verbs (page 201)

1. simile—found, hanging
2. personification—standing, see, leaping, springing, join
3. personification—gnawed
4. metaphor—striding, looming
5. personification—sang
6. personification—heard, screaming, felt
7. personification—tugged, strained, longed, racing
8. simile—turned, rolling

Section 4 (Chapters 11-13): Comprehension (page 206)

1. Old Mother tells the children to remember their oral tradition of stories and songs in order to give them hope and to keep them moving.

2. Some harsh decisions discussed in Chapter 11 include having to eat Rivo if food becomes scarce, giving the children only a little food and expecting them to hunt, and if help does not arrive Old Mother will wander out into the cold in order for there to be one less mouth to feed.

3. Maroo and Otak feel scared and lonely their first night in camp. It is their first night alone away from their family so they huddle together and talk through the night to build their confidence. Yet, although they are frightened of being alone, they are not frightened of their journey which makes them feel important.

4. Maroo falls into a crevasse in Chapter 12. She is saved by Otak who throws her a rope made of plaited hide. He ties the rope to his staff which he had driven deep into the snow and then winds the rope around his body. Maroo is then able to climb up the rope and out of the crevasse.

5. Otak brings the ibex horns as a reminder of his father.

6. Some examples that show the mountain spirits are against Maroo and Otak include Maroo falling into the crevasse, the blizzard approaching when they have no form of shelter in sight, and finding the prints of the mountain lion.

Answer Key *(cont.)*

Plurals and Possessives (page 207)

1. group group's groups groups'
2. ibex ibex's ibexes ibexes'
3. house house's houses houses'
4. lion lion's lions lions'
5. dress dress's dresses dresses'
6. drum drum's drums drums'
7. child child's children children's
8. goose goose's geese geese's
9. wolf wolf's wolves wolves'
10. rescuer rescuer's rescuers rescuers'
11. foot foot's feet feet's
12. spirit spirit's spirits spirits'
13. glacier glacier's glaciers glaciers'
14. crevasse crevasse's crevasses crevasses'
15. blizzard blizzard's blizzards blizzards'
16. bruise bruise's bruises bruises'

Section 5 (Chapters 14-16): Comprehension (page 211)

1. Old Mother's proverb is, "A thousand false throws are father to the perfect throw." This means you have to practice throwing and expecting failure until you finally get it right.

2. The mountain is personified with the sentence, "More than ever Maroo felt that it was the great black mouth of the mountain itself threatening to swallow her up."

3. Otak is angry at Maroo for killing the hare because hunting is a man's job. She had used his spear without asking, and even worse, she had been successful at hunting and he had not. This makes Otak feel very inferior when he was to be the "man" of their journey.

4. Maroo sets out alone because she knows this is the only way to save the rest of her family. She has no idea when or if he will return. She feels both angry and guilty because she knows it was her fault that he left to go hunting, because he felt that he had to prove himself a hunter now that she killed a hare.

5. Old Mother's wisdom helps by guiding their way using her descriptions, using her proverbs to make them feel better when they fail at something, helping Maroo to continue on without Otak in order to save the family helping Maroo to keep from panicking when she becomes lost, and finding the moon and stars which had woken her and made the mountain visible.

6. The mountain spirit is in the form of a lion. Maroo overcomes it by chasing it off with a torch lit from her fire.

7. Rivo saves Otak by bringing back food for him. Rivo did the hunting for a few days until Otak can walk. Then Rivo helps Otak find the way down to the camp.

Vocabulary (page 215)

1. spirit
2. flaying
3. tentatively
4. snarled
5. plait
6. clambered
7. brandishing
8. instinctively
9. desolate
10. meandered
11. pretense
12. merged
13. monotony
14. ebbing

Plot Problems (page 216)
Accept all reasonable responses.

Technology Bibliography

Videos

Blue Planet. (Shows how hurricanes, volcanoes, earthquakes, and people affect the Earth), 1990; Films for the Humanities and Science (Video Division), P.O. Box 2053, Princeton, New Jersey, 08543-2053; 1-609-452-1128.

Born of Fire. (National Geographic special that looks at how humans deal with earthquakes and volcanoes), 1987; National Geographic Society, 1145 17th St. NW, New York, New York, 10017; 1-213-210-1319.

The Building of the Earth. (Explain how the Earth is changed due to physical forces), 1988; Ambrose Video Pub., Inc., 381 Park Ave. S, New York, New York, 10016; 1-800-526-4663.

Earthquake! (Examines earthquakes and methods for predicting them), 1990; EME Corp., P.O. Box 2805, Danbury, Connecticut, 06813-2805; 1-800-848-2050.

The Fossil Rush: Tale of a Bone. (Compares/contrasts fossil hunters from the 1870's with those of today), 1991; Arts and Entertainment Home Video, 235 E. 45th St., New York, New York, 10017; 1-212-210-1319.

Glaciers. (Shows how glaciers are formed, and how they affect the land), 1983; PBS Video, 1320 Braddock Place, Alexandria, Virginia, 22314-1698; 1-800-424-7963.

Iceman. (Shows how scientists unthaw a prehistoric man who was trapped in a glacier), 1984; MCA Home Video, 70 Universal City Plaza, Universal City, California, 91608; 1-818-777-4300.

Mysteries of Mankind. (Shows recent evidence regarding evolution and anthropology), 1989; National Geographic Society, 1145 17th St. NW, Washington D.C., 20036; 1-800-638-4077.

Plate Tectonics, a Revolution in Earth Sciences. (Explains the theory of plate tectonics and answers questions about geology), 1983; PBS Video, 1320 Braddock Place, Alexandria, Virginia, 22314-1698; 1-800-424-7963.

Prehistoric World. (Tells unusual facts about mammals that lived during prehistoric times), 1987; Twin Tower Enterprises, 1888 Century Park E., No. 1500, Los Angeles, California, 90067.

Sandstone Secrets. (Examines sandstone as a source for paleontological information), 1983; PBS Video, 1320 Braddock Place, Alexandria, Virginia, 22314-1698; 1-800-424-7963.

The Story of America's Great Volcanoes. (Explains formation of volcanoes, and examines their importance in history and mythology), 1992; Questar Video, P.O. Box 11345, Chicago, Illinois, 60611; 1-800-544-8422.

Technology Bibliography *(cont.)*

Software

Bluegrass Bluff. (Simulates an archaeological dig); Apple II family; Available from MECC.

Creation Stories. (Tells stories about the creation of the world and humans); CD-ROM for MPC; Microsoft; In the U.S. call 1-800-240-4782; In Canada call 1-800-563-9048.

Dinosaur Discovery. (Shows clues from an explorer's diary that will help players hatch a fossilized dinosaur egg); Apple II family; Available from E.M.E.

Dinosaurs. (Interactive software shows how dinosaurs lived); CD-ROM for MAC or MPC; Available from Educorp, 7434 Trade Street, San Diego, California, 92121; 1-800-843-8487.

Fossil Hunter. (Interactive software in which students learn about geographical history using ancient plants and animals); Apple II family; Available from MECC.

Insight Dinosaurs. (Reference information about dinosaurs); Apple II family; Available from Optonica Ltd.

Interactive Archaeologist. (Interactive software allows players to solve archaeological mysteries based on clues from excavation sites); CD-ROM for MAC or MPC; Available from Educorp, 7434 Trade Street, San Diego, California, 92121; 1-800-843-8487.

Introducing the Humans. (Interactive software in which humans try to survive during prehistoric times); CD-ROM for MS-DOS; Gametek, Inc., 2999 N.E. 191st St., Suite 800, North Miami Beach, Florida, 33180.

LIFE map series. (Allows students to chart evolution by examining animals, animals with backbones, and organic diveristy); CD-ROM for MAC; Available from Educorp, 7434 Trade Street, San Diego, California, 92121; 1-800-834-8487.

Meso America. (100 photographs of artifacts from the Mesolithic period); CD-ROM for MAC or MPC; Corel Corp., 1600 Carling Ave., Ottawa, Ontario, Canada, K1Z 8R7; 1-613-728-8200.

SimEarth: The Living Planet. (Interactive software in which players control the evolution of Earth); MAC or WIN; Maxis, 2 Theater Square, Orinda, California, 94563-3346; 1-510-254-9700.

Time Navigator Around the World. (Players pick categories to move back in time); Apple II family; Available from MECC.

Volcanoes Delux Version 1.2. (Allows volcanoes to be predicted using scientific data); Apple II family; Available from Earthware Computer Services.

Bibliography

How We Learn About the Past

Aliki. *Fossils Tell of Long Ago.* Crowell, 1990.

Arnold, Carolyn. *Dinosaurs Down Under and Other Famous Fossils from Australia.* Clarion, 1990.

Arnold, Carolyn. *Trapped in Tar: Fossils from the Ice Age.* Ticknor and Fields, 1987.

Baine, Rae. *Prehistoric Animals.* Troll Assoc., 1985.

Batherman, Muriel. *Before Columbus.* Houghton Mifflin Co., 1990.

Baylor, Byrd. *If You Are a Hunter of Fossils.* Macmillan, 1985.

Benton, Michael. *Prehistoric Animals: An A-Z Guide.* Outlet Bk. Co., 1989.

Branley, Franklyn. *What Happened to the Dinosaurs?* Crowell, 1989.

Cork, Barbara. *Archaeology.* EDC, 1985.

Curtis, Neil. *Fossils.* Watts, 1984.

Day, M.H. *Fossil History of Man.* Carolina Biological, 1984.

Dixon, Douglas. *Be a Fossil Detective-Be a Nature Detective.* Outlet Bk. Co., 1989.

Gallant, Roy. *Fossils.* Watts, 1985.

Hackwell, W. John. *Digging to the Past: Excavations in Ancient Lands.* Macmillan, 1986.

Hoobler, Dorothy. *Lost Civilizations.* Walker, 1992.

Horenstein, Sidney. *Rocks Tell Stories.* Milbrook, 1993.

Lauber, Patricia. *Dinosaurs Walked Here and Other Stories Fossils Tell.* Bradbury Press, 1987.

Lauber, Patricia. *Tales Mummies Tell.* Crowell, 1985.

Leroi-Gourban, Andre. *The Hunters of Prehistory.* Macmillan, 1989.

Martin, Les. *Young Indiana Jones and the Secret City.* Random, 1990.

Martin, Les. *Young Indiana Jones and the Tomb of Terror.* Random, 1990.

Marton, Elsa. *Mysteries in American Archaeology.* Walker and Co., 1986.

Massare, Judy A. *Prehistoric Marine Reptiles: Sea Monsters During the Age of Dinosaurs.* Franklin Watts, 1991.

Norman, David. *Looking for Fossils.* Crescent Books, 1991.

Oliver, Ray. *Rocks and Fossils.* Random, 1993.

Pickering, Robert B. *I Can Be an Archaeologist.* Childrens Press, 1987.

Prehistoric Encyclopedia. Checkerboard Press, 1989.

Raintree Publishers' Staff. *Archaeology.* Raintree Pubs., 1988.

Rydell, Wendy. *Discovering Fossils.* Troll Assoc., 1984.

Sabin, Louis. *Fossils.* Troll Assoc., 1985.

Sandak, Cass R. *Living Fossils.* Franklin Watts, 1992.

Simon, Seymour. *The Dinosaur is the Biggest Animal That Ever Lived and Other Wrong Ideas You Thought Were True.* Lippincott, 1984.

Taylor, Paul D. *Fossil.* Alfred A. Knopf, 1990.

Whitfield, Phillip. *Macmillan Children's Guide to Dinosaurs and Other Prehistoric Animals.* Macmillan, 1992.

Bibliography *(cont.)*

Earth, the Early Years

Barret, Norman. *Volcanoes.* Franklin Watts, 1991.

Berger, Melvin. *How Life Began.* Doubleday, 1990.

Bisel, Sara Louise Clark. *Secrets of Vesuvius.* Scholastic, Inc., 1990.

Bramwell, Marty. *Glaciers and Ice Caps.* Franklin Watts, 1986.

Branley, Franklyn. *Earthquakes.* Crowell, 1990.

Cole, Joanna. *Magic School Bus, Inside the Earth.* Scholastic, Inc., 1989.

Crespo, George. *How the Sea Began.* Clarion, 1993.

Curry, Jane Louise. *Back in the Beforetime: Tales of the California Indians.* McElderry, 1987.

Fradin, Dennis B. *Continents.* Childrens Press, 1986.

Gallant, Roy. *Ice Ages.* Franklin Watts, 1985.

Goodman, Billy. *Natural Wonders and Disasters.* Little, Brown and Co., 1991.

Gorges, D.V. *Glaciers.* Childrens Press, 1986.

Hamilton, Sue L. *Mount St. Helens: Volcanic Eruption.* Abdo, 1988.

Hamilton, Sue L. *San Francisco Earthquake: April 18, 1906.* Abdo, 1988.

Humphrey, Kathryn Long. *Pompeii: Nightmare at Midday.* Franklin Watts, 1990.

Jaspersohn, William. *How the Universe Began.* Franklin Watts, 1985.

Kudlinski, Kathleen V. *Earthquake: A Story of Old San Francisco.* Viking, 1993.

Laskey, Kathryn. *Surtsey: The Newest Place on Earth.* Hyperion, 1992.

LeTord, Bijou. *The Deep Blue Sea.* Orchard Books Watts, 1990.

Markle, Sandra. *Earth Alive.* Lothrop, Lee, and Shepard, 1991.

Mayo, Gretchen. *Earthmaker's Tales: North American Indian Stories About Earth Happenings.* Walker, 1990.

Michel, Francois and Yves Larvor. *The Restless Earth: The Secrets of Earthquakes, Volcanoes, & Continental Drift in Three Dimensional Moving Pictures.* Viking, 1990.

Mitchell, Stephen. *Creation.* Dial, 1990.

Parker, Steve. *Charles Darwin and Evolution.* HarperCollins, 1992.

Schwarzbach, Martin. *The Father of Continental Drift.* Sci Tech Pubs. 1986.

Seddon, Tony and Jill Bailey. *The Physical World.* Doubleday and Co., Inc., 1987.

Simon, Seymour. *Earthquakes.* William Morrow and Co., 1991.

Simon, Seymour. *Icebergs and Glaciers.* William Morrow and Co., 1987.

Simon, Seymour. *Volcanoes.* William Morrow and Co., 1995.

Sotnak, Lewann. *Hawaii Volcanoes.* Crestwood House, 1989.

Stille, Darlene R. *The Ice Age.* Childrens Press, 1990.

Van Rose, Susanna. *Volcanoes and Earthquakes.* Alfred A. Knopf, 1992.

Walker, Sally M. *Glaciers.* Carolrhoda, 1990.

Waskow, Arthur, et. al. *Before There Was a Before.* Adams Pubs., Inc., 1984.

Whitfield, Phillip. *Why Do Volcanoes Erupt?* Viking, 1990.

Ziegler, Pieter. *Evolution of Laurasia: A Study in Late Paleozoic Plate Tectonics.* Kluwer, 1990.

Bibliography *(cont.)*

Early Humans

Anderson, David. *The Origin of Life on Earth: An African Creation Myth.* Sights Prod., 1993.

Andrews, P. J. and C.B. Stringer. *Human Evolution: An Illustrated Guide.* Cambridge, 1989.

Baroly, Jean-Jaques. *Prehistory, Australopithecus to Mammoth Hunters.* Childrens Press, 1987.

Beaude, Pierre-Marie. *The Book of Creation.* Picture Book Studio, 1991.

Brennan, J.H. *Shiva: An Adventure of the Ice Age.* HarperCollins, 1990.

Brennan, J.H. *Shiva Accused: An Adventure of the Ice Age.* HarperCollins, 1991.

Brennan, J.H. *Shiva's Challenge: An Adventure of the Ice Age.* HarperCollins, 1992.

Conder, Forest E. *You Are a Miracle: Why You Are the Way You Are.* F.E. Conder, 1989.

Cudoto, Michael J. and Joseph Bruchac. *Keepers of the Earth.* Fulcrum, 1988.

Gribben, John and Mary. *Children of the Ice.* Basil Blackwell, 1990.

Hamilton, Virginia. *In the Beginning: Creation Stories from Around the World.* Harcourt Brace, 1989.

Jasperson, William. *How People First Lived.* Franklin Watts, 1985.

Johanson, Donald and James Shreeve. *Lucy's Child: The Discovery of a Human Ancestor.* Avon, 1990.

Kindersley, Dorling. *Early Humans.* Alfred A. Knopf, 1989.

Lynch, Chris. *Iceman.* HarperCollins, 1994.

Macauley, David. *Motel of the Mysteries.* Scholastic, Inc., 1979.

Matus, Joel. *Leroy and the Caveman.* Atheneum, 1993.

McGowen, Tom. *Album of Prehistoric Man.* Childrens Press, 1987.

Millstead, Thomas. *Cave of the Moving Shadows.* Lascaux Press, 1986.

Nada, Yolanda. *Evolution of Man: Two Hundred Six Million Years on Earth.* Mark-Age, 1988.

Parker, Homer W. *Evolution of Man Since the Earth Was Created.* H.W. Parker, 1989.

Scieszka, Jon. *Your Mother Was a Neanderthal.* Viking, 1993.

Stanley, Steven. *Earth and Life Through Time.* W.H. Freeman, 1988.

Willis, Delta. *The Leakey Family: Leaders in the Search for Human Origins.* Facts on File, 1992.

Periodicals

"Iceman" by Leon Jaroff. *Time,* Oct. 1992, pages 62-69.

"Origins" by Alfonso Ortiz. *National Geographic*, Oct. 1991, pages 6-99.

"The Secret Life of the Neanderthal" by Shari Rudavsky. *Omni,* Oct. 1991, pages 43-44, 54-56.

"The Whole Evolution Almanac." *Omni,* Oct. 1991, pages 87-96.